How to Read a Graveyard

ALSO BY PETER STANFORD

How to Read a Graveyard

Journeys in the Company of the Dead

Peter Stanford

BLOOMSBURY

LONDON • NEW DELHI • NEW YORK • SYDNEY

First published in Great Britain 2013

Copyright © Peter Stanford, 2013

Paperback edition 2014

The moral right of the author has been asserted

No part of this book may be used or reproduced in any manner whatsoever without written permission from the Publisher except in the case of brief quotations embodied in critical articles or reviews. Every reasonable effort has been made to trace copyright holders of material reproduced in this book, but if any have been inadvertently overlooked the Publishers would be glad to hear from them.

A Continuum book

Bloomsbury Publishing Plc
50 Bedford Square
London WC1B 3DP

www.bloomsbury.com

Bloomsbury is a trademark of Bloomsbury Publishing Plc
Bloomsbury Publishing, London, New Delhi, New York and Sydney

A CIP record for this book is available from the British Library.

ISBN 978-1-4729-0918-3

10 9 8 7 6 5 4 3 2 1

Typeset by Fakenham Prepress Solutions, Fakenham, Norfolk NR21 8NN
Printed and bound in Great Britain by CPI Group (UK) Ltd, Croydon CR0 4YY

For my brother, Martin, who showed me a wider world

Contents

List of illustrations

'Let's talk of graves, of worms and epitaphs'

William Shakespeare: *Richard II*

Introduction

Beneath it all, desire of oblivion runs:
Despite the artful tensions of the calendar,
The life insurance, the tabled fertility rites,
The costly aversion of the eyes from death-
Beneath it all, desire of oblivion runs.

'WANTS' BY PHILIP LARKIN (1922–85)

I take the family dog for a daily walk around our local cemetery. Two circuits is my routine, one if the wind is biting. It is a habit that started by accident. I needed somewhere to exercise the pet I had reluctantly been persuaded to take on by my children – who, of course, insisted that they would attend to her but, equally inevitably, didn't and still don't. And the neighbourhood graveyard is the nearest green, open space in this over-crowded city. There are parks if I stretch my legs slightly further, but a few test runs showed them to be as busy as the high street. By contrast, in the cemetery, at most times of day, I can more or less be by myself – save for the dog, and the company of the dead.

It is tempting to congratulate myself on discovering a secret place others have been missing out on, but it is simpler than that. Most walkers and joggers recoil from the very idea of going into a cemetery on an everyday basis. 'Too morbid!', 'All those dead people!' are the standard responses when I reveal my daily destination. Even other local dog-walkers eschew it, and prefer instead a 40-minute round-trip by car to somewhere roughly equivalent in terms of greenery and space, but without the tombstones and the occasional hazard of ending up as an uninvited guest at a funeral. At least our dog is black.

As a society and a culture, we have grown squeamish about contact with death. We remember the dead but, we 'forget their fate' in that line from Dido's lament, 'When I am laid in the earth', from Purcell's opera that often plays in my head as I walk past the gravestones. Once we were so good at grief. We had patterns and protocols for it, jet necklaces, prescribed periods of mourning, passed down from age to age, the accumulated wisdom of bitter experience. They were structures that saw us through the agony of loss. Now we have only avoidance. We 'battle' with illness, as if it is a fight we can always win if we just try hard enough. We trumpet the efficacy of green tea and a positive attitude as weapons in holding death at bay. We browbeat doctors who know better, but dare not say so, into providing debilitating treatment that might, just might, delay our demise by a few days or weeks. Half of all chemotherapy provided on the NHS, a consultant friend told me recently, is absolutely pointless from a medical perspective. 'But what else am I going to say to my patient with a brain tumour? Ask them if they'd like to have a chat with me about death?' And so we fool ourselves, right up to the very last minute, that death is something that happens to other people, but not us.

Why, then, risk breaking the spell by wandering into a cemetery? I used to be as much a cemetery-avoider as the next person. Until we got the dog, it no more occurred to me to go for a walk there than volunteer to work in a hospice. I managed only the very occasional visit to my parents' grave. My excuse was that it was 200 miles away and that, anyway, they were always in my thoughts, in my heart, in my genes, in the way I react to everyday situations, in my essential beliefs: in short in the atmosphere around me. I didn't need to go through an elaborate ritual of journeying up to Liverpool to place flowers on their three-square-metre plot next to a dual carriageway. 'Flowers for the living', my mother used to say by way of explanation for her own habit of avoiding funerals. In other words, go and see people when they're alive, don't wait until they're in a coffin. But once the funeral was over, she'd wander along and pay her respects. I took the part of her legacy that suited me, and discarded the part that didn't.

And when I did finally manage to drag myself there, I knew why. I wept as I wiped the moss off the already discoloured white marble because a grave has an irresistible power in the midst of life to bring us face to face not only with our memories and our loss, but also with our own inevitable demise. So it is an invitation, many of us seem to have concluded, best avoided.

When both my parents grew up in the 1920s and 1930s, the Victorian ethic of mourning still prevailed – great public funerals, a 'decent' stone (the goal of a Co-op savings' scheme my grandmother contributed to all her adult life), a strict dress code as to what shade of black to wear in the months and years after bereavement, and regular visits thereafter to the graveside. They could both recall open coffins in the front parlour, next to the aspidistra, with the extended family gathering for a wake. Today, by contrast, we rely on undertakers and tasteful velvet curtains that close at the press of a button in crematoria to draw a veil over the physical reality of death. We return days or weeks later to collect ashes – or 'cremains' – in tubs that are so innocuous they can easily be used as a doorstop. Often, perversely, we now save our most flamboyant mourning and grief for those we don't even know, heaping cellophane-wrapped flowers from garage forecourts in remembrance of murder victims and lost celebrities.

The outpouring of national mourning over Diana, Princess of Wales, is just the most obvious example. Grieve for a woman who for many was a cardboard cut-out, known only for her good looks, humanity and a well-managed PR image, and death stops feeling too real, too flesh and blood, too close to home. And even when death does eventually visit our family circle, as it will sooner or later, we hold back from touching, holding or even seeing a dead body.

Traditional funerals, undertakers report, remain stubbornly popular in these sceptical times as much among non-believers as believers, presumably because alternatives more in line with a secular age have been slow to catch on. That, though, is now finally changing with new eco-burial sites opening at a rate of knots. A wicker basket is all you need for a DIY burial. They've even had one in *The Archers*. If you fancy something more flamboyant, there are craftsmen who will build you a replica of your favourite car, guitar or mobile phone to be buried in.

Among those who still opt for the time-honoured burial ritual, there is a pattern I have observed in my six years of dog walks. The freshly-covered grave will be drowned in flowers in the days and weeks and even months after the funeral, but eventually that high tide retreats, and the blooms wilt, die and rot into the ground, in parallel with the corpse beneath, at which stage the maintenance team discreetly removes the debris of dried-out green sponge letters spelling 'Mum' or 'Dad' or 'Grandma'.

Undertakers recommend a six-month period for the grave to 'settle' before erecting a stone. Many relatives prefer to leave it more like a year. If they get round to it, that is. Perhaps one in five of the new graves never even achieve this state of permanence. Only the simple wooden cross intended as a temporary marker is left, and eventually is dislodged by the mowers and animals who roam the graveyard after dark.

Around half do get a permanent memorial, but a year or two on these once shiny marble shrines, some decorated with pictures of the deceased in what was once a southern European Catholic fashion that is now increasingly popular here, are left stained by grass cuttings thrown up by the groundsman's strimmer. The plastic flowers in the built-in vase have been rudely scattered by a freak wind, and an air of neglect has set in. The final 30 per cent are carefully and regularly maintained, though even then the intervals between refreshing the flowers do seem to get longer. Rare is the figure of the daily or weekly mourner. They do exist and I do clock them, pulling back on the dog's lead to avoid them being disturbed in their vigil, but they are few enough in number to stand out. Research carried out by the funeral industry suggests that after 15 years most graves are no longer visited.

Only a celebrated handful of burial plots achieve a measure of immortality, still attracting attention 100 or 200 years on. Poets' last resting places seem to retain a particular pull, but for the rest that don't there is something sobering in the sight that greets me daily of so many graves untended year in, year out, especially the mausoleums, elaborate pillars and outsized angels once erected in sure and certain expectation that visitors would continue to come ever after.

However noteworthy we think we are now – to our families, in our careers, in the headlines, even – a graveyard teaches that such esteem is most unlikely to endure. If we went into cemeteries regularly, we'd be forced to pause and digest this basic lesson, a useful corrective to the look-at-me values that underpin so much of modern life and its aspirations. We would also be able to imagine the lichen on our own memorial, growing over the wording that recalls our best qualities, and picture the gravestone eroded at its edges by the weather, or worse tilting at a gravity-defying angle, or collapsed and propped against a wall somewhere at the back of the cemetery. On my daily circuits, I have started to find such sights comforting, the essential democracy of oblivion that levels out life's triumphs and setbacks once our bodies are laid in the earth.

In an age ever more taken up with the quest to enrich and prolong life at any cost – a fashionable new detox diet marketed every week, legions of health regimes, countless visits to the gym – there isn't much space or inclination to contemplate the passage of time. When I recently turned 50, everyone told me it was 'the new 40', a balm at that particular moment, I confess, but also a way of looking back rather than forward. Understandably, few hanker for death to come faster, and as medicine marches on those calculations we make change. If I'm 50, have I spent two thirds of my allotted time, or just a half? To think always of life in the context of death risks a paralysing morbidity, but that doesn't mean we can't, when in rude good health, occasionally spare a thought for our eternal fate, or allow ourselves on a walk round a graveyard to be reminded of it.

The decline of religion has played a significant part in what the poet Philip Larkin labelled 'the costly aversion of the eyes from death'. For it could be argued that the main point of religion has been to give us a language, a ritual and an impetus to confront suffering and death. Religious belief, in all traditions, covers this life *and* the next. It temptingly insists that there is a next. It may not offer answers – or, when it does, on the lips of fundamentalists, they tend to be paper-thin, platitudinous and unsatisfying – but it does provide a structure within which questions of mortality can be addressed and reflected upon. Yet now that so many have abandoned belief, and the churches have been elbowed out of the public square, all that is left is the cold comfort of death as oblivion. And that hardly invites reflection, debate or discussion, even if 1800 people are dying in Britain on an average day, 140,000 globally. So we put it off, turn the other way when we pass the cemetery gates.

Ancient Rome, the Greece of the philosophers, the Egyptians with their pyramids, all had rites and rituals that acknowledged the importance of mourning and remembrance. In Western society, Christianity distilled this cocktail of influences into a pastoral, ceremonial and theological approach that dominated the way death was treated for 1800 years. It became a Church monopoly, and a business. The stranglehold was broken – for good reasons – with the introduction of non-denominational, non-judgemental public cemeteries in the 1800s. Yet the result, 200 years later, is that a new orthodoxy has gripped us. Don't talk about death. Sweep it under the carpet. Get the funeral over with and then get on with the important business of living.

Within days of my mother's and then my father's death, well-meaning friends were telephoning to urge me to join them at the theatre or cinema or dinner – 'to take your mind off it', they explained. When I declined, wanting to be alone with my thoughts, they reacted as if I were Queen Victoria deciding to spend her last four decades in widow's weeds after the death of Prince Albert, or Charles Dickens, who wore for the rest of his life the ring that he had taken off the dead finger of his beloved sister-in-law Mary Hogarth when she died at just 17. For the first time I began to see Victoria's behaviour not as eccentric but just a bit extreme. I even wondered if there was an argument to be made for reviving the custom of wearing black as an unmistakeable sign of mourning. Perhaps people would leave me to my thoughts? More likely they would treat me as if I were mentally ill.

And so, by chance, it is my circuit round our local cemetery that has set me thinking. Each visit is different. Sometimes weather, mood, outlook and even the whims of my companion combine to make it depressingly bleak. The woodpecker's drilling reminds me that this noise was once regarded as the sign of Satan. But on other days, a bizarre inscription on a tomb I've never before noticed excites my curiosity, starts me off wondering. From this expanse of open space in the centre of one of the most densely populated cities on earth, I have therefore been prompted to embark on a wider journey in an attempt to answer some of the questions that have filled my head during walks. Who first thought of erecting individual memorials to the dead? When did we switch from burying the dead en masse in Neolithic barrows that still shape the landscape of Wiltshire and Sussex, to individual graves? What do those changes tell us about attitudes to death and mortality in those times? And what about the history of belief, and religious institutions? In short, how to read a graveyard.

The questions didn't come tumbling out in a neat list. Slowly, stutteringly, a plan formed in my mind, to travel round burial grounds, in Britain and beyond, to search for answers about the history of how we treat the dead, how we regard their memory, and, inevitably, how we face death. Or don't. Morbid? 'Half in love with easeful death', as Keats put it in 'Ode to a Nightingale'? I prefer to see my travels these past two years as simply a gentler way of dicing with death than the extreme sports and extreme speeds favoured by some in a society that deludes itself it is immortal.

The selection of locations, as in all such journeys, is very personal. Others will ask why I did not go here or there. I have simply tried to find places that tell their own intriguing, sometimes celebrated, sometimes neglected story, places that others may like to explore at their leisure, but which also encourage a more ambitious narrative, shaping and structuring a wider historical overview. That knowledge can then be applied to your local graveyard, if you are willing to risk paying it a call. And it really is worth it, I promise you.

The overall emphasis of what follows, since it is the world that I inherit, is on Western traditions and rituals. I make no claim to be comprehensive, but different perspectives are woven into the telling, in individual locations, and in the glossary at the end.

If you let it, a graveyard is the setting that can transform death and grief – our own and others – into an everyday event, unthreatening, there-if-you-feel-in-the-mood-to-think-about-it. Walking round a cemetery is rather like rummaging among the old socks that lie buried in frayed pillowcases. It sets us remembering, reflecting and puzzling.

Trying to explain what I have been doing, when questioned about my latest project has proved tricky. Is it history, theology, literature, anthropology or polemic? All and none. At a literary festival, when I mentioned in response to a question from the audience that I was writing this book, someone approached me afterwards with a kindly but worried smile to ask if I was terminally ill. In one sense, I suppose we all are, in that one day we will die. This trip has made me feel just a little more prepared, if not accepting. And that little is enough.

1

The Scavi, Rome

'The monument under Saint Peter's is the strongest single piece of evidence we have that ... the Christian community at Rome did indeed preserve the memory of Peter's death and burial among them, recorded not on paper or parchment, but in bricks and mortar in the corner of a pagan graveyard.'

PROFESSOR EAMON DUFFY, *TEN POPES WHO SHOOK THE WORLD* (2011)

Travel agents bill Rome as 'the Eternal City', a catchline usually taken to refer to its pivotal role in the history of Western civilisation for more than two millennia. And, indeed, on every street corner there is an ancient building, the remains of one, the site of a significant historical episode, or a repository of priceless frescoes, paintings and artworks.

Yet 'eternal' also has religious overtones, eternal as in 'eternal life', which makes it an even neater fit with Rome because this is also the capital of world Catholicism, God's business address on earth for 1.2 billion believers around the globe, and therefore a place with a keener interest than most in the hereafter. That religious resonance in the adjective 'eternal' may explain why Rome is so full of tombs. They are there, of course, in the floors and walls and side chapels of the city's unending procession of churches, some humble but most immodest. They are there too in gravestones and memorial plaques encased in secular walls, hidden down side streets in alcoves whose only function otherwise would be to house rubbish bins, in public parks that were once cemeteries, and in buildings that were once mausoleums. There is an abundance on the outskirts of the city in the 60 or so complexes of underground catacombs, some miles long, that line the main roads. Where better, then, to embark on a study of the forerunners of Western customs for remembering the dead?

Most cities prefer to shut away their dead in high-walled enclosures, behind forbidding locked gates (as if they might otherwise escape and haunt the living), or in anonymous suburbs, on the periphery, out of sight, out of mind, so as to avoid reminding the living that their pleasures are time-limited. Venice allots the dead an island all of their own, separate and separated from the here and now. Rome, though, stands apart by favouring an ostentatious display of death. Perhaps it is simply a function of its great antiquity, or the flip side of its fabled *dolce vita*, less a case of 'see Rome and die', but 'go to Rome to die', presumably in the belief (a rough parallel with those Jews who take literally the promise of the prophet Zechariah that to be buried on the Mount of Olives in Jerusalem will give you a front row seat when the Messiah returns) that if your body's final resting place is here in the city of the popes, your eternal soul will steal a march as it sets off on its eternal journey.

Whatever the cause, Rome and its environs boast some of the most significant formal burial monuments in Europe. Dating back to 500 BC, the elaborate Etruscan mausoleums on the outskirts of the city stand in a direct line that links them to the earliest burial chambers known on the continent, sites such as Maeshowe on Orkney, a Neolithic stone burial chamber for whole families, built above ground and then covered by a mound of earth, and surrounded by a protective ditch, or the dolmens – or portal tombs (of slightly later vintage, found in Ireland and elsewhere, where a single stone chamber was again encased in soil, though with time the mound has eroded and left the curious stone constructions exposed in the landscape).

Circular in form, and again covered by a mound or tumulus, the central burial chamber of the Etruscans' burial monuments was more elaborate than its forerunners. It was often surrounded by smaller rooms. But the most significant development of the Etruscans – whose city states dominated central Italy for 600 years until the Roman Empire came along – was to cluster their tombs together, gathering them on streets, creating cities of the dead. And since they believed those who had died were embarking on a lengthy journey to the next world, they decorated tombs as they would the homes of the living, complete with antechambers, furniture and precious objects. In this way, they hoped, their lost loved ones would not feel neglected, or be prompted to come back to trouble those left behind.

When he was in Rome in the 1920s, the novelist D. H. Lawrence was beguiled by the Etruscan tombs north of the city at Cerveteri and Tarquinia. '[They] seem so easy and friendly', he wrote in an account published after his death, 'cut out of rock underground … Death was neither an ecstasy of bliss, a heaven, nor a purgatory of torment. It was just a natural continuance of the fullness of life'.

*

I am walking one sunny April morning over the Ponte Vittorio Emanuele which bridges the Tiber between secular Rome and the holy city of the Vatican. The Castel Sant'Angelo, the looming presence ahead to my right, reminds me of that Etruscan taste for shaping their mausoleums in the round. The Romans borrowed much, in their pagan heyday, from the Etruscans, and in the second century AD the Emperor Hadrian commissioned this giant drum, once clad in marble but now stripped back to brick, as his final resting place. When the Catholic Church replaced the empire as protector of Rome, though, Hadrian's mausoleum was converted by the popes into a fortress where they could take refuge if the city was under siege. A golden archangel was placed on its roof to symbolize this Christian rebranding. To make the takeover complete, the urn said to contain Hadrian's ashes was transported the short distance to the baptistery in Saint Peter's.

I am retracing that journey. At the mother church of world Catholicism, I am hoping to unearth, almost literally, one of those sites that connects Etruscan and Roman approaches to honouring the dead with our own.

Even at this early hour, the crowds have already gathered on the Via della Conciliazione, the great wide approach road bulldozed up to Saint Peter's by the fascist dictator Mussolini in the 1930s, once he had made his peace with the popes. It is jammed with so many banner-waving pilgrims that it feels like walking up to Wembley Stadium on Cup Final day. After much ducking and diving in and out of the singing, sashaying, overexcited throngs, I arrive at Bernini's vast four-column-deep colonnade that stretches out like two welcoming arms from either side of the façade of Saint Peter's itself. In an instant the crowds seem to melt away. While they go straight on to see inside the basilica, I head off in a delegation-of-one to the left.

I have an appointment to keep inside the Vatican City itself. Though the Church insists repeatedly that it is no longer the secretive organisation of old – partly to counter the notions now harboured by the millions of readers of Dan Brown's religious conspiracy novels – it still keeps its inner workings hidden from public view. Getting inside the Vatican, the papal mini-state, is easier, say, than gaining admittance to North Korea, but it still retains a certain rarity value as the prize for the chosen few deserving of papal indulgence. And I therefore can't help experiencing my own sense of anticipation when a Swiss Guard, one of the pope's traditional army of protectors, bars the way between me and the inner sanctum of this 110-acre slab of sovereign territory ruled over by the pontiff as one of the world's last absolute monarchs.

The guard asks to see my papers. Clean-shaven and dressed preposterously in a medieval costume of blue beret, red, blue, orange and yellow knickerbockers and tunic with a high ruff collar (reputedly designed by Michelangelo), he puzzles at length over the documents I hand him. As I wait, all the newspaper articles I have ever penned questioning the pope's pronouncements on the authorized version of being a Catholic start cascading through my mind. Will someone, somewhere in the anonymous offices that I can spy peeping out from behind Saint Peter's, have noted such heresies and put my name on an Index of Prohibited Visitors? I start inwardly preparing to be unceremoniously turned back at Checkpoint Saint Charlie. A vain and immodest worry, perhaps, but the institutional Church has a long history of such vengeance, stretching up to the present day, even in the case of insignificant figures who dare to cross it.

After what feels like eternity, it turns out that I don't even register as insignificant. The guard looks up, manages a quarter of a crooked smile, and ushers me through the barrier in the direction of three arches that join an ornate administrative building to the waistline of Saint Peter's. I make my way, in as businesslike a fashion as I can muster, past a row of television outside broadcast trucks – the beatification of Pope John Paul II is taking place in two weeks time and they have arrived early to bag the best pitch.

The cobbled road is a slight uphill gradient, I notice, regretting my suit in the hot sunshine. It is a reminder that the Vatican was once a hillside on the other side of the River Tiber from the imperial beating heart until a vast basilica was plonked on top of it.

I'm heading towards the *Ufficio Scavi* ('Excavations' Office'). Here, three or four times a day during the week by appointment only, small groups gather to be taken underneath Saint Peter's to one of the most important, but curiously little-seen shrines in Catholicism, the spot where the first pope is said to have been buried. Jesus called Peter the rock on which he would build his Church and, when it comes to Peter's grave, Catholicism has taken this promise literally. Directly underneath the main altar in the basilica, deep down in the earth, is the tomb that the Church says contains what it believes to be the bones of its first leader.

When Pope Pius XI died in 1939, he requested in his will that he be buried in the galleries underneath the main altar of Saint Peter's which house the last remains of over 90 of his predecessors. These are known, somewhat misleadingly, as grottoes, conjuring up (for those familiar with the Irish countryside) images of miraculous appearances of the Virgin Mary. The official account states simply that, while accommodating Pius's wish, it was decided to strengthen and thus lower the floor of the galleries by a couple of feet because of the number of visitors who, it was anticipated, would want to go down there to pay their last respects to a popular figure who had taken an outspoken stand against the rise of Hitler.

A more colourful version – and Rome is a city awash not just with tombs and ruins but also with folklorish tales, some scurrilous (reflecting the native humour), some containing a grain of truth, and some both simultaneously – is that the elaborate sarcophagus made for Pius's body was just too big to fit into the low-ceilinged galleries, so the workmen were actually digging down to create extra headroom.

Whatever the truth – and when in Rome, it is definitely more enjoyable to enter into the spirit of the place and go with the embellished version – in January 1941 a labourer's shovel, some four feet below floor level in the grottoes, hit something hard and immoveable. On closer examination, it turned out he had accidentally exposed part of an ancient mausoleum. Some senior officials apparently suggested the hole should immediately be filled in and forgotten. This was wartime, after all, and the Church was under pressure from all sides as it tried to remain neutral in the conflict. It was not the time to embark on a programme of major excavations, least of all down to Peter's burial place.

But the newly-elected pope, Pius XII, (again in the embroidered version of the tale) had been greatly inspired by the opening in 1922 of the almost intact pyramid tomb of the Egyptian pharaoh Tutankhamun after almost 3000 years, and so he decided not to leave well alone, as a long line of his predecessors had done, but instead authorized more digging.

Guided by a team of distinguished archaeologists, ancient historians and architects, the works outlasted the war and slowly, over the next decade, brought to light one section of the pre-Christian burial ground that lies directly under Saint Peter's. These are the *Scavi*, or 'Vatican Necropolis', to give it what may have been its original name. This 2000-year-old burial site long predates Saint Peter's which in the fourth century was built on top of it, incorporating the existing structures in the foundations for the new basilica. A place of burial was thereby itself buried.

The reason for what appears at first glance an outrageous act of vandalism and disrespect for the dead was because the Vatican Necropolis had long been a site of pilgrimage for those seeking out the first pope's grave. As his cult had grown within the Church – the word 'pope' was not used in the early centuries of Christianity – numbers increased. Keen to root what was originally a Middle Eastern religion firmly in the otherwise foreign soil of Rome, the Church authorities endorsed the story that Peter had been buried here (still disputed by some historians), and so erected their mother church on the site.

Yet, curiously, for all the emphasis placed on that founding symbolism, for 1600 years until Pius XII (and including a complete rebuild of the basilica in medieval times), the popes kept the actual grave itself out of sight. It was treated instead as a voice off-stage in the theatre, capable of being heard clearly and powerfully, key to the plot, but never to be unveiled. What had previously been a place of pilgrimage was henceforth deemed unsuitable to be glimpsed by believers. In such a way the institution of the Catholic Church evolved.

Perhaps it was that fabled habit of secrecy, blossoming early. Perhaps it was the fear that too many visitors would destroy what was always described as a flimsy, delicate structure. Or perhaps – the sceptics say – there was very little to see, and the whole conceit that Peter was buried here, vital though it remains to this day to Catholicism's heightened sense of inheritance, entitlement and authority, was always more symbolic than real.

Whatever the reasons, Pius XII was the first pope to authorize excavations. And the works, as far as he was concerned, yielded the hoped for result. In his Christmas message for 1950, he announced to the world that, in the Scavi, the bones of Peter himself had been unearthed, a relic to eclipse every medieval saint's toenail or wisp of hair, clipped as they were martyred and thereafter the object of Catholic devotion down the ages.

*

My fellow explorers, assembling outside the *Ufficio Scavi*, are all smartly dressed, as stipulated when booking tickets. There is a dress code for visiting dead popes. Two sets of elderly American couples in peaked caps and sensible shoes line up next to what I take to be a father and his grown-up son (you have to be over 15 to go on the tour – the health and safety culture has reached into the heart of Catholicism). Then there are two young eastern European men, with matching casual shirts buttoned up to the neck, awkward in their skins and generally ill-at-ease, possibly trainee priests; and finally a young couple clearly madly in love, their efforts at being befitting failing to inhibit them from touching each other all the time, apparently unperturbed by the outsized statue of Saint Maria Josefa, a nineteenth century Spanish nun peering down disapprovingly from her niche on the side wall of Saint Peter's.

On the dot of nine, our guide appears. Magdalena is, she explains, an art historian from Poland. Her smile is set, her manner brittle, but her behaviour as studiedly correct as the Queen Mother patterned scarf knotted jauntily round her neck. She ushers us briskly through a door into the basilica. We pass at great speed through a procession of exhibition rooms, each containing extraordinary sarcophagi, decorated stone coffins, all around 1500 years old, which have been excavated from under the basilica. I slow down for a minute to examine the detail on one and try to spot which images of death and after-life they evoke – the Etruscans bequeathed their love of highly ornate carved tombs to the Romans – but Magdalena hurries me along with words of reassurance that what is here will pale next to what lies beneath.

Next we emerge into a busy corridor. There are priests and other male authority figures in suits with decorated lapels (Italian men love a uniform) busily talking earnestly as they go hither and thither, as if in a scene from *The West Wing*. We are, I realize, backstage in Saint Peter's. The priests are between sacristy and altar, and the men in suits are ushering them. The buzz of the crowds in the basilica beyond the heavy curtains filters through as incidental music, strangely anaesthetized in these well-scrubbed private quarters.

Magdalena directs us down a white marble staircase. At the bottom we begin to concertina together, like extras in a comedy film, in the small space in front of a closed glass door that has no handle. There is a brief, slightly breathless moment of panic and then, from behind us, with a gesture of unexpected theatricality, our guide announces that we are now entering the Scavi and presses a hidden release switch. The glass door slides away, allowing us to tumble through.

The contrast couldn't be greater if we'd just fallen out of the back of the wardrobe in C. S. Lewis' spare bedroom. The floor beneath our feet is no longer marble but crude and uneven, made up, to my untrained eye, of compacted dry mud with the odd bit of rubble mixed in as glue. It is as if we are outdoors, but we're not. There are walls pressing in from either side, made of rough, thin, reddish-brown bricks, while the ceiling – again of brick – brushes my head. I step forward tentatively, bent in a permanent reverential bow, trying not to feel claustrophobic in the heat. From the spring morning cool of the lofty service corridors of Saint Peter's, we have arrived in a humid, damp undercroft. As the glass door magically closes behind us, we are hermetically sealed in air that is earthy and musty and old, with just a whiff of human perspiration.

The whole area, Magdalena explains, has to be kept as close as possible to what would have been its natural, subterranean temperature in order to prevent the air from above ground seeping in and damaging the ancient building materials. She points with her infrared beam to evidence of the damage done to the delicate environmental balance below ground in the Scavi when they were first disturbed and exposed during Pius XII's excavations. Carbon dioxide got in along with other pollutants, causing a layer of salts to rise to the surface of the oldest sections of brickwork and leave a white stain. Today, organisms from above ground, she adds, risk destroying frescoes that have been pickled in mud down here for so long.

I wonder if she means human organisms – i.e. us. The heat generated in these closed quarters, she goes on as if reading my mind, by one normal-sized adult body – and I am already metamorphosing into a boiler – is the equivalent of leaving an 80-watt bulb burning day and night. The artworks will fade if numbers of visitors are not severely limited.

The whole group responds by making a conscious effort not to breathe. Or to do so as lightly as possible. We are led forwards and downwards along the enclosed passageway. Then, as quickly as we came into this funnel, we are spewed out into a wider, loftier space. If it wouldn't permanently damage the artefacts around me, I'd heave a sigh of relief.

In front of us, protected by a glass screen that doubles as its fourth wall, is a square room with the remains of a vaulted ceiling. This, our guide begins, her red-beam dancing around the details, is known as the Mausoleum of Egyptians because on its orange frescoed walls are depictions of the Egyptian god, Horus, identifiable by his traditional symbol, a hawk's head. In the Egyptian pantheon, Horus played a variety of roles – as the god of war, of hunting and of the sky – but more relevant here is his casting as god of protection, in mortal combat with the evil god, Seth. By including an illustration of Horus in this tomb chamber, that protection is being summoned in death as in life, for the Egyptians believed in an underground place of punishment for the deceased that they called Tuat, and which we would readily recognize as hell.

The Roman pantheon of gods was large, non-exclusive and effortlessly accommodated figures drawn from a range of earlier civilizations, including ancient Egypt. This mish-mash of borrowed and inherited beliefs is further emphasized by a depiction on one of the marble and terracotta coffins that line the walls of the tomb. It is of the Greek goddess, Ariadne, abandoned by her lover Theseus on the island of Naxos while she was in a deep sleep, and later found by Dionysus, who married her. The parallel between death and Ariadne's long slumber was a popular theme on both Greek and Roman sarcophagi carvings. It is the Greek word for dormitory that gives us cemetery. And that image of sleeping, so much gentler and more reassuring than the finite, brutal, usually abrupt message carried by the term death, has ever after been a part of funereal rites and religious language. The ascendancy of science should really have made it obsolete, but its emotional hold appears just as strong as ever. The 2011 English translation of the Catholic mass has restored the phrase 'fallen asleep' in one version of the Eucharistic Prayer, in preference to the plainer 'died'.

Our leader is keen to press on. She repeats her earlier promise of better things to come, though this time fulfilment is, she adds, even closer at hand. And, after following her round a couple more sharp turns in the next narrow, closed-in corridor, she delivers spectacularly.

We are standing in and on what feels like the main street of an abandoned film set for an epic picture about Graeco-Roman times. The enclosing walls have rolled back and the ceiling has lifted, as if the props department has pulled on a few ropes to remove them. In their place are façades of life-size buildings lining both sides of the road. Only these are not painted plyboard. They are stoutly built, sufficient to have lasted 2000 years. Each, though, has a curious lack of depth, explained by these being the entrances not to a home or shop or office, but rather to a family crypt.

Most feature a door in the centre, with lintels, thresholds and doorposts. There are ornamental windows to either side, and in some cases above, plus marble decorations, mostly crumbling. Many are topped by gabled roofs, picked out with elaborate edging stones. Blink and you could be looking at a line of abandoned neo-classical civic buildings on the high street of a North Country English market town – the library, the council offices, the court, the Temperance Institute.

This necropolis highlights again the influence of the Etruscans on Roman burial customs. At Cerveteri, for example, the seventh century BC graveyard features a very similar main street, fashioned to reflect the prevailing view of death as a continuation of life in its domestic, social and communal form.

There is suddenly so much to take in here under Saint Peter's that my eyes are darting round everywhere in the gloom, unable to rest for long on anything. But it is what is above the roofs of these tombs that finally causes my gaze to settle. Pushing down on them, as if trapping them in a flower press, are pillars of stone and brick and rubble, held in place by brick supporting walls, which join the tomb structures to the solid lid above us that is the floor of Saint Peter's. We are in a streetscape inside a Tupperware container with an elephant sitting on top.

'Listen', Magdalena instructs. Even the young lovers are still. 'If you are very silent you can hear the visitors above you in the basilica'. There is a low hum of something going on above our heads, nothing as distinctive as the sounds we'd heard earlier in the backstairs corridor, more an unmistakeable indication that there is other human life very close, but in another dimension altogether. The thought makes me shiver, despite the heat. 'If you can imagine', Magdalena challenges, 'look up and once you would have been able to see the blue sky. Then in the fourth century the sun stopped shining'. Because a basilica was built on top.

It is back again to the Vatican being a hill. In order to provide a flat base for the first basilica erected in the fourth century, the builders had to create a level site. In the crudest terms, they moved a mountain. Starting roughly half way up, earth was taken from higher up and used to fill in the shortfall lower down. Only it wasn't just a shortfall. It was a necropolis. So the existing mausoleums were treated essentially as unwanted cellars and filled and then covered with displaced soil and debris. Once that had been completed, supporting walls were piled on top of the buried necropolis as foundations for the new basilica, and finally a platform was created on which to start the construction of the first Saint Peter's.

The excavations of the 1940s are therefore best seen as a process of taking out what had been put in down here 1600 years previously. But wouldn't that risk making the basilica above fall down? 'They only went so far', explains Magdalena, 'because they were afraid that if they continued too much they would cause it to crack'. A crack, from where I am standing, would seem to be the least of their fears.

That knowledge that the whole of Saint Peter's was resting on such an unstable base may have been another reason why the popes left this underground world undisturbed for so long. When in 1506 a brand new basilica was commissioned to replace the existing one, even the celebrated architects and artists employed did not touch these makeshift foundations. Bramante, Raphael, Michelangelo and Maderno were seemingly content to rest their creation on top of this graveyard.

As I gaze up at the piers – to use the technical term – of rubble, brick and bits of old debris, the statistics that are regularly trotted out about the basilica above start to run through my head: the largest Christian church in the world, at 2.3 hectares in total area; the highest nave in the world; one of the most spectacular domes; and all that marble and gilding, the statues, the bronze doors and Bernini's giant *baldacchino* (canopy) over the main altar. How much does that all weigh and what stops it all coming tumbling down into the vacuum where I am now standing? A few props cobbled together from whatever was at hand. It makes you hanker after the rigours of a regime of modern-day building regulations.

Today's Romans, of course, are masters at building on top of the detritus of the past. Their whole city, because of its 'eternal' history, is literally layer upon layer of discarded buildings and monuments giving up their place to the next generation that is piled on top. And if you worry too much about investigating the foundations, you will never get round to putting up anything new. For the past 60 years, for example, efforts (so far only partially fulfilled) to give Rome a decent metro system have proceeded at a snail's pace because for every mile of tunnel drilled, the archaeologists then spend months if not years picking though what has been unearthed.

So the reasons why the architects of the second Saint Peter's left the original foundations undisturbed have become more obvious. But there may still have been a certain sensitivity, beyond the practicalities. The Vatican's own archives show that these late Renaissance builders were perfectly well aware there was an ancient graveyard entombed in the basement of the fourth century basilica they were replacing, but an instinct not to disturb the dead unless absolutely necessary appears to have kicked in, even if it meant potentially also forgoing the chance of unearthing the bones of Peter.

That failure, though, still puzzles me. For the Catholic Church of the 1500s remained as hooked as it had ever been throughout the medieval period on relics. Every major monastery would contain some relic of a saint, or a fragment of the true cross, with which to attract pilgrims. Long before people began to map their world scientifically, they developed what has been called a 'sacred geography', based on sites that boasted relics. Many were fraudulent – the Pardoner in Chaucer's *Canterbury Tales* claims to have in his bag a piece of the sail of Peter's boat – but that wasn't the point. The relic linked the human with the divine, the graveyard with the sufferings and struggle of the here and now, this world with the next.

There was also a financial incentive to the interest in relics. The Dutch Christian Humanist, Desiderius Erasmus, for instance, didn't take to the Marian shrine at Walsingham in Norfolk when he visited in 1512. He labelled it 'Falsingham', on account of the legion of salesmen he encountered there selling a square of tattered cloth to pilgrims by passing it off as the Virgin's veil, or a bottle of white liquid as her breast milk. If you had a relic, you could attract pilgrims, and with pilgrims came money. In the case of the construction of the second Saint Peter's, paying for it was a problem throughout the 120 years it took to complete the works. Indeed, it was Catholicism's decision to fund the project by the sale of indulgences – exemptions from punishment for sins committed – that tipped the German monk Martin Luther over the edge in 1517 and precipitated the Reformation.

So had the church authorities been able to claim that part of the grand scheme for a new basilica involved digging down to unearth Saint Peter's bones, the pilgrims would surely have flocked to the site and the need for indulgences – or at least the selling of them on an epic scale – might have been avoided. Yet, curiously, there is no evidence that this option was ever explored. Did they doubt the existence of Peter's tomb?

In pre-Christian Rome, the dead had to be buried outside the city walls. It was a custom considered so important that it was there in the Law of the Twelve Tables, the cornerstone of the constitution of the original Roman Republic, agreed by senators in 449 BC and engraved on ivory slabs displayed in the Forum. How to bury the dead – table 10 – sat alongside rules on marriage, crime, property, inheritance, parents and children and civil process.

Among the favoured sites outside the city was the Vatican, described by eyewitnesses back then as an area of brickworks, low-grade vineyards and marshes (infested, according to the Roman historian Pliny, with snakes big enough to swallow an infant child), stretching along the right bank of the Tiber. It was also a place where the Romans came to play – life and death co-existing side-by-side. The Vatican boasted pleasure gardens and a circus (or chariot racetrack) completed by the Emperor Nero (AD 54–68). At its centre stood the same obelisk, brought from Egypt in 40 AD on the orders of the Emperor Caligula, that is today in the middle of Saint Peter's Square.

Catholic tradition likes to describe the obelisk, as a 'witness' to the martyrdom of Peter, for this Vatican circus was also the place where criminals were executed. In 67 AD, again according to the annals of the Church, it was here that Peter, the apostle to whom Jesus entrusted leadership of his fledgling church, was crucified on the orders of Nero. Origen, one of the key sources on early Christianity, writes in the third century: 'Peter was crucified at Rome with his head downwards, as he himself had desired to suffer'. An upside-down cross is often the symbol of Peter, taken to mean that he did not consider himself worthy to die in the same way as Jesus.

Nero's wrath had evidently abated sufficiently to allow Peter's body to be cut down and handed over to his followers for burial. Several early sources (including the third century 'father of church history' Eusebius) insist that Peter was laid to rest in the graveyard that lay behind the Vatican circus, alongside the Via Cornelia, one of the arterial roads of ancient Rome. He was given a simple grave, it was said, in the midst of the sort of grander pagan memorials I can see on the street in front of me. His final resting place was marked only by a rock, but at some stage in the second or third century, a more formal pillared memorial was erected to Peter in the graveyard.

And it is towards that spot, deep underground, that we are now heading. Peter wouldn't have been allowed on one of the main avenues of the ancient cemetery such as the prime location where we are now standing. This was the preserve of the wealthy. Each ruin we pass has its own embellishments, displays of wealth and earthly power. In one, there is a staircase leading up to what would have been a roof terrace, where the family of the deceased would gather, on high days and holy days, for a picnic or wine (Magdalena tells us this with a note of disapproval in her voice, as if linking pagans with vice). And each mausoleum, though in area no bigger than a decent-sized sitting room, packs in its residents. The Caetenni family sepulchre, for example, elaborately decorated with terracotta panels of birds, flora and fauna, lists 120 individual names as resting there. Two doors down, the mausoleum of the Valeri, the largest on this block, four metres high, and the grandest with pilasters on its façade, trumps that by claiming 170 residents.

What appears to modern sensibilities to be a bad case of overcrowding is explained by the coexistence of two kinds of burial in ancient Rome. Originally the Roman Republic had opted for cremation, with the deceased burned on a funeral pyre, their ashes decanted into an urn, and then placed in a niche either within a family mausoleum, or in a purpose-built *columbarium* (building for housing urns). Later generations, though, began to favour burial – whether under the ground, or in sarcophagi stacked up in arched recesses (*arcosolia*) in the walls of a mausoleum. The switch seems to have coincided with the imperial age, which began in 27 BC, but both practices coexisted side by side, as the Caetenni and Valeri mausoleums demonstrate.

Elsewhere in their excavations of this necropolis, archaeologists have found coins dated AD 318, suggesting it was still in use when, in 313, the Emperor Constantine granted toleration to Christianity. So Christian graves would then have been mixed in with pagan ones. Yet even after Christianity was formally embraced as the religion of empire, pre-existing belief systems continued to be respected. So there must have been opposition, not least from those families with dead ones buried in the necropolis, when plans were announced to flatten it under a new Christian basilica. Why risk such a confrontation, unless there was a pressing reason to locate the church precisely here – i.e. the presence of Peter's grave? 'The decision to build is one of the most compelling pieces of evidence that Saint Peter was buried here', Magdalena confirms, articulating what is the official Church line.

We are now picking our way carefully round a wall that seems to mark the end of the street. Beyond it is a series of small, interconnected chambers, all apparently the remains of individual mausoleums. We walk through them, rather than round them as the headroom slowly diminishes. The floor of the basilica above is getting lower as we climb the slope of the original Vatican Hill. These chambers must have been decapitated when the site was originally levelled.

Some show the first signs of the public emergence of Christianity. In one, Magdalena indicates for us to stop and gather round. 'We do not have much space', she instructs, 'so if you could form yourselves into a circle'. Obediently we shuffle into the desired formation. The father and son lean back against a wall to let the elderly Americans squeeze pass. 'Do not press on the bricks', she barks. 'They are very old'. Fortunately the light is too dim to be able to see if the miscreants are blushing.

'In a minute, you are going to enter one by one into this passage here'. She indicates with her beam a narrow vaulted opening on her right. 'Take a look, and then reverse out so the next person can go in. You will not be able to turn round'. We pause to take in the instructions. 'You may begin', she adds with a hint of impatience.

As the human wheel starts to turn in this peculiar ritual dance, she explains what we are – or will be – seeing. I manage to position myself at the end of the line, preferring to know as much as I can about what I am looking at before I do it. The mid-third century mausoleum of the Julii family, which lies at the end of the corridor, is the only one unearthed in the Scavi that is entirely Christian. In others, some of the tombs have Christian markings alongside pagan ones, but this one contains what is believed to be the earliest ever depiction of Christ.

The words are still sinking in when the second of the young eastern Europeans emerges backside first from the passageway and gestures for me to take my turn. Head bowed even lower than before, I make my way along to the end of a short claustrophobic corridor. A sheet of glass guards a small vaulted tomb.

Archaeologists have found ashes in a niche covered over behind the back wall, which have led them to conclude that this may originally have been a pagan tomb, subsequently taken over by a Christian family – the Romans reused their graves. The bottom half of the rear wall is covered with a standard geometric frescoed design, but above it, in pale gold, blues and greens, is the figure of a fisherman – possibly Jesus or Peter – casting a line in the waters. Some fish are biting; some are not, which more or less sums up the position of the Christian Church in Rome at the time this was painted in the second century, attracting converts and persecutors in equal measure.

To one side is the prophet Jonah being swallowed by a whale – an episode from the Old Testament. God rescues Jonah, and this tale of resurrection/new life was evidently a popular one with early Christians in decorating their graves. But it is the mosaic on the vaulted ceiling that is most extraordinary. Again in golds, blues and greens, the tendrils of a flourishing vine circle round a central depiction of a heroic young male figure in a chariot pulled by white horses. The imagery is associated with the Greek god of the sun, Helios. He was often depicted with a halo, and holding a globe in his hand, but here the Greek imagery is mingled with Christian symbolism. For the head of the central figure is surrounded by nimbus rays of sunlight, a familiar image for Christians of Jesus 'the light of the world'. The combination in Christ-Helios of two sets of beliefs and symbols is striking.

The 1940s, Magdalena is recounting when I reluctantly drag myself away, was not the first time this particular mausoleum had been discovered. A small opening in its vaulted roof – that I had failed to notice – can be explained by an incident in 1574, recorded in the Vatican archives. Repair work near the high altar in Saint Peter's had to be stopped when 'a hole opened accidentally in the floor of the basilica'. But, the account continues, 'the ancient burial chamber was walled in without touching anything'.

We are now getting close to our final destination. The rear wall of the Julii mausoleum backs on to what is said to be the location for Saint Peter's grave. Yet, because of the convergence between the gradient of the hill, and the floor of the basilica above, we now have to embark on a detour up to, and then down from, the church to get there. Our first glimpse of what is called the *Campus Petri* – or 'Field of Peter', the name by which the ancient tomb is usually known – comes via a gap at the back of another mausoleum we pass through. Again we gather in a circle and move round in order to stand in the precise and only spot where a fragment of a white marble pillar can be seen, helpfully backlit in orange light.

This pillar, some scholars have concluded, is part of the simple memorial that according to various early Christian accounts was erected over the place where Peter had been buried in a pauper's section of the necropolis. Some suggest that it was the work of Pope Anacletus (AD 79–92), but brick fragments found around it are stamped with the date AD 150. This was, it is worth remembering, a time when the Christian community in Rome continued to face fierce periods of persecution followed by spells of relative calm. In such a climate a flamboyant shrine to Peter would have been regarded with

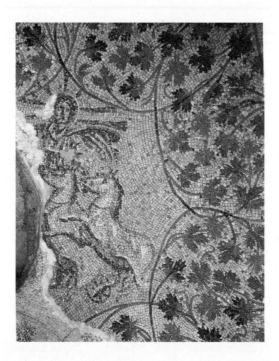

suspicion by the authorities, and indeed there are legends that the saint's remains had to be removed on several occasions from the grave and hidden in catacombs outside the city to stop them falling into the hands of officials determined to stamp out the Christian 'heresy'.

Artists' impressions of the monument at Peter's grave – sometimes called the 'Trophy of Gaius' after a late second century Christian writer who provides one of the earliest references to its existence – show something simple, in the shape of a high-backed chair, with the seat an altar and the rear panel decorated in red. There may also have been a room, or chapel, where Christians gathered, and a wall (possibly part of the chapel) where pilgrims to this sacred spot could scratch their own homage to the first pope, rather as Beatles fans today write on the wall outside Abbey Road studios in London, next to the zebra crossing where the iconic picture of the group was taken.

The tentative tone required of any description of the monument is the result of it being largely destroyed when the fourth century basilica was erected. Far from making it the centrepiece, as might have been expected, the builders sealed it in a bronze-lined structure topped by a golden cross. Directly above this tomb within a tomb within a buried graveyard was the main altar of the new basilica, where the Pope would celebrate mass as he stood on the grave of his predecessor. The symbolism made tangible the papacy's claim to an 'apostolic succession' – a link back through every holder of the office to Peter.

But why wasn't it incorporated into the altar of the new church? It is not as if Catholic Christianity has a tradition of shrinking away from such statements. In Lisieux, for example, in northern France, home to Saint Thérèse, the bones of one of her legs are on display in a glass case on the main altar of the basilica dedicated to her memory. Yet here we are asked to believe that the authorities opted for symbolism when they could have had the real thing.

Another explanation often quoted is that, back in the fourth century, to put any relic of Peter on such public show would make it a target for armies that besieged the city. The basilica was on the other side of the Tiber from the main fortifications of Rome and therefore was particularly vulnerable. Indeed, when the Saracens launched a raid in 846, they are said – bronze-clad protective casing or not – to have unearthed Peter's bones and scattered them.

Our detour is now complete and we have arrived in a simple underground room, just beneath the grottoes under the main altar. Behind a glass screen, there is a clear view of a section of another of the slender pillars of the Trophy of Gaius, plus a fragment of the 'graffiti wall' where in those early days pilgrims would scratch their prayers to the first pope. The engravings – principally the rather obvious words in Greek, '*Petros eni*: Peter is here' – have been dated and roughly coincide with the official narrative, but they demonstrate only that in those early centuries of Christianity there were plenty of people who *believed* this grave to be the last resting place of Peter, and who therefore made their way to the necropolis, then above the ground, to pay homage to him. What they do not prove is that Peter was actually buried here.

Believing and being are, of course, different things, and belief can often be the more powerful, especially if backed with the full force of the papacy. So when, in the 1940s, the excavations came to the remains of the sealed box-like structure built over Peter's grave in the fourth century, Pope Pius XII gave the go ahead for the team to continue digging. Hallowed ground or not, the final resting place of the leader of the apostles was no longer to be immune to modern curiosity.

Inside they found various fragments of bone. One story has it that until his death in 1958, Pius kept these bones in the papal apartment, even on his bedside table, so convinced was he that these were relics of Peter. Another – more cynically Roman – says that he deliberately kept them out of sight because he knew that they were animal bones, but he didn't want to disillusion the faithful.

Whatever the truth, the official line in 1950 was clear. Peter's tomb had been unearthed and that in itself was a cause for great rejoicing. The 'discovery' was used to tie Catholicism once again directly back to Jesus, a kind of one-upmanship in the competing claims of various branches of the Christian family. But no statement was made that these bones were actually the relics of Peter. It took another decade or so for that claim to be voiced.

In the late 1960s, the Vatican revisited some of the bone fragments that had been found hidden in a niche in the graffiti wall. They had, unaccountably given their potential importance, been left untouched in a cupboard since the time of the 1940s' evacuations. They were sent off to be examined by a distinguished Italian archaeologist, Professor Margherita Guarducci. She concluded that they were the bones of a 60–70-year-old man from approximately the first century AD. What she noted in particular was that there were no bone fragments from below the ankles. And Peter, of course, tradition has it, was crucified upside down. When he was cut down from the cross after his death, it is therefore perfectly possible that the guards simply chopped his corpse away from the cross above his ankles and handed over his body to his followers, minus his feet.

Supposition, but this argument proved sufficient for Pope Paul VI in 1968 to declare that these fragments were indeed, in his view, the bones of Peter. 'Believed to be' in that careful phrase used in all Church literature. Archaeology, it implies, isn't as straightforward as algebra.

'And here they are now', Magdalena announces with another flourish, though curiously modest next to her glass door trick. The beam of her torch hits a small see-through plastic container, smaller than a child's lunch box, containing shards of bone. There is a susurrus of awed mutterings from the rest of the group. 'The box was presented to the Pope by the US Air Force', she explains, 'and is made of special material to keep the bones protected'.

From what, I want to ask? The dangers of another Saracen raid had long since retreated. Perhaps an attack by a fanatic? Or decay? I glance questioningly at the rest of our party, but the American couple have already moved on to consulting their map for their next attraction and the young lovers are distracted. This grand finale – the box, the graffiti wall, and the fragment of a pillar – is not, after all, much of a spectacle. Perhaps that is why it was kept hidden for so long – to avoid disappointing breathless visitors.

It is tempting to be cynical and suspect that the low-key presentation is all about the fragility of the claims that these bones are indeed Peter's. But there is, I conclude as I stand looking on, a more positive way of thinking about it. When Saint Polycarp was martyred in a Roman arena in 156, probably around the same time that pilgrims were coming and writing on Peter's graffiti wall, Christians collected the remnants of his body, recording that they found them 'more valuable to us than precious stones and finer than refined gold'. Perhaps, in modern times the Church is rejecting the window-dressing of ornate medieval reliquaries (relic holders), and returning to the simpler, stripped down practices of the early Church. Leaving what it believes are Peter's bones in situ, in a graveyard, is arguably a thousand times more powerful than placing them in an elaborate receptacle and sending them off on a world tour. Moreover, it empha-sizes that essential connection between the living and the dead, ashes to ashes, dust to dust, yet still gives a particular power to the sacra-ments celebrated on the altar that lies directly above this small box, a link back to founding principles.

And, because this is a graveyard and not a shrine, it stresses the essential equality of death. Even the most celebrated and commemo-rated leader ends up as a small pile of bones. Given that we don't cope well with death in modern society, and try to push it out of sight, this modest display, kept in its original resting place, feels curiously like a rare invitation to look mortality in the eye – albeit with a microscope.

I don't feel quite up to sharing that thought with Magdalena, and anyway she is now intent on ushering us to the exit, via the main basilica, as quickly as possible. Her fixed smile slips for just a moment when the young eastern European seminarians ask directions to Pope John Paul II's tomb. The first pontiff, it seems, is less of an attraction than the 264th, but that is the way with graves. The more recent, the more visitors.

2

The Catacomb of Saint Callixtus, Rome

The Roman saw these tombs in his own age,
These Sepulchres of Cities, which excite
Sad wonder, and his yet surviving page
The moral lesson bears, drawn from such pilgrimage
LORD BYRON, *CHILDE HAROLD'S PILGRIMAGE*, CANTO 4:45 (1818)

Gianni loves history, he tells me, as we drive in his taxi out towards the Catacomb of Saint Callixtus on the Via Appia Antica, once one of the motorways of ancient Rome. Back then it was known simply as the Via Appia, and it was along such arterial routes in and out of the imperial capital that the dead were buried, in accordance with laws forbidding graveyards within the city walls.

The 'Antica' bit was only added in the eighteenth century, Gianni explains, when a '*nuova*' Via Appia was built nearby. Today most of the city's nose-to-tail traffic uses that new (in Roman terms) road, leaving the early stages of the original as more of a scenic route across an extraordinary funereal landscape. Cobbled in sections, lined in others by high time-worn walls, it is a parkland sheltered from the sun by pines, myrtles and cypresses. In the distance are the Alban Hills, framing a setting that has inspired artists seeking to imagine what heaven could look like. Most immediately eye-catching, though, are the monuments to the dead, principal among them giant ruined mausoleums such as the bloated turret that is the tomb of Cecilia Metella, a Roman noblewoman who died around 50 BC. The distracting frilly fortifications around its upper rim were added in medieval times, labouring the already romantic feel of the place, but it soon afterwards lapsed back once again into the decay that eventually wraps itself round all memorials to the dead. By the early nineteenth century, its distressed state, covered in ivy, inspired Byron to muse in *Childe Harold's Pilgrimage* on how quickly we forget:

> Where was this tower of strength? within its case
> What treasure lay, so lock'd, so hid? – A woman's grave.

Byron's interest – and his celebrity – briefly gave Cecilia Metella a second wind in history. There is even a restaurant named after her nearby. But contemporary tourists on the Appia Antica, when they are not jumping out of the path of Gianni's taxi, mainly head for the catacombs instead. First stop on their itinerary is the Basilica of Saint Sebastian, built in the fourth century next to what is thought to have been the original Roman catacomb. Its story is another key landmark in this chronicle of burial habits.

The site had once been a stone quarry but some time in the second century AD it was abandoned. Facing the same space problem that echoes down through the ages of what to do when the dead pile up but land is at a premium, the Romans opted ingeniously for fashioning the disused galleries of the quarry into a vast underground vault, digging down to add tiers to meet demand, linking it all by rough-hewn corridors and stairwells, and finally accommodating hundreds and thousands of bodies in individual niches carved in the rock and covered, once filled, by a stone frontispiece.

Many of those laid to rest here were early Christians. Their belief in the resurrection of the body on the day of Judgement made them prefer burial to cremation, as had been the Roman norm hitherto (though, as we have seen, this tendency changed around the second century AD, probably under the influence of Christian practices). There were practical reasons, too, why the early Christians favoured these catacombs. Property prices around imperial Rome were high, while many of the initial waves of converts came from the poorer sections of society. They couldn't afford lavish mausoleums like the Metella family, or those in the Vatican Necropolis. Instead, they adapted an existing Roman custom of burying the dead underground in vaults. '*Hypogea*' were an alternative in ancient Rome to a mausoleum, small, private, family vaults, of which there are also good surviving examples dotted in and around the Via Appia Antica. But the catacombs favoured by the early Christians were on an industrial scale.

The Romans can't claim this idea as their own. The origins of sculpting underground vaults to dispose of the dead can be traced back further in time to the rock-cut tombs of the first millennium BC in Asia Minor, and to the subterranean burial sites of Alexandria and Greece. The word catacomb, though, is distinctively Roman. The stone quarry that once stood on the site of the Basilica of Saint Sebastian (the present building is a seventeenth century replacement) had been known as '*Ad Catacumbus*' and so lent its name to this new-style public underground burial space.

*

The road surface on these early sections of Via Appia Antica is still a traditional Roman pavement, made up of blackened and flattened outsized cobbles, with chasms in between just waiting to break car axles. Gianni slows down and weaves his taxi from side to side as if on an obstacle course, but nothing stops him talking. He is, he explains, a self-taught historian. Self-taught and self-opinionated. His take on Roman history is decidedly anti-Church, typical enough of many Italians, despite their country playing host to the papacy and supplying, until recently, every incumbent on the throne of Saint Peter for hundreds of years. Or perhaps because of it. 'See those bare walls', Gianni gestures excitedly towards a wisteria-clad ruined mausoleum, 'the Vatican has stolen all marble from them to build its churches'. He laughs out loud at his own mischief.

In my schooldays, my Christian Brother teachers were also great story-tellers. The tales they used to regale us with, though, were rather more reverent, inspiring accounts of the early Christians, and notably of the catacombs. It was a saga of men and women so strong in their faith in Jesus that they refused to recant, even when, on the orders of wicked Roman emperors, they were being thrown to lions in the Colosseum, or tortured to death in the Circus Maximus. 'If you boys had a fraction of their courage', Brother Carroll would lament, small and shrunken with age in his neck-to-ankle black cassock, but still a powerful presence in the classroom. These sainted early Christians, he continued, not only buried their martyred confrères in the catacombs, they also lived down there with them, hoping that physical proximity would result in something of the martyrs' courage infecting them as they faced persecution by godless Imperial Rome.

It was such a resonant image that it stays with me to this day. I can almost feel the dark dankness, smell the bodily corruption, share the fear, and aspire to the faith of those early believers huddled together in makeshift homes alongside the graves of the recent dead. But the notion of finding a place of greater safety among corpses, under the ground, goes against all modern instincts. 'Like many pagans' – Brother Carroll had a way of spitting out the word – 'the Romans were very superstitious and so were frightened of disturbing the dead. They wouldn't go down into the catacombs and so the Church could flourish there, a real community with no barrier between living and dead'.

In the catacombs, he told us, lay our origins, the place from where the faith had been passed on to such a lazy, godless bunch as Form 1B in Birkenhead. Without the catacombs there might well have been no Catholic Church, no Christian Brothers and no Brother Carroll. It represented, at a suggestible age, a convincing logic.

However visceral the imagery, though, he was making it up. As – to be fair to him – were many other historians at the time who told the same story. Yet all the historical evidence that has been unearthed in recent decades points to the catacombs having been exclusively a graveyard, not a refuge for the living. The community may have gone down there to hold services, in the absence of churches of their own during a time of persecution, and out of a belief that they must honour their martyrs and get as close as possible to their remains. But they did not make their homes underground.

Like all successful organisations, Christianity has long been prone to embroider its own past to create inspiring legends that it judges an improvement on the truth, more effective in evangelising its chosen audience. And the catacombs are a prime example of that tendency to play fast and loose with history.

Gianni turns off through elaborate gates and up the long drive that leads to the Catacomb of Saint Callixtus. It claims to be the oldest official cemetery of the Christian community in Rome. So, for that matter, does the Catacomb of Saint Sebastian or, further afield, the Catacomb of Domitilla, but here the trump card is the 'Crypt of the Popes', a single chamber containing the remains of nine early pontiffs deposited here, side by side, in the late third century.

Callixtus himself, church tradition teaches, had been a slave, freed when his Roman owner converted to Christianity. Liberated, he followed his erstwhile master into the controversial new cult and rose to be principal advisor to Pope Zephyrinus (199–217). One of the tasks he was given by his leader was to oversee the catacomb where Christians were buried.

That the pope named one of his closest lieutenants to such a role – which today would better suit some cleric pretty low down in the hierarchy of sinecures for Vatican officials – reveals much about the paramount role of the dead, especially the martyrs, best of all papal martyrs, in strengthening the backbone of the persecuted early Christian church. Martyrs, as Professor Candida Moss of Notre Dame University in the States has shown recently in her study of the second and third centuries, were seen as 'other Christs' by besieged Christians, imitating him in both life *and* death. Their graves, therefore, were much more than simply places of remembrance.

As we go up the drive, Gianni is busy telling me another tall tale. It is late April and Rome is abuzz with internet-fuelled rumours that on 11 May a massive earthquake will strike the city. The source is a would-be astronomer, Raffaele Bendandi, usually dismissed by the authorities as a 'pseudo-scientist' and anyway dead since 1979. He is, though, still taken seriously by superstitious Italians – the superstition is the flip side of the anti-church prejudices exhibited by Gianni and his ilk. 'These catacombs, these holes in the ground you are going to see', Gianni explains, 'they will cushion Rome when the earthquake comes. They'll take the blow and we will survive. So make plenty of pictures. They may not be here after May 11'. With another laugh, he drops me off and disappears.

*

The above-ground modern infrastructure at the Catacomb of Saint Callixtus is modest and functional, as befits the gatehouse to a graveyard. There is a small gift shop-cum-ticket office, a toilet block, and a utilitarian pavilion that covers the original entrances that lead down into the earth. For some reason, it puts me in mind of a pithead.

When Pope Zephyrinus' turn came to meet his end by martyrdom, the fate of most early popes, Callixtus was elected to succeed him. He was, it is said, an enlightened leader for the five years he survived before also succumbing to the inevitable. There is some dispute, though, as to whether he was ever buried in the catacomb that carries his name. His sarcophagus was unearthed in the 1960s in the Trastevere district of Rome, cheek by jowl with the Vatican, but it may have been initially placed in this catacomb – alongside popes Pontian, Anterus, Fabian, Lucius, Stephen, Sixtus, Dionysius, Felix and Eurychian in their shared resting place – and then later transferred to a city centre church when burial fashions changed.

As indeed, ultimately, were all those buried down here, popes and paupers. By the eighth century every sarcophagus and stone memorial had been removed, along with whatever remained of the corpses that had been laid to rest. All were rehoused in the growing number of new churches being established in Rome, with elaborate tombs and displays for the more celebrated, and storage rooms or pits for the rest. Again it was part of the Church wanting to present its own history in a particular way, physically linking the trials and tribulations of the early martyrs of the catacombs to the new wave of churches being built now that Catholicism had become the official religion and a temporal as well as a spiritual source of authority.

Unintentionally the papacy therefore managed to sidestep a question that continues to trouble many when it comes to proper custodianship of ancient burial grounds such as the catacombs. There are twin and conflicting pressures. On the one hand, modern scientists, with their ever-expanding array of techniques for uncovering the past, argue that the remains found in graves thousands of years old can tell us much about our own origins. The chemistry of bones, for instance, is potentially a record of how people lived and died. Isotopes of carbon and nitrogen atoms in teeth can show who was a meat-eater and who a vegetarian. Skeletons can provide clues at to migratory patterns

But these remains, others object, are not just objects or curios. They are the bodies of human beings and should therefore be treated with dignity and respect, left in peace in their grave as had been intended when they were first buried. To exhume a recent grave, even for the purposes of scientific enquiry in, say, a murder investigation, is seen as a last resort and requires the permission of a court. Why should a different set of standards apply just because the graves are thousands of years old? The principle must remain the same.

The clash is seen most powerfully with those graveyards disturbed by nineteenth and early twentieth century colonialists. In clearing the land for the settlers to farm in, for example, Australia, pioneers unearthed whole Aboriginal burial sites, later shipping off the skeletons they had found, some of them thousands or tens of thousands of years old, to museums in Britain without a by-your-leave to the Aboriginals whose ancestors these were. For these native people, though, this was sacrilege.

Nobody listened to their objections back then. Graves were seen as fair game. Today, the pendulum has swung in their direction. They are listened to more sympathetically as they demand that the remains be returned for reburial because, according to their religious beliefs, they are 'souls in torment'. Laws have been passed to this effect in Australia, Canada and the US. In 2007 London's Natural History Museum agreed to send back 17 sets of remains of indigenous Tasmanians, in the face of protests from scientists who said that future opportunities to uncover the past, as new techniques were developed, had been lost.

Many Western museums now avoid displays of mummies or skeletons because of the difficult ethical questions that will be raised about proper respect for the dead. Curiously, in an age where we are reluctant to look our own death in the eye, we manage to get worked up about the rights of individuals who have been dead for thousands of years. Another present day manifestation of the same essential dilemma is the dispute over the remains of an Air France jet that crashed into the South Atlantic in 2009, killing all 230 passengers. The wreckage has been located three miles down on the ocean floor off Brazil. Some relatives – especially those from predominantly Catholic countries of South America – are supporting efforts to bring the bodies to the surface, so that they can come 'home' and have a 'proper' burial. Others insist that the wreckage of the plane should be seen as a grave in itself and so be left undisturbed.

Here in the Catacomb of Saint Callixtus, though, the dead are long gone. It makes this a very curious graveyard.

*

The intimate link of this catacomb with the history of the papacy means that I am back once again on Vatican sovereign territory. As well as the enclave around Saint Peter's, various sites and buildings in Rome, the catacombs amongst them, are designated parts of the papal mini-state. Vatican custodianship of these ancient monuments tends to ensure that they are carefully preserved and efficiently run, too efficiently to allow what I would really prefer, unaccompanied access, but it at least avoids the inexplicable closures for long lunch breaks that make visiting their Italian-controlled counterparts a lottery.

There is, at these Vatican-operated sites, a slightly old-world officiousness that I am always tempted to see, in its anxiety to tell people what to do, as a metaphor for the Church's relationship with

the modern world. 'We ask our visitors', reads a sign next to the ticket office, 'not to visit without a guide or to leave the group, not to use cameras or cine-cameras, not to smoke, to drop litter, to touch the frescoes or to write on the walls and not to interrupt the explanation of the guide'.

Perhaps a guided tour is the Church's way of showing proper respect to the memory of the dead who were once buried here, I tell myself as I inwardly rail at such restrictions, for the presence of the guide does also contribute to that modern affliction – the distance we like to put between us and the dead. Chaperoned tours round a graveyard make death itself into a museum piece, only dimly relevant to us today, and only to be confronted when accompanied by an expert.

At least Simonetta, the young Italian woman with a mini-microphone clipped to her face and a portable speaker in her hand, is a little more relaxed than Magdalena at the Scavi. Which may be a mistake on her part because, aside from me, the rest of our party is made up of a gang of over-excited nine- and ten-year-old school-children whose uniform yellow peaked caps denote an official outing. They seem to think they are about to walk on to the set of a horror film. As we go down the steep staircase into the catacomb, they begin making ghostly noises. At first they are amused by the echo their cries find in the tunnels below us, but the deeper we go down into the poorly-lit darkness, the more hysterical they grow.

Their antics remind me of an art historian friend who, when I told her I was visiting the catacombs, described a trip there aged 16 with her aunt. As a teenager, she was still very much in the mindset of her traditional convent school education, which is why, she explained, she had found the experience overwhelming and had disgraced herself – her words – by fainting. 'It was something about being in the presence of so many martyrs', she recalled. Presumably her teachers – like Brother Carroll – had painted such a vivid picture of the catacombs as the beating heart of the world's first underground church movement that she convinced herself she could feel their presence, even if their corpses had long ago been removed.

I steel myself against any similar swoon, but what I encounter is nonetheless remarkable. There is a mighty transition from the neat and ordered treads of the staircase down from the pit head – I could almost be going into the cellar at home to retrieve an old deckchair – to the cave-like environment of the catacomb. And it happens in an instant, between one step and the next, a journey from the twenty-first century into the third which this time requires no sliding glass door and theatrical flourish.

The browny-reddish *tufo* rock, on which Rome stands, and out of which the catacomb has been carved, looks rather like stale, congealed chocolate ice-cream, frozen in time as it oozes in from all sides to swamp us. There are even air bubbles in it, revealing its volcanic origins. Strong and malleable, *tufo* lent itself perfectly to the work of the catacomb builders, or *fossores* – *fosse* in Italian is the word for tomb or cave, and here covers both neatly – who were diggers *and* decorators in this natural crypt.

Tufo could be easily cut into any number of times to create *loculi* (or niches) in which to place bodies, without losing its core strength or imploding like a tower block under dynamite. And by way of a bonus, whenever a niche was carved out, the newly-exposed *tufo* would quickly harden on contact with the air.

Simonetta is digging in her coat pocket to find a beige knitted beret that she slips on her head. '*Fa freddo*' ('it's cold'), she mutters and shivers. She is the only one who has come prepared. I had been expecting a replay of the humidity of the Scavi, and don't even have a sweater. Here we are deep below the surface. In the medieval Christian imagination, hell with its raging fires may have been lying in wait beneath the earth's crust, but this underground resting space for the dead is more akin to the frozen final chamber of Dante's *Inferno* where the Devil waits encased in ice.

There was, though, I realize, ingenuity in the Romans' method when they built catacombs. In the absence of refrigeration, and facing the exaggerated highs and lows of a southern European climate, they consigned corpses to the one place available to them where the temperature was at least stable and cool, where the process of bodily corruption could therefore be slowed, and where the risk of infection of the living was in some small measure mitigated. In winter, one metre underground may have been slightly warmer than on the surface, but for the other three seasons of the year it was significantly cooler, at around 8–12 degrees centigrade. Days like today, indeed.

We start to make our way tentatively along the corridors on the second tier down. The passageways, hewn out between the pitted walls of *tufo*, are narrow and cramped. At intervals, they give on to small square chambers, or *cubicula*, lined floor-to-ceiling with niches, sometimes the exclusive preserve of one family (some wealthy Christians chose to be buried in solidarity with their poorer co-believers, as their religion demands), but more often a collection of strangers was packed in to every available inch as in a dormitory.

At least in the cubicles there would have been a kind of tranquillity. The only visitors would have been those who had a reason to come in. By contrast, to be buried in a niche cut into the wall of one of the main corridors – and there are 10 kilometres of them down here – would have been the equivalent of finding yourself laid out next to a main road as mourners went back and forth, day and night. The image makes me think of the constant buzz of traffic near my parents' graveyard. If death is sleep, theirs will be fitful and disturbed.

The early Christians may have been inspired by the memory and example of the dead, but when they came down here, to bury what some historians have estimated to be 4,000 martyrs in this catacomb alone, it would have been the stench of bodily corruption that assaulted their senses. There was almost nothing between them and the dead. Bodies were often wrapped only in a sheet and the opening in the wall then covered over with a thin piece of stone. Even with the natural chilling system, there would still have been a terrible pong from all those decaying corpses in such a crowded and airless space. The only relief would have come from placing a candle or terracotta vase with sweet smelling spices on the tiny ledges above or beside each niche.

It is impossible, as we follow Simonetta's slight, be-hatted figure, to get any sense of perspective. There is simply no room in the narrow corridors to step back and take in the bigger picture. But at various corners and junctions where passageways intersect, and where there is a vast main shaft rising up above us to a cover at ground level to let in air and light, there is just a hint of the scale of the layer upon layer of niches on tier after tier.

It is quite unlike anything I have ever seen before. The closest analogy I can manage is a composite one, halfway between the underground shelf stacks of books in copyright libraries that seem to go down and down forever, and a kind of multi-layered giant bunk bed, fashioned by Fred Flintstone.

The catacombs remained in use into the fifth century. The cult of martyrs continued, even when the persecution of the Church had stopped, and so the catacombs changed slowly from being working graveyards into sites of pilgrimage. Guidebooks from the seventh and eight centuries still exist, but they make clear that by then the corpses had been removed.

As well as the symbolism, there were sound administrative reasons for this. As the power of Imperial Rome crumbled, outside forces increasingly targeted the city. Outlying areas, such as the Via Appia, could not be defended as easily as what lay within the walls. And Lombard, Saracen and Goth raiders all displayed a victor's delight in desecrating the graveyards of the vanquished and scattering their contents.

The transfer of the remains into Rome hastened the eventual neglect of the catacombs. Why would pilgrims head out here when everything that the Church increasingly held up as valuable – the relics of saints and martyrs with their reputed power to heal – was on hand in the new breed of city-centre churches?

This abandonment of the catacombs continued until the early seventeenth century and the advent of Antonio Bosio (1575–1629).

Sometimes called 'the Columbus of subterranean Rome', Bosio had been born in Malta into a wealthy family and came to the city as a young man to train as a lawyer. Instead he found himself utterly caught up in the new science of archaeology. An entrance to an underground crypt had been discovered north of Rome, on the Via Salaria – once the imperial route to the Adriatic coast – and Bosio set out to find more.

Reading and re-reading the early Christian texts, he culled as many clues as he could and then embarked on a search of the terrain, eyes peeled for a hidden staircase or the overgrown top of a light shaft. The local peasant farmers, who by then were using the abandoned funereal landscape around the Via Appia for their animals and crops, provided him with a wealth of helpful information. Eventually he was able to distil details of the 30 rediscovered catacombs into his book, *Roma Sotterranea* (*'Underground Rome'*), published five years after his death.

It even lists the frescoes and carvings left behind in these underground burial chambers. Which is just as well, for Bosio's scholarship had an unforeseen consequence. His book became a looters' guide. They followed his directions and plundered everything of value from the catacombs, stripping them to the bare state they are in today. It took until the nineteenth century for the Vatican to set up an effective custodian, the Pontifical Commission for Sacred Archaeology, to protect these burial sites.

Bosio's pioneering work inspired the other key figure in the revival of the catacombs, Giovanni Battista De Rossi. An archaeologist working in the Vatican Library, he was responsible in 1854 for re-opening the corridors I am now walking along. The Catacomb of Saint Callixtus, he claimed, had once contained the graves of 50 martyrs and 16 popes.

And it is to the 'Crypt of the Popes' that we are now heading. The cold is starting to make the school children restless and grumpy as we proceed in single file behind Simonetta. A few more robust stragglers dart in and out of the various cubicles, but most are trudging silently. Some of the side rooms are shut off by glass screens to protect the remaining crudely executed frescoes, presumably judged worthless by the looters.

In one, there is a depiction of a feast, with women under trees laden with fruit, and exotic birds in the sky. It is most likely an image of heaven as a paradise garden, standard in Christianity then as now. In another there is an illustration of shepherds watching their sheep, another familiar Christian theme. 'Sheep May Safely Graze' is still regularly sung at funerals.

Most prized amongst these smaller chambers is the 'Crypt of the Sacraments', where the individual niches are surrounded by a rough frieze depicting the sacraments of Baptism and Eucharist. Elsewhere, though, the remaining decorations are of flowers and fauna, the sort of motifs you would also find in pagan tombs of the same era, shared and transferable symbols of life amid death, and of the hankering for rebirth into eternal life.

Two images crop up repeatedly: the fish symbol and the letters XP. The first – two intersecting arcs, crossing at one end to form what looks like a fish's tail – is known as the *ichthys* (from the Greek word for 'fish'). The early Christians were as fond of fish imagery as the New Testament with its stories of fishermen who became 'fishers of men'. They used the *ichthys* as a secret code, both to identify themselves to others of similar disposition, and as a signpost to their secret meeting places.

Some say that the word *ichthys* is also an acrostic – that each of its letters refers to the first letter of the phrase (when said in Greek) 'Jesus Christ God's Son Saviour'. Though it fell out of use for many centuries, the symbol was revived in the latter part of the last century, and is today especially favoured by American Evangelical Christians. They have it on a sticker attached to their car bumper as a sign of highway solidarity against what they perceive as a hostile, secular world.

The XP – or 'Chi Ro' – symbol is again based on Greek. Chi and Ro are the first two letters in the Greek word for Christ. By overlapping them, the resulting shape invokes the cross on which Jesus died. Not as popular with the early Christians as the *ichthys*, it came into its own later when the Emperor Constantine embraced Christianity in the fourth century, inspired, it is said, by a dream in which he saw the symbol.

In another of these underground burial sites, there is a much more controversial surviving fresco. The Catacomb of Saint Priscilla features an early third century illustration with seven figures, one if not all of them women, celebrating the Eucharist by re-enacting the Last Supper. For supporters of women's ordination in the Catholic

Church (which refuses to recognise their vocation), here is clear but buried evidence from the past that the priesthood knew no gender bar in the early centuries.

That image of a funeral banquet, of women in charge in the Church, mixes in my head with the scene before my eyes now, of the slow procession of schoolchildren along the corridors, following our very own female guide/shepherd, towards the 'Crypt of the Popes'. Modern dress to one side, we could be participants in one of the rituals which would have passed this way 1600 years ago, mourners parading reverently in the depths of the earth behind our priest, heads bowed in prayer, to bury friends, family members or martyred leaders of our besieged community.

Brother Carroll may have misled us about there being a resident community down here, but evidence has been found in the catacombs that they were used regularly for services, prayer meetings and even for what we would today call Mass. I hesitate to use the term because it only appears around the end of the fourth century, in the writings of Saint Ambrose. And very little indeed is known about the burial rites in the early centuries of the Church. One of the first surviving accounts on the subject – written by Saint Jerome in the early fifth century about the burial of Saint Paul the Hermit – speaks only of there being hymns and the reading of psalms. Another glimpse, 100 years earlier, comes from Saint Augustine, a key figure in the development of Church doctrine, when he records in passing the burial of his mother, Saint Monica. He describes a Eucharistic celebration as part of proceedings.

As with much else in their evolving rites and rituals, it seems likely that the early Christians, down in these catacombs, would have adapted local customs to their particular needs and beliefs. Some sort of ceremony to say farewell to the dead is part of every religion, and the overlaps between each variation are many. What the Romans offered the Christians, by way of a template from which to borrow, was an elaborate set of funeral ceremonies that began when the soon-to-be-deceased's family would gather round the death bed and the closest relative would kiss the dying one so as to retain the soul that it was believed abandoned the body with its last breath. The corpse would then be ritually washed, perfumed and anointed, after which there was a wake. A procession followed, with mourners all in black, sometimes accompanied by musicians, to the pyre where the body would be cremated, or, as became more popular in the later years of empire, buried. Sometimes wealthy Romans would hire professional mourners – *praeficae* – to weep so as to make a public show of grief, part of a tradition of employing designated lamenters that was seen in Egypt, Mesopotamia and Greece, and which survives there to this day with the *moirologistres*, or female mourners, who will chant and sing

at funerals in the Mani peninsula of the Peloponnese region. They put into words and music the pain that families cannot express.

Finally there would be a funeral banquet. In many catacombs, a large communal space for just such a feast was located near the entrance. In the Catacomb of Saint Callixtus, this room is called the 'Crypt of Refrigerium'. With the underground chill now getting into our living bones, I am tempted to see this name as a reference to a place where the temperature was lowest – a kind of naturally occurring refrigeration unit or morgue – but in fact it comes from the rites of *refrigerium*, a commemorative meal held by Roman families on the day of burial, then again on the ninth day, and thereafter annually.

The Romans were good at regular attendance at gravesides and mausoleums. They liked to pay homage to their dead on various flower festivals – such as *Rosalia* when the roses were in full bloom in May – when the temples would close, work would be set aside, and grieving families would make a ritual return to lay sweet-smelling buds. This, it is thought, may be the origin of the Christian habit of placing cut flowers on a grave (not something done by Jews, for example), and even of the 'Day of the Dead', or *Dia de los Muertos*, in Spanish-speaking cultures (usually on November 1 or 2) when graves are cleaned by relatives and decorated with sugar skulls, marigolds or the deceased's favourite food and drink. In other Catholic cultures – notably the French who traditionally mark the same period as *La Toussaint* – remembering the day can include taking a celebratory picnic to the graveside, thus narrowing the gap between living and dead and helping to banish the sad faces.

*

Our underground procession is at its destination. Simonetta's tone is that of one who has left the best to last, and the 'Crypt of Popes', larger, wider and higher than anything we have seen so far, is certainly a contrast to the *tufo*-lined corridors and crowded, crushed spaces of the rest of the catacomb. It is more buried church than hewn-out cave. Its brick-lined walls, containing the outsized niches where the nine popes were buried, along with eight bishops (three from Africa), were once clad in marble, but it has been looted over the ages, presumably not by the Church, I make a mental note to tell Gianni when I re-emerge into the daylight. Why would it strip its own shrine?

De Rossi was convinced of the paramount significance of this crypt. He called it 'the little Vatican, the central monument of all Christian cemeteries'. Which may be overstating it somewhat, the thrill of discovery leading him to over-egg his language. It certainly contains the earliest and largest collection of papal tombs; there are a few others dotted elsewhere around the catacomb, off the tour route. And, as such, it could indeed be regarded as the forerunner for the grottoes that lie directly below the main altar at Saint Peter's – 'the big Vatican'. They today confer an aura of historical continuity on the mother church of world Catholicism. In their time, the collection of papal sarcophagi in this space may well have served much the same purpose: the dead leaders and their burial place shaped the beliefs of the living. Yet, without them there, it is hard to summon up the effect. It feels like nothing more than an abandoned church, another set of ruins in a city with more than enough already.

Much of what we are looking at was recreated by De Rossi, in what appears to have been a fairly crude attempt to attract pilgrims once again. The marble slab that was installed on the back wall features an ode allegedly written by Pope Damasus (366–84) in honour of his predecessor, Sixtus II, one of those buried here. Sixtus (257–58) had been leading a service in the catacomb, the story goes, when some Roman soldiers overcame their antipathy to entering graveyards and arrested him and four of his deacons. All were tried the same day, found guilty and beheaded on the spot.

If you are looking for, know that here lies a host of the Blessed.
The venerable sepulchres enclose the bodies of the Saints,
but the royal palace of heaven carried off to itself their sublime
    souls.
Here lie the companions of Sixtus who bear the trophies won
    from the enemy.
Here the group of the elders who keep guard of the altars of
    Christ.
Here the bishop who lived through the long peace.
Here the holy Confessors sent to us from Greece.
Here the young men and children, the old men and their chaste
    nephews
who preferred to keep their virginal purity.
Here too, I, Damasus, confess I would have liked to have been
    buried
were it not for fear of vexing the holy ashes of the Blessed.

The verse and its use down here both feel clumsy, distracting from
the unadorned simplicity elsewhere. A few original features did
survive De Rossi's renovations. One catches my eye – a fresco of two
indistinct figures, etched in orangey-brown, almost Lowry-like with
their matchstick bodies. In their antiquity and simplicity, they do
have a curious power, reaching back to a time before Christianity
built basilicas and commissioned great works of art. They are labelled
'Christ and the Good Samaritan'. It is pretty much a stab in the dark
as to their theme. Less would be more. But that is not always the way
of the Church when it comes to its own history – even the history of
its dead martyrs, saints and popes. The power of the burial ground
cannot here be left to stand unadorned.

3

Saint Margaret's Church, Burnham Norton, Norfolk

Beneath those rugged elms, that yew-tree's shade,
Where heaves the turf in many a mouldering heap,
Each in his narrow cell for ever laid,
The rude Forefathers of the hamlet sleep.

'ELEGY WRITTEN IN A COUNTRY CHURCHYARD' BY THOMAS GRAY (1750)

It reveals much about our contemporary confusion about the reality of death that so many continue to hanker after 'a grave with a view', as if they are going to spend eternity sitting up in their coffin, lid cast casually to one side, gazing out over the top of their pit towards a sunlit panorama. One eccentric American socialite once requested that she be buried not in a coffin, but in the seat of her favourite car, with it tilted back at a comfortable angle so she could look out, as if through the windscreen when driving, at what was going on around her. No matter that she would be six feet under.

The view to the far horizon where sea merges with sky may be the closest that most earthbound imaginations can stretch in visualizing eternity. It has, after all, been a favourite all the way back to the fifth century, when Celtic monks would stand half-immersed on the shoreline, gazing out to where, they believed, lay various heavenly 'Isles of the Blessed'. Such a desire in perpetuity for what one Victorian matriarch of my acquaintance liked to refer to as 'pretty peeps' is, of course, rooted firmly in the hopes of this world, and in our projections of what after-life might be like, based on what we have experienced already. No matter that such pictures go entirely against both science, which can quote chapter and verse on the physical corruption of the body after death, *and* against the theology of Christianity, with its stated belief that heaven is ineffable, beyond words, and hence also our wildest dreams.

There is no official template. So why not, I suppose, when seeking out a final resting place, find what each of us regards as the most perfect corner of the planet and use it as our chosen backdrop to eternity? Fra Angelico's 'Last Judgement' shows angels leading the saved through a beautiful garden towards a shining city. And Stanley Spencer's 'Resurrection: Cookham' has the risen Christ returning to the graveyard of Spencer's local church, Holy Trinity in Cookham on the Thames, amid coffins thrown open, with their inhabitants climbing out.

Spencer's projection was set in the landscape he loved. Cookham was his birthplace, somewhere he labelled 'a village in heaven'. He worshipped in its church and in 1959 was buried in the adjoining graveyard. So he invested the everyday details of otherwise unexceptional Cookham with a mythical significance – 'angels and dirt' was his phrase for it. In our own less visionary ways, we are doing something similar when we select our burial plot.

I've already picked mine (in my head at least and on the basis that my paramount wish is to be buried with my wife). This is the first time I've committed it to paper which feels uneasily like a milestone. It is the graveyard of Saint Margaret's, Burnham Norton, on the north coast of Norfolk. Clustered next to an ancient church with a distinctive round Saxon tower, rare elsewhere but common in this county, it is a graveyard with both a timeless quality – the Christian presence here dates back to before the Norman Conquest – and a view to die for, if you'll excuse the pun. Standing atop a gentle rise, it faces out under a famously big blue Norfolk sky, past a picture-postcard windmill, to the salt marshes, sand dunes and creek at nearby Burnham Overy Staithe, thence on to Scolt Head Island, and thereafter to the sea that stretches to forever. The wind that blows in uninterrupted from the Arctic carries into the churchyard a gossamer thin coating of salt and the soothing scent of water.

Part of the appeal is familiarity. This is a stretch of the coast I know well, where I have spent – and hope to spend more – happy times, and where I have come to feel at home in an extraordinary landscape.

Being buried here has a natural momentum. These are, of course, the
same reasons why one might choose to buy a house in the area, but
a grave is a different kind of property holding. And hence my choice
is more about how, for me, this place manages to capture the two
often-conflicting hankerings that arise on those rare occasions when
our modern sensibilities allow a discussion about death and burial:
the wish for some sort of idealized, permanent resting place; and
the expectation, real or imagined we cannot know, that we will be
embarking on a journey.

Saint Margaret's scores highly on location. As a side, short-term
consideration, surely that will encourage my nearest and dearest to
come and put flowers on my grave, once in a while, perhaps longer
than the 15 years of visits that research allocates each of us. And it
certainly has permanence. Like many medieval country churches,
Saint Margaret's speaks readily to that yearning for something that
has lasted, and will go on enduring even when generations die out
and family trees end without issue. It has been in use as a place of
prayer, worship and burial for so long that it explodes any illusions I
may have picked up over half a lifetime of my own significance, just
as standing next to a 400-year-old cedar of Lebanon makes me realize,
as few other objects can do so readily, that I am nothing more than
a ring on its trunk. This is a church where people have been seeking
meaning in life and death for a thousand years or more. Its round
tower is the centre of a wheel whose spokes stretch out to infinity.

What, though, of Saint Margaret's as the embarkation point on an
eternal journey? The landscape that spreads out in front of me now, as
I stand in the quiet lane outside the church, is perpetually in motion.
It is never the same one day after another because this particular spot
is one of the planet's crossroads, somewhere the natural relationship
between land, marsh, sand, sea and sky is daily in flux. One high tide
and the 'Hard' – the solid bit of ground at Overy Staithe where I park

my car – turns into a bay. Another inch or two on sea levels and the houses will be under water. Back in 1953, during the infamous floods that claimed 300 lives, the waves were lapping at the foot of the hill up to the churchyard.

Eternal rest here, then, would never be static, still or simply dead, but instead a process of merging into something forever alive and on the move. There's a strange comfort in that, a powerful sense of being part of (returning to?) nature, of creation and hence – at least from my own perspective (but I accept not others') – of the sacred. How many caveats we have to enter when we finally broach the subject of death!

Once, I reflect as I walk through the unexceptional gate into Saint Margaret's churchyard on this late summer's afternoon, it must have seemed more straightforward. Death was a routine part of daily life. This entrance could have been a lych gate, still a common feature in other local medieval churches, the place where corpses, wrapped only in a shroud, or winding sheet, knotted at top and bottom, would be delivered on a bier by family and friends and consigned to the eternal care and protection of the Church, as symbolized by the priest who waited there to receive them. It was an unadorned community ritual. There was no attempt to hide the reality of death with coffins and sweet-smelling flowers. This was a time when the sight of a corpse and the stench of bodily disintegration was all too familiar.

By contrast, I was 38 before I saw a dead body, partly the blessing of growing up in a generation that hasn't lived through a world war. And I only saw one then because, wrong-footed by grief, I mistook a funeral director's invitation to 'view' my mother in the chapel of rest for a summons. In a converted garage behind the parlour – the Victorian language persists – the chapel was filled with tanks of goldfish, presumably because they have 15-second memories and the emphasis was on forgetting the pain of grief as quickly as possible.

Hideously made-up, a slack lower lip attached to the rest of the familiar face by a clumsy stitch, my mother's body was sanitized, odourless, thanks to the formaldehyde, and deserted. It was a shock, but at least I knew for sure she'd gone.

*

Saint Margaret's today stands alone in splendid isolation – part of its appeal – a good half-mile south of the village it serves. It is closer to neighbouring Burnham Market (which has two medieval churches of its own) than to the community Burnham Norton, now perched as it is uneasily on the edge of the salt marshes, behind a sea wall.

Once, though, there were dwellings around this church. Bones, oyster shells, medieval pottery and other signs of settlement have been found in the field that lies behind me. There are many explanations for this odd state of affairs. The most popular is the suggestion (disputed by historians) that this dislocation of church and church-goers came about because of the Black Death. When plague swept across Britain in the 1340s, the story goes, the village around Saint Margaret's was decimated. Those who survived – and, throughout Europe, this epidemic claimed the lives of 30 to 60 per cent of those who were stricken – naturally wanted to distance themselves from what they regarded as polluted ground, and so rebuilt their settlement a good few fields away. But the church, already ancient, was too big and too venerable to move, so it stayed put.

The relocated villagers would have had a longer walk up to church services, but they kept coming nonetheless for, in medieval times, the house of God played the key role in local communities such as this. And underpinning that was its pivotal place in handling death, and deciding the fate of souls. There was none of our present public debate and agonizing about belief, the drawing of fine distinctions between denominational attachment, agnosticism, 'cultural Christianity' and atheism. Instead, there was simply an acceptance that, when you died, if you wanted eternal life, then your corpse had to be accepted at the lych gate for burial in consecrated ground. Refusal meant damnation to hell forever. And hell, in the medieval imagination, was real and appalling.

I'm now inside the churchyard, a regular haunt. Usually I do a round of visits, in this pastoral enclave of the dead, at various graves with familiar names inscribed on them. It is an instinctive ritual that I cannot remember ever learning. I just followed in the footsteps of my parents as a child as they did it. One very clear picture is of walking across the graveyard around the rural churchyard at Quatt in Shropshire where my grandmother had been buried, watching as my father and his brother – who lived nearby – crouched beside the unmarked lump in the ground and chatted away affectionately to their 'Ma'.

And then one day I found myself having a one-way conversation at my own parents' graveside. As a habit, it carries with it a comforting vision of after-life as reunion with friends and family who have gone ahead before us, as tombstone inscriptions often put it. 'They'll be saying what's taking you so long', my mother would say when we went to Old Fletton graveyard in Peterborough where my father's beloved maiden aunts were buried. No matter that notions of heavenly reunion, when considered in a less emotional landscape, feel too simplistic, a balm to apply to our wounds rather than a realistic prospect. In the moment, they soothe.

Today, though, my socializing with the dead is interrupted by the presence of someone else alive and breathing in the churchyard. Derek Woodhouse is sitting contentedly on a bench, his old bicycle propped up nearby. A local man, probably in his late 60s (but it is hard to judge because he looks so pink and healthy), his family can trace back through the generations its history in the Burnhams, the collection of villages on this coast dotted around the twisting course of the River Burn as it approaches the sea. Since 1977, Derek tells me, he has dug all the graves here and in neighbouring parishes. He's grown old amongst the dead and knows with a forensic precision what lies beneath every sod of the lumpy grass surface of this place. He is reported to be adept at finding gaps to accommodate the latest arrivals.

He stands up as he greets me, a smile on his weather-beaten face. As we chat, he points over to where his great grandparents are buried, right up next to the church. And then he runs me through the family, and where each branch is located in this graveyard. That's why he likes sitting here, he explains. It brings them back. They live in his head. He has his own plot singled out, he adds, gesturing towards the 'newer' overflow section, so new that it was added in 1900. Though still spectacular, its view isn't quite so fine as in the original, but that doesn't seem to worry Derek, better versed than most in the earthy reality of death. There's room for four more rows, he estimates, which at the current take-up rate should last about 40 years. 'And that will definitely see me out', he adds as he resumes his vigil. Spencer would, I'm sure, have approved

*

That figure of four short rows lasting for 40 years niggles away afterwards in the back of my mind. Even with the general depopulation of rural villages, the local newsletter still continues to contain an average of three or four In Memoriam notices each edition. At that rate, those four rows should be full before the end of the year.

Many, though, now opt for cremation, common in ancient Rome but banned thereafter in the Christian West for 1200 years. The given reason was that to burn a corpse denied that individual the prospect of resurrection in body *and* soul on the day of final judgment, as promised in the New Testament. The rule was on occasion waived – when, for example, large numbers of bodies had to be disposed of after a battle, or in times of plague – but the general prohibition on cremation endured until the late nineteenth century. Church objections melted away, and today cremation's share of the 'market' has risen to three quarters.

Some still want their ashes buried in a traditional grave or, more usually, added to an existing one. Of the remaining quarter who continue to opt for a coffin and burial, many prefer to be laid to rest in the network of non-denominational municipal cemeteries – there is one ten miles inland at Fakenham, without a view, but equally without the oversight of the Church. Derek's figure is beginning to make more sense.

Then I have to factor in how few regular worshippers use this church on the one Sunday morning every month when the vicar is here. This churchyard is, after all, specifically a place for those of faith and, in our increasingly sceptical, secular society, individuals who fit that description, or are prepared to be shoe-horned into fitting it, are dwindling. Meanwhile, those without, or undecided, who once might have simply gone along with the whole business of being a Christian to ensure a 'decent' funeral and burial, have plenty of other options. And it is that element of choice that has caused the great shift in attitudes to burial these past 200 years, away from that landmark of the English countryside, the churchyard, and away too from the idea of sacred ground administered by institutional religion.

It is of the history of burial in those earlier Christian centuries that Saint Margaret's speaks most eloquently. Once the Church of Rome had emerged out of shadows and out of the catacombs in the fourth century, churchyards such as this started to develop a monopoly on the business of death in the West. Private and public, Church and state, the individual and the collective were all brought together in a single ending in this one place. As the official religion of the Roman Empire, Christianity steadily assumed ever greater political and social authority, along with responsibility for day-to-day administration, filling the vacuum left as old imperial structures grew corrupt and crumbled in the face of assaults from outside.

The Church took to itself the custodianship of the bodies of the dead. It was a public-spirited, humane impulse, but it had broader consequences. For the ecclesiastical authorities did not leave it there. They also saw fit to impose their own ideas on how the dead should be regarded, treated and, most importantly, judged. As well as outlawing cremation, they abandoned the Roman habit of burying corpses outside city walls, away from the living. The early years of the fifth century saw the establishment of the first graveyard in the centre of Rome. By the seventh century such places were the norm.

Like the Romans, the pre-Christian belief systems of Europe had preferred to bury the dead at a distance from settlements, in groves, funeral mounds and barrows. The landscape, in such creeds, was regarded as having a holy purpose – wells, rivers, trees such as oak and rowan all carried a heightened spiritual significance. Hence burial was in blessed ground, in theory closer to the gods.

The early Christian Church appropriated this concept of a sacred acre, but stamped its own authority by demanding that such sites be well-ordered, regulated plots next to its churches. So some existing burial mounds and groves in the countryside were annexed for Christianity. The churchyard at Ogbourne St Andrew in Wiltshire, for example, close to the prehistoric sites of Salisbury Plain, contains a Bronze Age round barrow, a bowl-shaped burial mound and surrounding ditch. And at the English Heritage site at Knowlton in Dorset, there is a ruined Norman church that had been built inside a Neolithic henge monument. Elsewhere, the 'conversion' was cruder.

Often the simple expedient of erecting an outsized cross slap, bang in the middle of an ancient burial ground was deemed sufficient.

Building a wall around the plot was also popular. Separating the churchyard from all that lay beyond may have started as a sensible way of controlling the sorts of disease spread by rotting corpses, and of excluding hungry animals who might disturb graves (the advent of walled enclosures is said to have contributed to the long-term decline and extinction of the wolf population in Britain), but it also sent out a powerful message about the need to line up alongside the Church to enjoy its protection in death for body and soul.

In its fledgling years, the Church had been strengthened by the cult of martyrs' graves. Once it moved mainstream and martyrdom became a memory, Christianity nevertheless continued to make a link between tombs, altars and churches, but the emphasis was subtly different. For the self-avowedly missionary Church now had ambitions to extend its everyday influence over believers, and the moral codes of society as a whole. By taking to itself the central role in burials, it realized it could achieve its larger goals in bending society to its will.

From the pulpit, congregations were told that the only route to salvation and eternal life after death lay in following the Ten Commandments, set out in Saint Margaret's, as in many ancient country churches, on a painted board. Those judged to have followed the commandments – and the Church was clear that, on earth, it alone was competent to make this particular judgement on behalf of the Christian God – would earn burial and sanctuary in the sacred ground of the churchyard, and hence take at least the first step on the journey to heaven. Those who didn't would be denied a church burial, cast out of the churchyard, and denied God's mercy in perpetuity.

If eternal salvation was the carrot dangled to encourage submission in all things to the authority of the Church, then the presence right outside the church door of the graveyard was the stick. The words from Genesis, 'Remember thou art dust and unto dust thou shalt return' may only have been pronounced from the altar each Ash Wednesday, at the start of Lent, but they echoed throughout the liturgical year and the life of the medieval parish church. The graveyard would often be lit at night by a lantern. In a practical, superstitious way, the light it spread was meant to keep unquiet spirits at bay, but symbolically it also served as a reminder for anyone going about their business of their mortality and the judgement that lay ahead.

The overriding concern in the medieval period, when it came to death and burial, was for the collective fate rather than the individual. Prayers would be offered in church each day for all the souls of the dead of the parish, rather than for any particular one among their number. Once a corpse had been accepted at the lych gate and given a Christian blessing, it would be consigned in its shroud to the common pit in the churchyard. Some wealthier members of the community might merit a wooden or even a lead coffin (which replaced the stone sarcophagi of ancient Rome), especially since such containers were thought to slow decomposition and increase the chances of still having a body to resurrect come Judgement Day (which many, at this time, continued to believe was imminent).

When the common pit was full of bodies to a level of six feet from the surface – deemed sufficient to prevent disease spreading, but often ignored or ineffective as a guideline – it would be covered with soil and quicklime and then left. A new pit would be dug elsewhere in the churchyard. When, in its turn, it was reaching its capacity, the old pit would be uncovered and the bones that were left moved to an ossuary or charnel house, sometimes in a covered cloister or gallery of the church. The first pit could then be reused. It may have been brutal and, to modern sensibilities, ghoulish, but it was, compared to later fashions, very efficient in terms of land use.

Originally seen only in Orthodox Christianity, charnel houses came to Western Europe in the twelfth century. They were at first just store-rooms, but at monasteries and in large city centre churches they developed into places of pilgrimage, the skulls and bones arranged in patterns, even decorated, to draw visitors in. Pilgrims were invited by the spectacle to reflect on the meaning of death and their own prospects for eternity. In Rome, the crypt of Santa Maria della Concezione, a seventeenth century church on Rome's fashionable Via Veneto, still contains to this day the bones of thousands of Capuchin friars, arranged along the walls in the five rooms, embellished with macabre works of art. It was in active use as late as 1870. In Britain, by contrast, few charnel houses or ossuaries survive, the triumph of Protestant ideas after the Reformation sweeping away such features of Roman Christianity deemed superstitious and manipulative. A rare exception is found in the crypt of the thousand-year-old church of Saint Leonard's at Hythe on the Kent coast. In this basement charnel house are 2000 skulls and 8000 long bones (mainly thighs), some from adults, others from children, and a fair number, subsequent scientific tests have shown, from the other side of the Channel.

*

There is no reminder in Saint Margaret's churchyard today of any of the thousands of parishioners who would have been buried here in unmarked graves in medieval times. Even the rich seldom felt the need for a tombstone, and only the very grand indeed would merit a memorial, initially usually within the church building itself or underneath in specially built crypts.

To the medieval mind, the absence of individual grave markings and stones – even for the prosperous – would not have seemed at all odd. It was a time dominated by one immediate worry – that after death the Church would give its blessing to your corpse and accept it. Once that had happened, the corpse itself became unimportant. There was little weeping and gnashing of teeth by relatives at the edge of the common pit. Instead, they stayed inside the church to pray, with the rest of the parish, for the collective souls of the local dead.

In this spirit many medieval churches had a 'burial guild', made up of parishioners who volunteered to oversee both the fate of the corpses received, and the organization of masses for the dead on the third, seventh and thirtieth days after burial, and then again after 12 months, the origin of the phrase 'year's mind' still in use today. The guild would encourage local people to attend such masses in memory of the dead. If there was no prospect of a decent congregation, the guild would fill the pews with the offer of food afterwards, or even cash – echoes of the professional mourners and lamenters of Greece and Rome.

Horrific and unhygienic as the pit now sounds – with all those rotting limbs intertwined and noxious gases escaping – there was a worse fate. The body could be rejected by the local priest. Though Common Law may have upheld a right to burial in your local churchyard, the resident cleric's discretion in applying that right was total. Legal grounds for refusing admittance to God's acre included suicide – directly contrary to Church law – or excommunication, or more generally the 'sin' of living a life at odds with Christianity's norms. In reality, it tended to come down to the priest's judgement or whim, and how susceptible he was to inducements to overlook the deceased's misdemeanors.

Refusal could be qualified. The priest might permit the next best thing to the graveyard, the smaller pit usually at its furthest extremity and reserved for unbaptised infants who were deemed by Christianity to be consigned eternally to Limbo, a concept only officially abandoned by the Catholic Church in 2006. For the most part, though, those denied sacred ground were shut out altogether of the embrace in death of Mother Church, symbolized by the walls round the churchyard, and instead had to be disposed of by their families, in makeshift graves, or simply left to the elements.

As the ambitions and power of the Church grew, it steadily strengthened its grip in such matters. From the ninth century onwards, it actively discouraged and eventually forbade even the wealthy from making their own arrangements for burial on their land. Instead the Church wanted them to find a resting place in the local church, or churchyard. The family plot behind the family home was no longer allowed – unless, of course, the family in question built a church there.

Not every landowner, however, either wanted to or could afford to build his own church – especially in a county such as Norfolk already so well endowed with them. And so instead, the gentry began to build memorials first inside, then underneath and later outside their local churches. Graveyards as we now know them started to develop.

So in parish churches such as Saint Margaret's, tombs started to line the floors and side chapels. These graves usually took the form of a shaft in the earth, lined with masonry. Tomb slabs were aligned with the altar. In some grander churches, there was a return to the fashion of earlier ages, with stone sarcophagi appearing in recesses to house a dead benefactor. Decorated coffin-lids were sometimes carved with a full-length figure of the deceased, especially popular with bishops in their cathedral. Pavement slabs had elaborate enamel or brass inlays, and became part of the decoration of the church building. Funerary art grew in stature as more and more families of means craved their own stand-out memorial.

Not everyone approved. The seventeenth century English diarist, John Evelyn, described his father-in-law's disgust at the 'novel custom of burying everyone within the body of the church and chancel, that being a favour heretoforth granted to the martyrs and great persons, the excess of making churches charnel houses being of ill and irreverent example and prejudicial to the health of the living, besides the continual disturbance of the pavement and seats, and several other indecencies ...'. He makes it sound like the modern plague of roadworks, with the aisles and nave forever being dug up and diversions in force en route to the altar.

The Christian emphasis on the collective experience of death was fading and being replaced by an ever greater concentration on the individual. This trend was in line with Renaissance ideas from the fifteenth century onwards which emphasized the essential worth and potential of each person, as opposed to medieval Christianity's tendency to stress that everyone was part of a single lump of putty in God's hands. And with individualism, older ideas, soundly based in theology and the gospels, about the need for humility and charity in life, and of the equality before God of all in death, were eclipsed by ever more showy personal or family memorials.

Saint Margaret's crop of such commissions is modest – another point in its favour as far as I am concerned. In the south aisle, a series of unobjectionable flat or 'ledger' stones in the pavement date back to the seventeenth century and recall the Thurlows, a local family of prosperous landowners from Polstead Manor, who rose so high as to include in their ranks at least one Lord Chancellor. John Thurlow, 'gentleman', (1619–84) was laid to rest under the same stone as his aunt Bridget (died 1655) and uncle William (died 1630). 'All three lineally descended from the Thurlows' ends the epitaph.

In the opposite aisle is a plainer floor stone, recalling in sloping script Mary Flight, wife of Richard Flight, who died in 1680, a quarter of a century before the oldest surviving stone in the churchyard outside records burials there. One other pair of ledgers exists indoors – a mid-nineteenth century addition in memory of William Mack and his descendants – plus a further one that has been so eroded by time that not a single detail of its inscription remains.

There are no wall tombs or plaques in Saint Margaret's. The most eye-catching memorial in the church, though, is its wineglass pulpit (so-called because of its shape), with its hand-painted panels. It was a gift in 1450, a small plaque records, from John and Katherine Goldale – their choice of a memorial that would not just serve their memory but would also be of use to those who came after them. (Later generations would follow the same impulse by founding hospitals and almshouses in memory of dead relatives.)

The Goldales were not, it should be noted, your traditional gentry. Records show that John, four years earlier, had been prosecuted for stealing oysters from the salt marsh. Presumably this repentant thief had then gone on to make his fortune and this memorial was his way of repaying a debt to his community. Graves can reveal something of the changing social and economic patterns of a community.

*

Many have tried, down the centuries, to capture the essence and appeal of the English country churchyard. Amongst the most successful was Thomas Gray, who composed his celebrated 'Elegy', a fragment of which is quoted at the start of this chapter, in the churchyard of Saint Giles' in the village of Stoke Poges in Buckinghamshire, where he was later buried in 1771, next to his mother.

Poets and churchyards seem to go hand-in-hand, an affinity to be explored in more depth later in this journey. Saint Margaret's exerts a strong pull on the locally-based, but internationally-acclaimed poet and writer of children's stories, Kevin Crossley-Holland. He too has chosen Burnham Norton churchyard as his final resting place. 'I am not a scatterer', he tells me when we meet there on a warm August early evening, 'otherwise I might think of having my ashes scattered on Scolt Head'. We both turn to face out towards the island nature reserve that sits between the salt marshes and the sea.

Kevin often comes to Burnham Norton churchyard to write, he confides, finding inspiration in a place he experiences as 'humming with spirituality'. There is, he believes, a special if ill-defined power in the spot. 'It has something to do with a building of consequence being here, a building whose origins are mysterious, a building that people still want to visit. It is not neglected, the churchyard is not overrun, but neither is it regimented'.

That element of dialogue – between the living and the dead, between any particular instant and the timeless moment, between landscape and the sacred, between the collective weight of a community's history and those who have inherited it – is present in some measure in all graveyards. At Saint Margaret's it is just more tangible.

We wander round as we talk. Every churchyard has its noteworthy 'names' and, here on the coast one such is Richard Woodget, master and captain of the tea clipper, the Cutty Sark. Kevin leads me towards Woodget's large, still strikingly white memorial, located alongside the simpler plots of his parents. Erected after his death in 1928, it is topped by a beached anchor, and appears to have been placed so that – in our imaginations at least – he could sit up and watch the boats passing on the horizon.

Over the centuries, this churchyard has allowed few obstacles to blot out that view. It welcomes the outside in; rather than sheltering behind high walls and artificial barriers, or seeking to create its own aesthetic within its boundaries. There is a row of slightly puny, hunchbacked cherry trees, battered and bent by the prevailing northerly winds that regularly sweep up across this ridge. They stand between the original plot and the newer section, where I had previously bumped into Derek Woodhouse, the gravedigger. To the west and south are beeches and limes, though none of them to my untrained eye ancient or venerable.

Medieval Christianity preferred its churchyards uncluttered and unobstructed. Not only did this exclude any symbolism that might be construed as borrowed from the earlier nature-worshipping creeds that had been squeezed out of existence, it also maximized space for burials, emphasized the *tabula rasa* devastation of death and thereby trumpeted humanity's reliance on the Church in the next life as in this one. There was, though, plenty of variation on this overall ambition. In the south of France, for example, the planting of rosemary in churchyards was popular because its fragrance was said to cover up the smell of rotting flesh in the summer heat.

For much the same reasons the humble yew tree found favour in graveyards further north. Its pungent scent was able to mask unpleasant odours. Perhaps the absence of a yew here, at Burnham

Norton, is explained by the presence of a sea wind just as well suited to dispelling any stink.

The yew had been regarded as sacred in pre-Christian times, though less so than the oak or the rowan (the latter particularly popular with the Celts), and so it was retained as part of the inheritance when the Church absorbed older burial sites. Legend has it that when he landed in Kent in 597, sent by the papacy to convert the English, the monk Augustine, the first Archbishop of Canterbury, conducted a ceremony in which he showered a yew with holy water in order to bring the whole species over to Rome.

The yew's ubiquity in places of mourning was noted by Robert Blair, like Thomas Gray one of that group of mid eighteenth century figures, so fond of reflecting on mortality in churchyards that they are known to history as the 'Graveyard Poets'. In 'The Grave' (1743), Blair writes:

> Well do I know thee by thy trusty yew,
> Cheerless, unsocial plant! that loves to dwell
> 'Midst skulls and coffins, epitaphs and worms

The yew also boasts additional benefits over and above other trees that ensured its survival in churchyards once Christianity felt confident enough to shake off and then expunge its inheritance from pagan customs. Its foliage is toxic. If a medieval farmer allowed his animals to wander in, they risked being poisoned when they nibbled at the yew. And its branches could be adapted for use in various religious festivals: in Spain they are laid on graves on the Day of the Dead, and in English churches, before the global market with planes carrying goods all over the world, and easy availability of anything that takes your fancy, they were used in place of palms on Palm Sunday.

Most significant of all, though, was the ability of the evergreen yew to go on and on and on for centuries if not millennia. It therefore made for an unrivalled symbol of eternal life. Two yews vie for the title of the oldest tree in Britain – one in the churchyard of St Dygain's in Llangernyw, near Conwy, in north Wales, the other at Fortingall in Perthshire, Scotland. Both are said to be between 2,000 and 5,000 years old, stretching all the way back to the Bronze Age. What social history they could tell if they had words.

Often yews were also endowed with legends that linked them with the dead. Commonly these revolved around the idea that the souls in purgatory sat in their branches, or that their ancient roots reached down so far into the earth that they silenced the screams of the tormented way below in hell. So at Llangernyw an ancient, pre-Christian spirit called Angelystor is said to reside in the yew and emerge every Halloween (All Hallows' Eve, the Christian festival that immediately precedes All Saints and All Souls Days) to announce those in the parish who will die in the coming 12 months. Meanwhile at Fortingall, the churchyard lies next door to a Bronze Age burial mound – Cam na Marbh ('Cairn of the Dead') – and is therefore a prime example of Christianity superimposing its claim to custodianship of the souls of the faithful departed over and above thousands of years of funereal practices by other belief systems at the same site.

During the fourteenth century, the tumulus at Fortingall was apparently broken open and reused to bury plague victims. A stone records this event, describing how the dead were 'taken here on a sledge drawn by a white horse led by an old woman'. It is an image to inspire a poet.

Kevin Crossley-Holland has produced his own small collection of verse based in Saint Margaret's churchyard. *Swarm and Honeycomb*, published in 1998, was penned in memory of Lady Margaret Douglas Home, a member of the parish who is buried here under a simple, elegant flat stone. A celebrated translator of Anglo-Saxon poetry and reteller of Norse myths, in addition to his other achievements, Kevin evokes in the collection an England 'a-buzz with saints', missionaries travelling the length of this east coast to bring Christianity. And in 'Jesus of Norton' he captures the magic of this churchyard next-the-sea that inspires him as much as its equivalent at Sète, in southern France, did Paul Valery's 'Le Cimetière Marin' or the Quaker graveyard on the island of Nantucket, Robert Frost:

Infant of the bubbling spring
well in my heart.

Child of the sighing marsh
breathe in my head.

Son of the keen light
quicken my eyes.

Rebel of the restless creeks
tumble in my ears.

Disciple of the rising tide
dance in my heart.

Teacher of the gruff salt-wind
educate my tongue.

It brings us back to the idea of this graveyard's special something being because of its location at a crossing place. 'If you look down to Marsh Farm', Kevin says, directing my gaze once more outwards towards the village of Burnham Norton (Nor-ton – 'north town'), 'it stands only four feet above sea level. So this view that we see is in jeopardy. As are we. And so being here, and looking out to the blade of sea on the horizon somehow manages to call into question all of human life. There is an endless argument going on in this most tranquil of places'.

*

After Kevin has departed, I stay on, waiting for what promises to be a spectacular sunset. There are, for those with the patience to seek them out, stories aplenty in the stones in any graveyard. J. C. Loudon, the inspirer in the nineteenth century of Britain's new breed of manicured urban Victorian cemeteries, delighted in the lessons he found in older country churchyards. 'To the local resident', he wrote in 1843, 'poor, uncultivated by reading, the churchyard is their book of history, their biography, their instructor in architecture and sculpture, their model of taste, and an important source of moral improvement'.

Twenty-first century schooling and communications systems may have made aspects of his claim redundant. 'Moral improvement' is no longer a widely-held ambition, but his bigger point continues to resonate. No budding novelist, I reflect, need ever be short of names for their characters if they happen upon a graveyard. Or soon-to-be-parents' possibilities for naming their unborn child. Morbid? I prefer to see it as part of that human chain that links one generation to the next.

The only impediment to such trawls is where time has worn away inscriptions. In its more legible sections, this churchyard tells of the amazing continuity of local families, a counterpoint to our own age of mass migration. There are the graves of various Uttings, Howells and Grooms, some of them dating back to the eighteenth century, all bearing surnames that are still in daily use in nearby Burnham Market over the door of the greengrocer's, butcher's and baker's.

And though it seems at first glance random in its arrangement, once I take time to study it, there is also a precise geography of death here. The earliest graves are on the east side of the church. Through the orange and yellow lichen that cling to one headstone, I can just about make out the date 1707 and the name R. Ballis. A few plots along William Goude, who died in 1732, is more legible among the group of crumbling, lopsided markers that followed the custom of their age and faced the origin of Christianity in the Holy Land.

By contrast, to the north of Saint Margaret's, there are remarkably few plots. This is because traditionally this side of a church was shunned in still superstitious times for fear that the Devil was lurking in the darkest, gloomiest section of the graveyard. Scared by the sunshine, he would lie in wait there in the shadows to steal souls. All but one of the graves here date from very recently, when shortage of space and the abandonment of old superstitions have presumably overcome older scruples.

I search in vain, though, for any sign that Burnham Norton, like other medieval churches, ever stood at the end of a designated 'lych way' – known popularly as 'corpse roads' – that would have connected it with outlying churches or chapels in the surrounding area that did not have burial rights of their own. There was, as in most medieval church matters, a financial element in such classifica-tions. If the larger churches wanted to keep up the income that came with burials, they had to deter people from choosing to be laid to rest in the grounds of smaller rivals. So they would mark out 'lych ways' to their gates, often lined at intervals with 'coffin stones', where the bearers could rest their load. Where such paths remain – the one between Rydal and Ambleside in the Lake District is an outstanding example, now used by ramblers – it is claimed that they were among the first public rights of way. Once corpses had been carried down a route, the logic seems to have gone, it belonged to the community.

One curiosity I do spot in my search for signs of a corpse road at Burnham Norton is that, when standing in a particular spot in the upper part of the graveyard, there is a direct eye line first to the spire of Saint Clement's at nearby Burnham Overy Town, and then onwards to Saint Withburga's at Holkham. The three ancient churches are lined up like soldiers on parade.

The sun is taking its time to set, and the clouds are arriving late to spoil the show, but my wait is rewarded by a steady stream of visitors who come and go at Saint Margaret's. Some are tourists, on their way back from the beaches, curious about the spire they have spotted while munching their sand-filled sandwiches. Most, though, are local, including the couple who walk up from Burnham Norton with the outsized key that locks the church door at 6 p.m. We exchange greetings and they chat about their connections here. It is a spot that remains, I conclude as I take my leave, for now at least, a meeting place for the community, even in our secular and sceptical times. It may not quite rival the local shop, pub or post office, but this classic English churchyard continues to serve the community of the living, as well as of the dead.

4

Greyfriars' Kirkyard, Edinburgh

The peaks and troughs of Edinburgh city centre disorientate me on a crisp, blue spring day. As I cross the Royal Mile in Old Town, my two-dimensional map isn't up to the task of deciphering the relationship between the grand, elevated street I am walking along and the parallel basement universe of pedestrians and cars I can see way down below in the gaps between the imposing buildings. Somewhere between the two tiers, presumably suspended in mid-air I can't help thinking, is Greyfriars' Kirkyard, but quite where the entrance might be, I can't fathom.

I stop a woman coming out of a café. She's the first person I've seen for a while who isn't carrying a guidebook, so I'm hoping for a local. 'I'm trying to find Greyfriars' Kirkyard', I explain. She smiles encouragingly. 'It can be tricky but you're almost there'. She points up the street. 'Can you see Greyfriars' Bobby?' She is indicating an iron statue of a dog that looks from this distance like Tricky Woo, the pampered pooch beloved of the eccentric Mrs Pumphrey in the TV adaptation of James Herriot's *All Creatures Great and Small* that filled so many Sunday evenings of my childhood. 'It's just away there down an alley to the right'.

'Greyfriars' Bobby' is one of this late sixteenth century kirkyard's two magnets to attract tourists' attention in a city that is a cacophony of competing claims from the bag-pipe(d) music oozing out of shops which promise to identify visitors' clan tartan to the austere seriousness of the elaborate Central Library building on my right as I head 'away there'. Bobby was, the plaque below his life-size model reads, a Skye Terrier who guarded the grave of his night watchman owner, John Gray, known (almost inevitably) as 'Auld Jock', in the adjoining graveyard. Dates are given. I quickly do the maths. Bobby managed just two years at Auld Jock's living, breathing side, or heel, and then spent 14 keeping a lonely vigil over his master's last resting place (only one short of what most humans apparently manage). Quite a feat of devotion, but apparently not so lonely because, when Bobby died in 1872, those who had observed his canine mourning ritual arranged for him to have his own burial spot in the kirkyard, just by the East Gate, since he was not eligible, as a dog, for interment in consecrated ground.

The compromise neatly gets round the double-think in Christianity about animals. In its more crowd-pleasing versions, the Church embraces modern sentimentality about animals, especially those like Bobby believed to possess *Lassie Come Home* special powers of communication and empathy with their owners. Staying with friends in Sussex one weekend, we – and our dog – were taken to their local top-of-a-chocolate-box village church where the vicar, in all seriousness, was holding a blessing service on the main altar for local pets. Yet, in their theology, the mainstream Christian churches relegate the animal kingdom and, indeed, the whole of creation, to the role of serving and sustaining humankind (an attitude found, too, in Islam but not in the older animist traditions, such as Shinto). At its simplest, Christianity holds that animals don't have souls – though I'm sure Mrs Pumphrey was confident, whatever her Yorkshire vicar said to the contrary, of eventual heavenly reunion with Tricky Woo.

As would have been the Duchess of Bedford in the 1910s, when she built a temple of Corinthian columns in the grounds of Woburn Abbey, her family seat, to house a bronze model of her beloved deceased Peke, Che Foo, or 'Wuzzy'. The Chinese, she would have pointed out, had long honoured the memory of Pekes, seeing them as a cut above other animals. And the provision of pet cemeteries, though seen as a modern phenomenon/indulgence that started in France in 1899, has a much longer history. The Egyptians laid out animal graveyards next to the Nile in 1000 BC.

Bobby may not have merited anything quite so grand as Wuzzy's mausoleum, but he makes up for it with quantity. He has not one but three memorials – the iron statue on the main street that doubles as a signpost, a pub named after him next to the alleyway that leads into the kirkyard, and then, greeting me as soon as I enter it, a traditional tombstone in coffee-coloured marble. It was unveiled in 1981 at the behest of the Dogs' Aid Society (Scotland) by HRH Duke of Gloucester (that's what minor royals do). The inscription ends with an arresting flourish of pulpit oratory: 'Let his loyalty and devotion be a lesson to us all'. It apparently still manages to strike a chord because there are several freshly cut bunches of daffodils and tulips placed on the ground in front of the monument.

*

Thanks to the legend of Bobby, this kirkyard has become one of the sights of Edinburgh and so there is no need to root around unaided to uncover its stories. Directly opposite Bobby's grave, and sounding a rather different note, is an outbuilding trading under the name 'The Creepy Wee Shop in the Graveyard'. A variety of walking tours is advertised on posters edged with flames and pinned to blackened windows. This is the cemetery-as-horror-show/tourist attraction par excellence.

The ghoulish displays reveal the second contemporary USP for visitors to Greyfriars' Kirkyard. One group is just setting out with a guide, ready to be entertained and chilled in equal measure. First stopping off point is in the shadow of the ancient Greyfriars church itself, a large, plain structure, softened slightly by being painted in a sandy-coloured wash. It sits on the site of what was once, pre-Reformation, a Franciscan friary. 'Welcome', begins their black-clad leader as I edge forward to eavesdrop, 'to the most haunted spot in Edinburgh'. Cue the sharp intake of breath and nervous laughter.

Graveyards naturally lend themselves, by dint of containing so many corpses, to tales of nocturnal haunting and unquiet souls rising from coffins to terrify those among the living who are foolhardy enough to stray into their environs late at night. There is a religious basis to this. Part of the original purpose of most burial rituals was to contain the dead – i.e. to make sure their spirits did not return to trouble the living – either by covering the hole dug in the earth by stones, rocks, mounds of earth, and/or by building elaborate structures above the ground with gates that could be barred. And so fevered imaginings about the paranormal activities of the dead have long been part of the human condition.

The ghost of Pharaoh Khufu, begetter and tenant of the Great Pyramid at Giza from around 2500 BC, is said still to wander Egypt's Valley of the Kings at midnight, in his full regalia, seeking to make atonement for his cruelty in life. It is a tale gainfully employed today to give an edge to the itinerary of visitors, lest the achievement and endurance of the pyramids is judged to be insufficiently compelling for modern attention spans. That same uneasy relationship between commercialization and preserving the sacred nature of burial grounds is also on display here in Greyfriars' Kirkyard.

A casual glance around the tombs in the area near the gate immediately confirms that this is a cemetery that contains more than its fair share of skull and crossbones decorations, in contemporary culture the stock-in-trade of tall tales of things that go bump in the night. There's even a complete, half-life-size skeleton, etched in stone, on a monument leaning against the east end of the kirk itself. The bright March sunshine notwithstanding, such a cluster of motifs manages to give the place a decidedly sinister edge.

Skull and skeleton decorations have been present in funerary art from Ancient Rome through the Renaissance and on into post-Reformation times. They held a particular appeal for those of a

Puritan Protestant disposition, well-represented in Scotland, when it came to burying their dead, a shorthand reminder of their belief that only a small number of 'the elect' stood any chance of making it into heaven, leaving the rest to rot. And when it comes to the history of seventeenth century Puritanism, Greyfriars' Kirkyard can claim a central role.

In the south-west corner, in a dogleg attached to the main cemetery by a broken-pedimented gateway, is the Covenanters' Prison. To get there, I circle round the tour party. 'Does anyone have a problem', the guide is asking them, in the sort of throaty, cracked voice favoured by maverick detectives in *noir* thrillers, 'walking over dead bodies?' A brittle titter spreads through his group. 'Because here you are walking on 100,000 bodies'. Gasps. 'Once this was the only burial ground in Edinburgh and they packed them in'. I can almost hear the bones of the skeletons cracking under my footsteps in the silence that follows.

The gates to the Covenanters' Prison are secured by a large padlock. Beyond them is a long grassy corridor flanked on both sides by substantial eighteenth and nineteenth century memorials, all of similar design, each bearing an outsized inscribed plaque shaped like the façade of a Roman villa and containing the details of the deceased. All are fronted by a curiously suburban low-walled garden, albeit minus the privet hedge. It looks as peaceful as the corner of any other city centre graveyard and, if it were not separated by locked gates, would be indistinguishable from the rest of the kirkyard. Yet back in the winter of 1679–80, this was where some 400 captured prisoners, all Puritan Protestants from the Covenanters' Army that had taken on the Crown over matters of religion and been defeated, were held in such appalling conditions that many met long-drawn-out and gruesome deaths. Their still suffering spirits are reputed to be well-represented among those who continue to haunt this infamous corner of Edinburgh.

Such is the reputation of the old Covenanters' Prison on the multitude of websites that exist for those keen to swap paranormal experiences that special permission is required to go in. It feels like a tacit endorsement by the local authority that runs the kirkyard of the claims that this section is haunted.

'Myself and my husband went there in 2006', writes Emmie, a self-diagnosed 'conductor', on one of the most popular websites. 'My parents had been on the tour previously and said nothing had happened and that it was a great laugh and we should go. So we did. Going around the graveyard and hearing stories was interesting and fun, then the serious bit as we get to the gates of the prison. I made sure my husband was standing behind me. We were near the back. My arms were by my sides and he was holding my hands. Then, as the guide was speaking, I experienced a tightness around my arms, like a band was put around them. Then my fingers in unison started to go numb, little fingers towards the thumb. Then I couldn't breathe and started to go woozy and could not stand up. My husband took me outside. Just before I could step out of the gates, something behind me kicked me at the back of the knees and my legs went from under me. I can only describe the sheer despair and hate and terror within my body. I wailed the place down like a banshee. But the strange thing was, it didn't feel like it was coming from me. It was almost like feeling the tortured souls of the prisoners, and the crying was a type of relief or expression. Mad I know [but] the next day I was left with bruises on my arms and legs that looked like finger marks'.

My first instinct with such tales is to dismiss them with a smile. And my second and third. Hauntings, ghosts, troubled spirits are in the eye of the beholder. If you are predisposed to feel, see or imagine – delete as appropriate – such paranormal manifestations, then it is not surprising if a visit to a graveyard, especially one that markets itself as creepy, gets you going. But a note of caution. While I have never, consciously, seen anything that might count as a ghost, and therefore essentially must lack the requisite predisposition, I have on occasion been in rooms, houses, and dips in the landscape that make me shiver involuntarily. There was one house I once visited near Newcastle that had an atmosphere so malign, I had to leave. Isn't that the first step on the same paranormal journey? And while the mainstream churches generally pooh-pooh reports of spirit and demonic possession, and refer those claiming to be in the sulphourous claws of the devil to psychiatrists, they also maintain a network of exorcists.

*

The Covenanters took their name from the pledges or covenants made by Puritan Presbyterians from the 1550s to 1580s to keep the Church of Scotland exclusively Protestant and resist the Catholic encroachments of Mary, Queen of Scots. On that occasion, they prevailed and continued to hold sway after England and Scotland were united under Mary's son James VI/James I in 1601. However, when her grandson, Charles I, started to pick away at the religious settlement at the behest of his Anglican bishops down south, a large crowd gathered in Greyfriars' Kirkyard in February 1638 to defend the covenants against the Stuart king's encroachments, an act of defiance which led to the Bishops' Wars of 1639–40.

Again the Covenanters came out on top and remained so after the defeat and execution of Charles I by Parliamentary forces led to Cromwell's Puritan-influenced Commonwealth. The restoration of the Stuarts under Charles II in 1660, however, challenged their spiritual and political hegemony in Scotland and finally led to the defeat of the Covenanters' Army at Bothwell Brig in 1679.

Of the 1200 prisoners taken, a third were confined in this strip of land, alongside the kirkyard, presumably intending to teach them a very public lesson by returning them to the site of the original

1638 rebellion. Internment camps are something that, nowadays, we associate with unenlightened overseas regimes, but those held here were given little food and inadequate shelter in the hope that deprivation would persuade them to renege on their loyalty to the Covenant. A handful did yield and were released, but the majority stuck to their guns. Some were transported to penal colonies. The rest were tortured – literally torn limb from limb, according to some accounts – into submission. Their broken bodies were then piled up in mass graves, with their severed heads put on display on the walls of the graveyard to deter others from imitating their defiance.

The principal tormenter was Sir George MacKenzie, 'Bluidy MacKenzie' in folklore, a local lawyer, staunch defender of the royal prerogative in public and religious life (though evidently in private a gentle, bookish figure, given to setting up libraries and penning essays on how to lead a moral life). By one of those ironies of graveyard geography, his own grand, circular and now near derelict domed stone mausoleum today stands on the south wall of the kirkyard, no more than 20 yards from the scene of his appalling crimes. It is the largest monument in the whole cemetery (more imposing even than the square mausoleum built close by to remember the Adam family, creators of eighteenth century Edinburgh's elegant built environment) and gives absolutely no hint of remorse or repentance. Quite the opposite.

If MacKenzie and his family intended his memorial to be the last word on his outstanding and wholly positive contribution to history, they have been disappointed. They were pushing against the tide. A simple rule of graveyards is that, however emphatic, celebratory and triumphant the monument, it can never stop the past misdeeds of the great, good and not-so-good resurfacing. First, historians challenged the authorised version and painted a negative picture of MacKenzie and his deeds. And, more recently, in the 'creepiest place on earth' caricature that has been imposed on this kirkyard, MacKenzie's mausoleum has been given the tag 'black'. Eye-witness reports say it is haunted by a poltergeist believed to be the man himself, his conscience too troubled for him to rest easy on the other side. And so it is twinned with the nearby Covenanters' Prison as inexorably as the wicked witch is with Snow White.

I position myself outside it and watch as a young couple break away from the main tour group to take playful photographs of themselves on its crumbling steps, underneath the buddleia poking out of the neglected roof. It certainly has the air of a building auditioning for a part in a Christopher Lee film, but that may simply be my imagining. A 2004 court case added to its legend by giving the monument its own peculiar place in legal history. Two local youngsters, 17 and 15 at the time, were found guilty in the High Court of the ancient crime of 'violating a sepulchre'.

It was the first such case in over 100 years. The pair had broken into the MacKenzie Mausoleum, encouraged no doubt by its reputation for darkness, opened one of the coffins contained in the circular inner room, taken out the skeleton, and then detached the skull. Reports vary as to what they did with it, from sacrilege to silliness. 'What lies behind this offence, and always has done', the presiding judge told them in passing sentence, 'is the notion that in any civilized society there should be respect for the dead'.

Which brings me neatly to what is arguably Greyfriars' Kirkyard's most important contribution to an understanding of the history of how we treat the dead – and also, a relatively minor part (to judge by its time allocation on the guided tour) of its 'spooky' reputation. A few paces from the MacKenzie Mausoleum, nestling near the wall of the kirk, are two otherwise undistinguished graves. 'Sacred to the Memory of Anne Craigie Lindesay died May 1838' reads the plaque on one. The words are engraved not in stone – as everywhere else in the kirkyard – but on iron. The plaque is in the centre of a long, low cage of bars, freshly painted in black, that covers the grave. It is padlocked to matching iron fastenings set into the ground round the grave. This is – to use the technical term – a mortsafe and one of only a handful remaining in their original location in Britain. The mortsafe was a solution to a pretty universal problem – grave-robbing.

*

In medieval times, the skills of a surgeon were usually learnt on the job, often by untrained practitioners known as barber-surgeons, who would treat the war-wounded in makeshift hospitals on the battlefield. (They are the precursors of today's barbers, the red and white pole that still is displayed outside a traditional barbers' shop having originally been the mark of a barber-surgeon, the choice of colours a reflection on the bloodletting that went with their efforts to save life on *ad hoc* operating tables.)

There was, however, always some kind of covert trade in the dead bodies required for medical research. It is hinted at on the grave of William Shakespeare, at Holy Trinity Church, Stratford-upon-Avon. His dates (1564–1616) are followed by a verse that ends: 'Bleste be the man that spares thes stones, And curst be he who moves my bones'.

By the mid eighteenth century, surgery was developing and fast becoming a regulated professional calling. In 1745, George II gave his blessing to the establishment of the College of Surgeons. Those who wanted to join its ranks were required to undertake formal training in the arts of dissection, which required them to practise on recently deceased cadavers. Any shortage there had previously been was as nothing to the clamour for corpses that now resulted.

The traditional source of supply was criminals sentenced to death. From 1752, English judges were given powers not just to order those guilty of serious (and some not so serious) crimes to be hanged, but also to rule that the defendant's body should be used thereafter for medical purposes. It was a curiously high-minded combination of moral approbation and dedication to medical progress. In the same spirit, the resulting dissection would often be undertaken as a public entertainment, with the surgeon, surrounded by his students, centre stage and local citizens looking on from the gallery as he wielded the knife.

An insight into how casual attitudes were to dead bodies then is provided by the case of a Bristol man, John Horwood, hanged for murder in 1820. In 2010, one of his descendants discovered, when researching the family tree, that parts of his skeleton, left over after his corpse had been dissected in front of students at Bristol Royal Infirmary, were being stored at the city's university in an understairs cupboard. The rope was even still in place round the neck, but what distressed them most was that his skin had been tanned and turned into a book binding. The resulting volume was kept in the local Records' Office and was regarded as such a treasure that the family's request to have it handed back, as remains of their relative, was refused. The skeleton was returned and a formal burial was arranged alongside other Horwoods in a local churchyard.

By the early nineteenth century, judges were becoming more lenient in their sentencing, though, and the supply of corpses from the gallows was falling from a peak of several hundred in the mid 1700s to just 50 a year in the 1820s. By 1831, it was reported that in London there had been only 11 bodies for the estimated 900 student surgeons in training at the city's hospitals.

Enter the Resurrectionists (*'les corbeaux'* or 'the crows' in France) who would creep into graveyards after dark and exhume newly buried bodies so as to sell them to the local medical school or school of anatomy. Jerry Cruncher, in Charles Dickens' *A Tale of Two Cities*

(1859), is a 'Resurrection man' by night and a bank porter by day (as well as a wife-beater, a nasty habit that he renounces at the same time as giving up his illicit trade).

In the absence of refrigeration, the cadavers had to be no more than a couple of weeks old to be fit for purpose. Too much decomposition would render them useless for the students. So the body-snatchers would operate in the big cities, close to the medical schools. Their activity was illegal, but was regarded by the authorities as a necessary evil and so was punishable only by a fine. Oddly, if the body-snatcher also turned his hand to grave-robbing, he risked an altogether more serious punishment from the magistrates.

Elaborate techniques were developed to avoid detection. One consisted in the body-snatchers digging a tunnel from somewhere outside the graveyard. It would then run under the ground at roughly the same level as the coffins had been buried. In the best case scenario, their target could be dislodged from its last resting place, pulled along the tunnel and out of the cemetery, without the top soil of any grave being disturbed.

If the law took a relaxed attitude to such activities, grieving relatives did not. For the six-week period when a body was considered sufficiently intact to be of value to the students, there were various precautions a family could take. For the rich, there was the option of encasing it in a mausoleum, such as those that line the walls of the kirkyard, or laying it under a slab of stone so substantial that it would defeat even the most resourceful body-snatcher.

For the poor, without the money to pay for such peace of mind, it was often a question of taking it in turns to guard the grave 24 hours a day. Some graveyards, especially those near medical schools, even installed watchtowers, just as now we would have recourse to closed-circuit security cameras. In Glasgow a society of grave-watchers was established that at one stage amounted to 2000 members. But the nightwatchman could succumb to sleep, or be frightened away by the diversionary tactics of the body-snatchers. A safer option, therefore, was the mortsafe, popular from the early years of the nineteenth century. It could be hired from the churchyard authorities for six week periods, fitted and then secured by a padlock over a standard grave.

There were various models. The cage arrangement, covering the whole grave, as seen here, was the most popular. In London's Science Museum, there is a variation that is more like a metal envelope that fitted tightly round the wooden coffin to stop anyone gaining entry. And at Udny Green in Aberdeenshire, a morthouse was built in the graveyard as a kind of specially protected vault. Behind its locked doors was a large turntable on which seven coffins could fit at any time. The theory was by the time one had completed a full circle on the turntable, the contents would be so decayed that it would be of no interest to grave-robbers and hence safe to bury in consecrated ground unprotected.

The prevalence of mortsafes in Scotland intrigues historians. They do exist elsewhere but they seem to have caught on here as nowhere else. One suggestion is the prevalance of Puritan/Presbyterian beliefs with their marked preoccupation with resurrection, come Judgement Day, both of the soul and the body. So protecting the corpse was of paramount importance.

The popularity of mortsafes in Edinburgh is more easily explained. The city was a pioneer in the training of surgeons. The Faculty of Medicine at the city's university was founded in 1726, while its School of Anatomy was so popular that in 1764 a 200-seat Anatomy Theatre was opened close to Greyfriars' Kirkyard in Old Town to accommodate all the students keen to observe their teachers dissecting dead bodies.

Science and religion found themselves in fierce competition against the backdrop of the eighteenth century scientific enlight-enment, of which Edinburgh was a particular centre. Surgeons, on the one hand, would say that they could save more lives by perfecting their techniques using the bodies of those already dead. Churchmen, for their part, blocked this laudable aim because it would cut across deeply held beliefs in the nature of the afterlife.

Their debate is a variation on the same battle seen today between scientists, keen to keep hold of unearthed remains from thousands of years ago for experiments that, they say, will reveal ever more about the origin of the species, and the God-fearing descendants of those whose bodies were so crudely carted away, anxious only to reinter them in line with their belief systems. Or again, the opposition of some more evangelical Christian groups to the now widespread practice of carrying organ donation cards. To bequeath your heart, kidneys, lungs, or corneas at your death, which science can now use to prolong, or improve, the life of another, is still seen, in such Church circles, as giving up your chance of bodily resurrection.

*

The Greyfriars' Kirkyard mortsafes are also a reminder – as the tour guide is now busy telling his group – that it was in Edinburgh that the most notorious of all body-snatchers operated. Brendan Burke and William Hare, both Irish immigrant labourers, began in November 1827 by selling for £10 the body of a lodger in the boarding house run by Hare's wife to Dr Robert Knox, an extramural anatomy lecturer at Edinburgh Medical School. The old man in question had died of natural causes. Their success made them grow bolder. Their next victim was another lodger in the same house, sickly but still alive when Burke and Hare smothered him. Thereafter they picked up the homeless and rootless off the streets of Edinburgh, or in public houses around the city, plied them with drink, invited them back to the lodging house, and then killed them. Among those they targeted were a grandmother and her blind grandson.

By the time the tally of corpses the pair had delivered to Dr Knox reached 17, they were apprehended. In October 1828 another lodger in Mrs Hare's rooming house had grown so suspicious that he called in the authorities. Hare confessed everything in return for immunity from prosecution. Burke was tried, found guilty and condemned to be hanged. Some 20,000 people gathered for what took on, the *Scotsman* reported, 'the lively aspect of a gala day'.

His dead body was used for an anatomy lecture – though not by Dr Knox (who seemed to suffer no other consequences for his part in the crimes). The queue for seats exceeded all expectations. A crowd of 24,000 gathered and most were finally admitted only when the lecture had ended. 'The corpse was stretched out on the dissecting table in a state of nudity', according to the *Scotsman*, 'and, though the skull had been taken off to allow the lecturer to expose the brain, the eyes were more than half open, quite bright and the features were so little distorted that they were recognised by numbers to whom he had been previously unknown by name. The sight, on the whole, was very far from being agreeable ... Incredible as it may appear, it is nevertheless true that seven females pressed in among the crowd'. No squeamishness about dead bodies back then.

Despite Burke's fate, he and Hare inspired others. The 'London Burkers', a group of men operating out of the slums area that is now the fashionable Columbia Road Flower Market in the East End, is believed to have murdered anything up to 500 vagrants to supply Saint Bartholomew's, Saint Thomas's and King's College schools of anatomy with corpses at £8 a time. They were eventually captured and executed.

Parliament was roused to frame a response. The 1832 Anatomy Act set up a licensing system for teachers of anatomy and identified new sources of corpses among unclaimed bodies and those who had died in the workhouses – another reason why such institutions struck such terror in the hearts of the poor.

The story of Burke and Hare – subsequently popularized in Robert Louis Stevenson's fictional account of their deeds, *The Body Snatchers*, which was in its turn made into a classic horror film of the same title in 1945 with Boris Karloff and Bela Lugosi – is another contributory factor to Greyfriars' current ghoulish reputation. But even that is evidently not quite enough for the tourist guide, as he passes close by the mortsafes. Or perhaps he is just trying to lighten the mood with a bit of twenty-first century banter. The kirkyard, he is telling his group, with an air of authority in his gravelly voice, is 'the second most popular place in Edinburgh for public sex'. I wait in vain for someone to ask him which location tops the charts.

In more seemly mood, the authorities have at least provided a notice-board to distract visitors' attention away from all this voyeurism. It notes the famous – rather than infamous – names buried in Greyfriars' Kirkyard. These range from James Douglas, Earl of Morton, Regent of Scotland, who died in 1581, to William McGonagall, poet, who departed in 1902. But perhaps the best antidote to thoughts of death and desecration is an uplifting scheme running in the kirkyard, in co-operation with the kirk itself. Local young people are being trained for the jobs market in workshops on the other side of the north wall of the cemetery. Some are restoring old wooden pews and some learning about gardening. The fruits of their labours – literally – have been planted between the tombs, softening the landscape and introducing new life into the place of shadows and ghosts.

So, in front of the tombstone of John Ritchie and his extensive family (they are, as the guide had warned, packed in tight here), there is a small bed edged with new bricks and containing a variety of herbs. Each is described by a slate slab, in chalk handwriting: 'Fennel – Foeniculum Vulgare, stewing herb for flavour, can be eaten as a vegetable. Ancient Greek slimming aid'. And further round, nearest the largest of all the monuments, to Elizabeth Paton, is a bed of 'Fragerna vesca – wild strawberry, a regular delicacy at the court of James IV. A tea from the leaves is said to be a good tonic for convalescence'.

Convalescence perhaps from too much Hammer horror. Next to all these skulls and crossbones, tales of torture and body-snatching, the beds offer a modest counterweight, not that the group now heading back for the 'Creepy Wee Shop' is pausing to take much notice.

5

Père-Lachaise, Paris

*'Show me the manner in which a Nation or Community cares
for its dead and I will measure with mathematical exactness the
tender mercies of its people, their respect for the laws of the land,
and their loyalty to high ideals'.*

ATTRIBUTED TO WILLIAM GLADSTONE (1809–98)

There can't be much peace with Oscar Wilde as your neighbour – even in a cemetery. Pity then the Papeils, whose family plot is next door to Wilde's grave in Père-Lachaise. They were here first and duly erected a solid, dignified, no doubt expensive, but pretty standard for its time marble plinth on their regulation three square metres.

Neither epitaph nor history records the Papeils' achievements, but their choice to be buried in Père-Lachaise at the end of the nineteenth century suggests they were haute bourgeoisie and ambitious. You paid to be here, over and above the rates charged by other cemeteries around Paris, because of the company you were keeping in death – Balzac, Chopin, Delacroix, Ingres and so on. It was, one wag suggested, like purchasing the *Légion d'honneur* in death, hardly a new concept since the medieval Church had peddled indulgences to ensure speedy boarding for the soul of your dear departed into heaven. Here, though, in this new variation, the emphasis was firmly on earthly immortality. A plot in Père-Lachaise carried with it the promise of getting you noticed by visitors ever after, drawn as they were and are to what is today routinely called 'the celebrity cemetery'. Divine judgement in eternity here rubs up against the more tangible verdict of subsequent generations. In theory the latter should be more controllable, but the Papeils seem to have disproved this theory. They have got rather more than they bargained for.

In 1909, Robert Ross purchased the plot next door on behalf of his one-time lover, Oscar Wilde, who had died in exile and in disgrace in Paris nine years earlier. The passage of time tends to eclipse the literary reputations of most writers, however lauded in their day, but Wilde is one of the few for whom it has done the opposite, allowing his enduring worth as a writer to triumph over passing sensation. In 1909, though, the memory of Wilde's notoriety was still fresh. He was as known for his published works as he was for his imprisonment in Reading Gaol for gross indecency, a very public humiliation that had precipitated his early death, at the age of 46, following an operation for an ear infection picked up in prison.

In 1914, any concerns the Papeils' descendents may have had over the character of their new next-door neighbour were confirmed when the adjoining plot was filled to bursting point in all three dimensions with a monument quite unlike anything else seen up to then, or since, in Père-Lachaise. Which, indeed, is going some, since this cemetery contains just about every style and architectural variation on the theme of a memorial.

Thanks to a gift of £2,000 from Wilde's friend and admirer, Helen Carew, Ross had commissioned the newly fashionable sculptor, Jacob Epstein. He must have seemed an appropriate choice since he was at that time in the midst of the sort of prurient public scandal that Wilde knew all too well. Epstein's frieze of naked and semi-naked figures for the headquarters of the British

Medical Association in London had been condemned by some as pornographic.

The tall, thick, squared-off shoulder-high block of stone he carved for Wilde is decidedly top-heavy and features a huge winged figure, half human, and half beast, like a mythical creature about to fly away from the stone that attaches it to the ground. Epstein variously said that this beast had been inspired by ancient Assyrian tomb sculptures he had seen in the British Museum, or by Wilde's little known poem about the Ancient World, 'The Sphinx': 'a beautiful and silent Sphinx has watched me/through the shifting gloom./Inviolate and immobile she does not rise she/does not stir'. The best guess is that it was a mixture of both.

Were this monument a building in the city of the living, rather than a tombstone in the city of the dead, the Papeils, as neighbours, would undoubtedly have had a Rights of Light claim, since their own premises are put in the shade, in every way. But it was not the size or shadow cast that caused Epstein's creation to be hastily covered up in a sheet once it had been put in place. It was the naked birdman's genitals. The cemetery authorities received complaints (possibly from the neighbours) that it was an indecent and inappropriate exhibition for a graveyard, as judged by the standards of the time. And these required modesty, even in death. No matter that the Book of Job promised, 'naked I came from my mother's womb, naked I shall return'.

After prolonged haggling a compromise was agreed whereby a fig leaf was placed over the offending parts, returning to the vandalism of previous ages when various statues and frescoes in the Vatican, including Michelangelo's *Last Judgement*, had been similarly amended to spare prudish blushes. This particular clash between one person's definition of the modesty appropriate to a place where the dead are buried and another's demand that a free-spirited writer be remembered by a free-spirited sculpture rumbled on until the 1920s, when a group of anti-censorship protestors tried to chisel off the offending fig leaf and ended up inadvertently carrying out a castration. It could be a scene from a farce. Legend has it that the detached lump of stone was thereafter used as a paperweight on the cemetery superintendent's desk.

True or not, the tale has only served to push Wilde's grave to the top tier of the list of 'most visited' sites in Père-Lachaise, at least when I go to the cemetery to conduct a poll on a grey June morning. There is a decent-sized gathering of 25 or so clustered around Epstein's sculpture, all individuals and couples and family groups, not a single coach party. One is sitting on the Papeil tomb, as if it were a park bench, another using it as a vantage point to get a better angle with his camera on Wilde's memorial. There are also a couple of rucksacks propped up against it and, later, one young girl, with long flowing hair, uses the top as a writing desk while she scribbles in her journal. Such is the daily indignity of being Wilde's neighbours, a sure case of be careful of what you wish for. In any other less-celebrated Paris cemetery, they could have rested in peace.

As I approach the gaggle, two young women walk up to me brandishing a camera phone and pointing to Wilde's tomb. They apparently speak little English but are gesturing that they want a photograph of them with it as a backdrop. I duly oblige. One holds up her finger, as if to say 'one more'. I nod and am about to press the button when I notice them backing towards the monument itself. Both bend forward, eyes pointed at the camera but heads turned towards the stone and plant a lipstick kiss on it as I take the shot.

This is one of those curious customs that grows up around famous graves. Its origins seem to lie in that row over the fig leaf. Before it was hacked off, it had been covered with red kiss marks. Since its removal, these lipstick bouquets have spread all over the lower portions of Epstein's sculpture. The imprint is evidently hard to clean off because of the oil in the cosmetic, which has pitted the surface of the stone. Guide books warn that a guard is in position to stop them 'defacing' the memorial – usually a surefire way of encouraging any tradition – but there is no sign today of the ban being policed. Hounded out of England in life by people spitting at him in the street, and on occasion marching up and slapping him, in death Wilde is apparently more publicly and ostentatiously loved than any of the other famous names here.

(*I made my visit before, in the autumn of 2011, a modest restoration was carried out to remove the lipstick marks. A barrier is now in place to deter those who wish to continue the custom. It may also bring the Papeils a little more peace in their eternal slumber. But I wouldn't count on it.*)

Originally, the grave, with its epitaph from 'The Ballad of Reading Gaol' – 'And alien tears will fill for him/ Pity's long broken urn/ For his mourners will be outcast men/ And outcasts always mourn' – was treated as a shrine by the gay community, seeing in Wilde's imprisonment for 'the love that dare not speak its name' (copyright Lord Alfred Douglas, Wilde's partner) a mirror of the enduring prejudices they faced. That is still one part of its appeal to judge from messages scratched on its rear. 'Thank you for all the inspiration, you were right', reads one. 'For your information Stephen Fry loves you in case you didn't know, love Tony', says another. (Fry, an outspoken critic of homophobia, especially in the Catholic Church, played Wilde in a 1997 film.)

But the circle of those drawing inspiration from Wilde's grave has also widened (as anti-gay prejudice has retreated in the West) to embrace all outcasts, and at the same time has been diluted by being conflated with traditions attached to other sites in Père-Lachaise. The grave elsewhere in the cemetery of the thwarted lovers, Abelard and Héloïse, for example, used to be the place to leave *billets doux*, but there are a good few propped up against Wilde's tomb today.

What brings you here? I ask my two subjects as I hand back their camera phone. They evidently understand enough English to reply in unison, 'Oscar Wilde'. I can almost hear them adding 'duh', or its equivalent in Japanese. But what is it about Oscar Wilde? I persist. Their English is broken but should be up to answering this one. Yet they just shrug. His plays, his novel, his sayings? I prompt. They look blank. I'd lay money on them not having read more than the verse that serves as his epitaph. Perhaps they've seen the Stephen Fry biopic.

After we've said a fond farewell, they insist on taking a picture of me too; I pause next to the Papeil tomb by way of counterbalance. I resist the temptation to perch on it, though they must be used to it by now. So Wilde, among some visitors to Père-Lachaise, is now remembered for being remembered. That is one purpose of a graveyard, I suppose, especially a celebrated one, and even more so when your friends erect a striking and controversial monument over your remains (Ross's ashes were placed in there too in 1950). It is also the logical development of the whole Père-Lachaise story and its deliberate policy of seeking to house the graves of the famous. Don't bother building libraries or museums to honour the memory and promote the works of dead writers and artists. A tomb that people can visit demands so much less by way of time or knowledge. Its focus is the life – or at least the barest outline of the life conveyed in dates and a single quotation, if that – rather than the work. It is a depressing thought.

But Père-Lachaise has a more important claim in this tale of how to read a graveyard. It was the first modern municipal cemetery. And it is also the classic example of the cemetery as a political statement, in this case of anti-clericalism and, hard though it is to believe it now, egalitarianism.

*

It is ironic that the pioneer in breaking the Church's stranglehold on public burials is named after a Catholic priest. François de la Chaise, better known as Père-Lachaise, was a Jesuit and King Louis XIV's confessor. He died in 1709 but he and his extended family were popularly associated with a large Jesuit property in the east of Paris, on the Mont Louis hill, so called after Louis XIV came to visit his confessor there. It was therefore known as Père-Lachaise. When the Jesuit order was suppressed by the papacy in 1763, the property was sold off but the Père-Lachaise name stuck. During the French Revolution the land was confiscated and passed to the city's municipal authorities.

The state of churchyard cemeteries in Paris had long been a matter of public outrage, mirroring concerns in other expanding cities across Europe. Only five per cent of the urban population managed to avoid their corpse, wrapped in a simple shroud, simply being thrown into the pit – or '*fosse commune*' – which lay open all the year round next to the church. It was, as in Burnham Norton, the fact that it was located on consecrated ground that mattered, not the manner of disposal. Here, though, to accommodate the burgeoning population, the pits would be 20 feet square on the surface and go down to a depth of 30 feet, a hell of tangled, rotting corpses. Most were covered, when not being used, by rough planks that did little to keep in the smell or disease. When the pit was full, often to bursting, it would be covered with quicklime, to rot the flesh, and then a layer of soil. It took two years, it was believed, for bodies to be reduced to bone at which point the pit could be reopened, the skeletons removed to an ossuary, and then reused.

It was a brutal, unsentimental practice, and few felt it right or proper, but they had no voice. It was only with the rise of the bourgeoisie in the early years of the eighteenth century that protests began to be heard, amplified by Enlightenment figures who objected on grounds of public health, out of an anticlerical distrust of Church control over burial, and also because philosophically they held to the egalitarian position that each individual was worth more than simply being thrown in a common pit when they died.

The travel writer, François-Marie Marchant de Beaumont, mixed high principles with high disdain in describing the churchyards of Paris in the early 1700s. 'The remains of the vulgar masses went incessantly to stuff the vast communal pits. Putrid miasmas struck neighbourhoods with epidemics as if to punish the living for lack of respect for the dead'.

The public health risks were highlighted in learned reports throughout the century. In 1713, Marc-René D'Argenson, lieutenant general of the Paris police, was prompted to look into practices in cemeteries by complaints about the polluted air in certain parts of the city. At Clamart, next to the Royal Botanical Gardens, he recorded that two open pits, created to hold just 10,000 bodies each, contained 13,000 in one case and 18,000 in the other. Descriptions of piles of corpses stacked so high that dead limbs could be seen over the churchyard walls are not unusual.

As a result of D'Argenson's report, a new regulatory regime was laid down in statute, limiting the pits to 500 bodies, but there was no way of enforcing it in the face of opposition from the Church which enjoyed the protection of a privileged position at the royal court. It saw such efforts by civic authorities as an encroachment on its internal affairs, and on its ability to raise funds via burial fees. To those who complained about the smell, it liked to reply that rotting flesh was a sacred odour that concentrated the mind on the prospect of eternal life – and sent people scurrying back to Church in fear of ending up with the devil.

Subsequent reports in 1734 and 1763 to the *Parlement* of Paris were likewise ignored, but by 1776 this legislative body, though still far from democratic, had grown sufficiently in muscle (thanks to the campaigns of the middle classes and Enlightenment thinkers) to force Louis XVI to close the unsanitary cemeteries of Paris. It was decreed that all burials were hitherto to be redirected, on the model of ancient Rome, to sites outside the city limits.

The king did, however, insist on exempting the graveyard next to the Church of the Saints-Innocents, the largest in Paris and dating back to the tenth century. He was acting, it was said, at the behest of the Archbishop of Paris, but it was a decision he came to regret. In 1780 the sheer weight of bodies dumped in mass pits near the cemetery walls caused these boundaries to collapse and spill their contents into the cellars of neighbouring houses. The scandal that ensued added fuel to the popular fire that the monarchy and the Church were both corrupt and incompetent. Too late did Louis order the closure of the Saints-Innocents graveyard (later the site of a vegetable market) and decreed the transfer, under the supervision of the Royal Society of Medicine and usually at night to avoid causing further public distress, of some six million skeletons from it and other now defunct city centre cemeteries. The horror of the degradation of the Saints-Innocents, with its resident prostitutes and avaricious clergy, is explored in Andrew Miller's award-winning 2011 novel, *Pure*, as it chronicles the emptying of charnel pits that are as deep as mines.

The displaced remains were placed into a new burial chamber that had been fashioned to the west of the city out of former limestone quarries. This vast new ossuary was christened the 'Paris Catacombs' in 1786 by Archbishop Leclerc de Juigné. It was, he said, a revival of the Roman Catacombs that had housed the early martyrs.

If de Juigné was hoping to present the Catholic Church as the victim of a similar persecution, he would have regarded events three years later as proving his point. Revolution swept the country, cost the king and queen their lives, and saw the Church officially abolished. Anticlericalism was still the dominant mood when, in 1804, the First Consul, Napoleon Bonaparte, unveiled his plan to open a ring of out-of-town cemeteries around Paris. They were to practise the highest standards of hygiene and be open to all, regardless of their standing with the Catholic Church. Burials within the city's 11 central *arrondissements* were henceforth banned. Battered and broken by the Revolution, the Church was in no position to object.

Napoleon is right up there among the most significant reformers of the manner in which we treat the dead. Sanitary, regulated grave-yards appealed to that same sense of good order that produced the Napoleonic Code to end feudalism, sort out local government and streamline the administration of justice. A return to the practices of ancient Rome in separating out the living from the dead, moreover, chimed with Bonaparte's view of himself as the natural successor of the Roman emperors (soon after giving the green light to Père-Lachaise he was proclaimed Emperor by the French Senate). And, despite agreeing a concordat with the Church in 1801 after the Revolutionary upheaval, he was firmly of the view that practical matters (such as burial) should be the domain of the state not bishops. As an advocate of religious freedom – passing laws that tackled discrimination against Jews and Protestants – he found intolerable the untrammelled authority hitherto enjoyed by the Catholic Church over the earthly fate of the dead of all creeds.

As Napoleon's empire spread across Europe, so too did the model of his reform of graveyards. In 1805, for example, he was crowned King of Italy, in which role he passed a decree banning all further burials in the over-crowded and disease-ridden churchyards of Venice. He replaced them by joining the outlying islands of San Michele (formerly a prison) and San Cristofero della Pace. The canal that separated them was filled in and the land enclosed behind high walls familiar to any tourist who today has travelled on a vaporetto in the Lagoon. Special funeral gondolas have subsequently carried out to the Cimitero di San Michele thousands of bodies, including Stravinsky, Diaghilev and Ezra Pound.

So exclusive control of burials finally passed out of ecclesiastical hands and, in Paris, into the control of the municipality. Originally the new Parisian graveyard on the Mont Louis was to be called Cimetière de L'Est, but the name never really caught on with local people. They continued to call the site Père-Lachaise. As we do today.

*

When space is tight in cities, the tendency is to build upwards, and this city of the dead is no exception. So as I join the cemetery's

main Avenue Circulaire via a side gate by Père-Lachaise Métro, I immediately find myself on a rising cobbled street lined by nineteenth century graves, all of which are surmounted by tall, thin 'house-tomb' structures, standing to attention, each with a front door enclosing a mini-altar, a plaque and sufficient space for one mourner to stand and say a prayer, kneel at a squeeze, but no more. They have the look of a grand outside toilet cubicle, or a garden shed intended to double as a quirky folly.

Others – with ornate wire mesh over the frosted glass of their entrance – are a dead ringer for the lift cubicle in the Parisian apartment block where I am staying. Climb in and press the buttons. The image of a lift going down into the depths feels curiously appropriate here in a graveyard and suddenly puts me in mind of a childish fear I used to have (no doubt induced by my Christian Brother teachers with their ready talk of the torments of Hell) that one day I'd get into an elevator and it would descend interminably until the doors suddenly slid open to reveal the devil waiting in his fiery lair to claim my sinful soul.

I dispel the memory with a shake of my head and turn right into the Avenue de la Chapelle. The very precise, almost suburban layout, with kerbstones, cobbles and cast iron signposts at every junction is – presumably by design – the antithesis of a churchyard burial ground. Ordered, manicured and reassuring, it speaks of the business of death rather than faith in an after-life. The graves are six or seven deep on each side, most with their ungainly monuments plonked on top, every one straining to catch my eye among the crowd by a twist in the detailing or a daring reference to something in the canon of architecture. One variation, entirely fashioned out of cast iron, suggests (accidentally, for it predates it by decades) Dr Who's Tardis. Several need only a lick of red paint to transform them into old-fashioned GPO phone boxes, the part-glazed doors on three

sides leading on to a blank back panel with the details of the deceased where the telephone and money slot would be. This is not as fanciful as it sounds. The neoclassical architect, Sir John Soane, came up with a design for his family tomb in Old Saint Giles' burial ground in London's Saint Pancras that topped it with an unusual shallow dome. This is said, in the 1920s, to have inspired Sir Giles Gilbert Scott's iconic design for the standard GPO red telephone box.

The memorials appear to get more and more bizarre as I make my way up the hill. One that causes me to gasp out loud is the by now standard lift cage design, this time for the Famille Chasles, but extended even further upwards by adding a huge classical sarcophagus on the top, like an outsized roof box atop a Smart car. A case of nearer my God to thee, or stealing a march in the clamour for attention?

What makes the whole landscape so dense is that there is almost no room at all between the monuments – in most cases hardly enough of a gap for a squirrel to slip through. They are cheek by jowl, which emphasises both their differences and their similarities. Most of the tall 'house-tomb' designs feature some fragment of glass in the front door – stained or not – that affords a glimpse of the small altar inside and a list of names of those buried underneath. Some are better kept than others. For every well-swept, carefully secured front entrance, with polished glass and a prominent padlock, there is another with its door swinging open on its hinges, broken panes revealing the dust and dirt inside.

Those that are abandoned can, in theory, be removed by the authorities. Part of the innovation of Père-Lachaise in 1804 was that it allowed plots to be reused. By moving towards a system of individual burial, the cemetery may have been reflecting the value of each and every person buried there – as against lumping them together in a common pit – but it then had to accommodate the consequence, namely that a great deal more land would be required than hitherto in churchyards. Demand seems to have taken the authorities by surprise, for Père-Lachaise was extended five times in its first 50 years until it reached its absolute limit, save for demolishing the homes, shops and apartment blocks that surround it.

To cope with this voracious appetite for ground, Père-Lachaise retained one key element of the old churchyard system – that land could be recycled a certain number of years after burial. It applied this with a good deal more delicacy than previously, and gave the arrangement a clear legal basis. Relatives of the deceased – or the deceased if they had seen ahead and made plans for their death – could chose from a number of options. The lease on a plot could be bought forever – the most expensive – or for as short a time as ten years. Once that ten years had expired, the authorities would contact the leaseholder, or his or her descendants, and offer an extension. If they declined, the monument would be removed, the bones taken to the cemetery's own ossuary, named Aux Morts ('To The Dead'), and the plot resold.

To this day, the system – subsequently much imitated in every modern cemetery thereafter – remains much the same. Standard leases run for between 10 and 50 years. There is a right to renew, but if descendants cannot be traced, the grave is tagged, inviting anyone with a connection to the family to contact the cemetery authorities. If still no one replies within two years, it can be reused.

Père-Lachaise therefore remains a working cemetery, quite an achievement given its popularity. There is now a waiting list, since most leases are still renewed, but the charge for a plot is approximately £1,000 for ten years. Leases in perpetuity – priced at £15,000 – are rarely available any more as a matter of policy.

The early decades of Père-Lachaise coincided with a new appetite among the prosperous middle classes for an undisturbed final resting place rather than the indignity of the churchyard. Many of its first rush of customers therefore paid up for perpetuity. Their graves, no doubt well-tended in the aftermath of their deaths and for years later, have long since been left, but with the lease in place, they cannot be touched.

The cemetery is built on a slope and, seen from the foot of the hill, the monuments in this 'house-tomb' section appear as if stacked in terraces like a filing system. Originally there was a much greater feeling of space. The vision of the architect, Alexandre-Théodore Brongniart, was to marry classical good order with an Arcadian sprinkling of winding paths, foliage and groves such as might be seen in the admired works of the seventeenth century landscape painter Claude Lorrain, or – to return to the source – on the Via Appia with its ruined mausoleums. The planting of poplar trees and shrubbery was therefore carefully planned to create serene, Italianate vistas. Garish flowers were outlawed. But so popular did the result prove to be among would-be purchasers of plots that very quickly the very air of manicured calm and good taste that had so attracted them was overtaken by the demand for space from those anxious to take up residence.

Brongniart may have taken credit for the look of Père-Lachaise – Napoleon was so pleased with the result that he commissioned him to design the Paris Stock Exchange building, known to this day at the Palais Brongniart – but after his death (and burial here) in 1813, his place was taken by Etienne-Hippolyte Godde, retained as the cemetery's in-house architect, and in that role the creator of its solemn, outsized neoclassical main entrance gates on the Boulevard de Menilmontant and its chapel, abandoning the pyramid design originally envisaged by Brongniart in favour of something more conventionally church-like.

Success at Père-Lachaise was achieved on all sorts of levels – architectural, secular, commercial and in terms of public health. The municipal authorities managed to make a non-judgemental, sanitary

graveyard pay for itself, but in its early years its fate lay in the balance. In 1805, its second year of operation, just 14 new graves were added. Yet ten years later, it was nearer 2,000 in twelve months.

What changed? Arguably the authorities' best marketing ploy was to arrange – with great and unmissable ceremony – for the transfer of the remains of Molière, La Fontaine, and Héloïse and Abelard to rest within the walls of Père-Lachaise in newly-designed and splendid tombs. When Molière had died in 1673, shortly after collapsing on stage while performing in his own play *Le Malade Imaginaire* ('The Hypochondriac'), he was refused burial by the ecclesiastical authorities because he was an actor, then considered a disreputable profession. It was only the personal intervention of his widow, Amande, with Louis XIV, that persuaded the Church even to allow him into a section of his local cemetery usually reserved for unbaptised infants, destined according to official teachings for Limbo.

Molière's post-mortem earthly limbo, though, ended with a striking new grave here, next to another recent arrival, La Fontaine. Close by is the Gothic *baldacchino* under which, in 1817, Abelard and Héloïse were reunited in death. (Some, though, persist in claiming their reburial was simply a scam, that this eye-catching monument is an empty shell, and that the remains of one or both lie elsewhere.)

Whatever the truth, and indeed whatever the dubious ethics of disinterring and reburying any individual to gain a commercial advantage, the welcoming of such 'names' into Père-Lachaise made it suddenly fashionable. Architects were commissioned by the wealthy to create memorials to stand proud next to those already there, and indeed to stand out. These new splendours were sketched and reproduced in magazines across Europe in the 1830s and 1840s. In 1829, for example, Augustus Charles Pugin, father of the architect of the Palace of Westminster, provided illustrations for a book called *Paris and its Environs* that included several views of tombs in

Père-Lachaise. So popular did they prove that he was subsequently able to sell individual prints of these drawings.

That cachet remains with Père-Lachaise to this day. As a final benediction on a life in the public eye, especially in France, it remains without equal. In its well-kempt *divisions* and *secteurs*, the graves are like books on a library shelf, familiar names mixed in with those that stubbornly refuse to ring a bell. There is not a 'celebrity corner', an area akin to Beverly Hills in Hollywood where the rich and famous cluster to make their homes (in the case of Père-Lachaise, their final home) and the public file on organized tours to point and stare. Here, in Paris, the crowd-pullers are sprinkled like gold dust across the whole 44 hectares. And none of the freshly-painted signs points to individual graves – that would be too vulgar.

I veer between following everyone else, each of us clutching the fold-away '*Plan illustre*' purchased at local newsstands, or taking neglected paths in what is ultimately a futile effort to conjure up the illusion of being lost in this land of the dead. Père-Lachaise is too much of a grid for that to be possible.

Every few minutes, there is a grave that stands out, usually because people are gathering round it, or because it has obviously been tended recently. Singer Edith Piaf's otherwise unremarkable tombstone dominates its low-rise *secteur* because admirers of 'the Little Sparrow', who died young at 47, continue, almost 50 years later, to cover it with the bright chrysanthemums and lilies banned by the original designers. By contrast, the artist Delacroix, feted forerunner of the Impressionists, has an eye-catching classical sarcophagus in black marble with gold letters that is so austere it would most probably wither on contact even the most tasteful floral tribute.

If I ever wanted to compile a dictionary of gravestone types – or better still a pocket guide to every different architectural style known to humankind – I couldn't do better, I reflect, than to base it on a walk round Père-Lachaise. There are Gothic towers, Celtic crosses, table-tombs copied from antiquity, neoclassical urns, Egyptian slabs, Art Deco 'house-tombs', mini-medieval fantasy castles with turrets, Greek columns, and enough busts and carved figures to fill several sculpture parks. Moreover, moving between the cemetery's various areas is to trace the changing fashions in funerary art. The nineteenth century house-tombs eventually give way to table-tombs as I move into the early twentieth century, and then to the floor-level graves as I reach its second half. Ornament yields to scale and then to simplicity the closer I get to nowadays. Granite is supplanted first by shiny white marble and then – most recent of all – by sleek black. The decline of religion in France, once called 'the eldest daughter' of the Catholic Church, is told – albeit skewed in a graveyard determinedly secular and non-denominational – by the dwindling number of crosses in the newer arrondissements.

A few designs are just so odd that I stop to take a closer look – the grave of nine-year-old A. Nicoud (what must that Christian name have been that it couldn't even be recorded on his tombstone?), near the crematorium, for instance, topped with a sculpture of him and his dog. Sentimental, yes, but it still brings a tear to the corner of my eye. The double-sized plot of the 'Famille de Raoul Duval', just a little further on, takes me back to pagan tombs in the Scavi under Saint Peter's in Rome with its *trompe l'oeil* staircase, appearing to go down into the ground to a crypt. And 13-year-old Marguerite Poccardi's family paid tribute to her abbreviated life not with the traditional single broken Greek column, but a whole circle of them at differing heights, gathered as if the ruins of a temple transplanted from the shores of the Mediterranean to the grey skies of northern Europe.

It says something about human nature that there seems, in general, to be an inverse proportion between the size of memorial and the size of enduring reputations, with the exception of Oscar

Wilde, of course. As I approach the monument to Baron Louis-Félix de Beaujour (1756–1836), I am convinced my map is wrong and I have stumbled upon the crematorium and its tower. On top of a round circular chamber rises what might variously be mistaken for a chimney, a lighthouse or a gigantic phallus. The inspiration seems to have been a brief revival in the 1830s of the appetite for 'tower-tombs', themselves loosely based on a reworking of the pyramids, and first seen in ancient Rome. In the history books, the architect of this monstrosity, Cendrier, merits a line or two for his work elsewhere on railway station buildings, and Baron Louis-Félix himself, it is recorded briefly, was a diplomat. His one real claim to immortality, though, is his tomb, the tallest in the whole of Père-Lachaise.

Compare that boast with Jim Morrison's squat, bland gravestone. Even its grey marble looks as if it may be concrete. Yet, outflanking

even Wilde, it is the most popular destination in Père-Lachaise, today as every day. So much so that since 2004, barriers have been put up around it and the security guard, promised but absent at Wilde's tomb, is here present and correct to ensure some minimum standards of decorum. The lead singer of the much-feted rock band, the Doors, Morrison died young (27) in Paris in 1971 from a suspected heroin overdose. His actual funeral, one eyewitness reported, was 'pitiful', poorly attended, over in minutes and with just a desultory bunch of flowers thrown casually on the ground. The grave was left unmarked.

But Morrison has not been allowed to rest in peace. The crowds began arriving to pay tribute to their hero. At first it was a trickle of youngsters with their wild flowers and weeping, but the vigil soon developed a momentum and an age-range all of its own, with mourners vying to outdo each other. They daubed messages on neighbouring gravestones, left their empty wine bottles and syringes, underwear and even used condoms as if to echo Morrison's own lengthy catalogue of rock star excesses. Which is when the cemetery authorities began to take measures to control the crowds. Again, inevitably, such efforts simply encouraged yet more outlandish behaviour.

In 1981 a bust of Morrison was placed on the grave but it quickly suffered the same fate as the memorial to Oscar Wilde. People began chipping bits off it. And, being smaller than Epstein's bird-man, the inevitable happened in 1988. Someone simply cut it off its mounting and walked off with it, creating yet more interest.

The cult around Morrison's grave is an intriguing one. While I stand watching, most of those who come up to the barriers to pay their own tribute weren't even born when he died. Their given reason, when I engage a few of them in conversation, is that they want to acknowledge his genius. 'He was more than just a singer', a Belgian teenager tells me. 'We're nostalgic for a time we missed', says another of his friends. An American couple in their twenties are more precise.

'We want to join Jim for a drink on the other side', they say, 'probably in Hell'. Their cackle is self-conscious.

One couple have brought their guitars and lead a chorus of 'Light My Fire'. It sounds appalling, but once they get going after a stumbling start, I find myself wanting to join in, even though like them I am too young to remember him.

Morrison's music, like Wilde's writings, lives on. He wasn't – as in the case of Wilde – a martyr for any particular cause, but rather like James Dean appears to mirror the desire of each and every younger generation before and since to express themselves in ways that their parents and elders try and usually fail to control or understand. In that sense, his memory is something bigger than his achievements, and his memorial therefore more a symbol of the need to emerge from your parents' shadow than an invitation to dwell on Morrison himself.

There are, though, particular factors behind this cult. Because the circumstances of Morrison's death were never satisfactorily explained by the only witness, his girlfriend, Pamela Coulson (who died herself three years later), there are those who claim he is still alive and that the grave is an elaborate ruse to win his freedom from the trappings of success. He had, after all, come to Paris in 1971 in an effort to get out of the spotlight. For such conspiracy theorists, then, the grave is an inevitable starting point.

*

Historically Père-Lachaise may mark an important turning point in attitudes to dying and death, but this cemetery – perhaps because of its renown – also plays a wider national role in France, as spelt out by a series of collective monuments that it hosts. The most significant, on the east side, is the Mur des Fédérés, or 'Communards' Wall', which recalls the 147 supporters of the Paris Commune executed here on 28 May 1871, with their corpses thrown into an open trench. These defenders of the radical government that took over Paris after an uprising in early 1871 had chosen the Père-Lachaise site to take their stand against the forces that wanted to restore the old order. Some might have seen their decision to make a graveyard a battleground as a desecration, others an anticipation of failure. There wouldn't be far to carry their dead bodies to burial.

Ever afterwards their deaths took on a bigger significance for the radical Left in French politics, and more broadly for the workers' movement. The wall became a shrine to their ideals and the emotionally-charged backdrop for their gatherings and rallies, further cementing Père-Lachaise's place in the national consciousness. It is quite an achievement, I can't help thinking, to be both a radical shrine and the last resting place of the rich and famous, but typically this unique place has managed to accommodate both simultaneously.

And to evolve. After the Second World War, the significance of the Communards' Wall developed when it became the setting for a series of Holocaust memorials – from a Giacommetti-like sculpture of twig-like figures recalling those who died at Auschwitz, to larger, more block-like carvings in remembrance of Dachau. Some 75,000 French Jews were deported to the Nazi death camps during the Second World War.

And unlike most graveyards, Père-Lachaise has never lost its relevance to the wider world outside. It has added memorials to more recent tragedies, including a row of monuments to those killed in various air disasters.

*

I am making my way back to the Metro, past the domed crematorium, which remains in regular use. As I walk past, a woman in black, clutching an urn, is heading towards a parked car. A young man I take to be her son has his arm around her shoulder and she is sobbing. In that moment, the tourist trail feels slightly tawdry.

6

Il Cimitero Acattolico, Rome

'The cemetery is an open space among the ruins, covered in winter with violets and daisies. It might make one in love with death, to think one should be buried in so sweet a place'

PERCY BYSSHE SHELLEY: *ADONAIS: AN ELEGY ON THE DEATH OF JOHN KEATS* (1821)

Some words just don't translate. The Italian 'Il Cimitero Acattolico' is usually rendered in English as 'The Protestant Cemetery' or 'The English Cemetery', but neither quite captures the native description of this corner of Rome. 'Protestant' is plain wrong as there are Hindus, Jews, Buddhists, Zoroastrians and Orthodox Christians buried here in the dappled precincts of the 1800-year-old Aurelian Walls that enclose the city. And many nationalities (almost as many Germans as English) are represented among the inhabitants – another odd word, since all have arguably ceased to inhabit anywhere on this earth, but one more case of the shortcomings of language. When it comes to death, most tongues fail to come up with something that isn't either brutally specific (corpse, cadaver), shoddily redolent of marketing-speak (customer, consumer, client) or cloyingly coy ('the loved one' in the title of Evelyn Waugh's 1948 satire on the American funeral industry).

'Acattolico', though, gets straight to the point. For this cemetery evolved, at first informally, and then from the 1820s with official blessing, as a burial ground for anyone who wasn't Catholic. Another of its names, increasingly popular, is 'The Non-Catholic Cemetery', but I still prefer the Italian, 'acatholic', rather than 'Non-Catholic', for the former somehow conveys the sense of standing apart from the crowd, rather like the modern use of asexual in a world otherwise soaked in sex.

And in the early years of the nineteenth century, when Rome was not just the spiritual capital of world Catholicism but also a city ruled over temporally by the Pope, to be 'acatholic' made you very unusual indeed. If you weren't of the state religion, you were banned in death from all Catholic graveyards. And that was the only sort of official graveyard there was since the Church insisted on a monopoly, believing it alone offered the prospect of eternal salvation.

Friends and relatives charged with disposing of the corpses of those who dissented religiously were therefore left with two equally unappealing options. The body could be transported slowly, in the heat, without refrigeration, and at great cost, the 150 or so miles north to Livorno (renamed Leghorn by the English when they established a naval base there in the sixteenth century) where there had long been a Protestant cemetery, beyond the ken of the popes. Or it could be furtively buried under cloak of darkness in the unconsecrated ground of out-of-the-way places. The pleasure gardens and orchards at the foot of the Pincio Hill, otherwise frequented by prostitutes, was one such favoured location, and this spot at the foot of Monte Testaccio was another (an alternative name for the cemetery is 'The Testaccio').

Many, know it though, as 'Keats' Graveyard' for it was here in February 1821 that the Romantic poet John Keats was buried. He had travelled to Italy in the autumn of 1820 in the hope that its milder climate might bring him some advantage in his battle with tuberculosis, but an ill-fated journey and colder than average temperatures in Rome when he finally got here in November had instead precipitated his death at the age of 25 in a room next to the Spanish Steps. He did not live to see his poetry widely recognized, and his disappointment at his failure to make a mark led him to insist that his name should not appear on his tombstone. He wanted only the words 'Here lies One Whose Name was writ in Water' but his friends added a brief explanation (and subsequently regretted doing so): 'This Grave contains all that was Mortal of a Young English Poet, Who, on his Death bed, in the Bitterness of his Heart at the Malicious Power of his Enemies, Desired these Words to be engraved on his Tomb Stone'.

Today there is no longer any need to bemoan Keats' 'malicious enemies'. Their reputations have been eclipsed and their criticisms forgotten, while his name is high up there on every list of immortal poets. The presence of his grave in the Cimitero Acattolico – as well as the spot where the ashes of his friend and admirer Percy Bysshe Shelley were buried after he died the following year in a boating accident off Livorno – has made this a shrine for lovers of literature, Rome's unofficial Poets' Corner. There is something unique about the combination of its layout, under cypresses and ilexes, at once both Italianate and redolent of an English churchyard, and about its setting, below the great grey walls of Imperial Rome, dominated by the huge 40-metre-high triangle of the time-silvered Pyramid of Gaius Cestius, erected as a pagan burial monument in the latter half of the first century BC.

Add to that the romantic melancholy that is part and parcel of many a graveyard. Then there is the final ingredient – the tragedy of promising lives cut short, and burials in foreign ground forever far from friends and lovers. 'Sweet are the gardens of Rome; but one is for Englishmen sacred;/Who, that has ever been there, knows not the beautiful spot/Where our poets are laid in the shade of the pyramid lofty' wrote the Victorian poet, Eugene Lee-Hamilton. Henry James, novelist and frequent visitor to these parts, went further when he wrote of the Cimitero Acattolico as 'the most beautiful thing in Italy … tremendously, inexhaustibly, touching – its effect never fails to overwhelm'.

*

The entrance to the cemetery is in a quiet side street, close to the Porta San Paolo, reputedly the gate out of the city used by Saint Paul on his way to execution (though since the Aurelian Walls were only built 150 or so years later, this is another Roman attribution to take with a pinch of salt). The high walls that now surround the cemetery were completed in the 1870s, with a main gate and a castellated portico that proclaims in confident block capitals 'Resurrecturis' – 'for those about to rise again'. By the time this was chiselled out, the Catholic Church's political control of Rome had been finally broken, and so it was possible, as never before, to trumpet the claim that other religious roads might also lead to heaven.

I step inside, out of the dusty early summer heat of an otherwise non-descript and ramshackle urban street, and into the cool of a large, well-ordered garden. The gravestones lie between tall, thin, bare tree trunks. High above my head, the foliage they support acts as a canopy from the warm mid-afternoon sun. Perhaps it is the boast on the entrance portico that has planted the seed in my mind, but the scene immediately conjures up the *pairidaeza*, the walled garden of ancient Persian kings, an oasis of shade, peace and beauty in an otherwise parched and exhausting landscape, that is the origin of our word paradise and the blueprint for Christian imaginings about the landscape of a heavenly after-life. All that is missing is the tinkle of a fountain.

The cemetery is made up of two distinct sections, pre- and post-legalization in 1821. That was the date when Cardinal Ercole Consalvi, Secretary of State to Pope Pius VII, gave the stamp of official approval to the burial ground that had already existed here for a century. Inside the main gate is the larger post-1821 part, still occasionally used for burials to this day, with its tombstones neatly in rows, the symmetry softened by bushes and roses and exotic flowers, and a chapel far away to my right. To read this graveyard in its correct historical order, however, I must first head off through a gateway to my left, next to the small visitor centre – more of a glorified summer house – and into the Parte Antica.

Once again on this journey, there is that curious sensation of before and after. One moment, I am in the hooded, regimented garden of remembrance, the next I am in an open meadow of ankle-high grass, patrolled by stray cats and giving on to an exotic pyramid. The trees are sparse and the shade intermittent. Save for the few scattered monuments that litter this pastoral scene, it would be the perfect place to spread out a picnic rug but, unlike the ancient Romans who once feasted in the mausoleums now buried under Saint Peter's, modern convention usually forbids eating on or near graves, originally for reasons of hygiene, but subsequently overlaid by concerns about showing 'proper' respect. Death and the dead must always be treated with solemnity.

Yet here, in this meadow where what became the Cimitero Acattolico began in the early decades of the eighteenth century, solemnity feels about as appropriate as a scarf and gloves on such a warm day. Perhaps it is the enduring spirit of the place eclipsing the mood created by its more recent usage. The Testaccio was for 2000 years an informal playground for Romans, an untended, unmani-cured public open space – the 'Prati del Popolo Romano' or 'Roman People's Meadows' as they were known. Here city dwellers could

wander as if in the *campagna*, visit cafés, watch plays and entertain-
ments, drink to excess, assemble daisy chains and make love. These
pursuits continued into the 1700s when the lack of official supervision began to turn it into another of the sites around the city where
'acatholics' could be secretly buried. The bump their graves left in the
meadows was soon flattened by roaming Roman feet and the hooves
of the sheep who grazed here.

With this mingling of dead and living, the Testaccio became a
kind of Elysian Fields, the paradise of the ancient Greeks, located by
the poet Homer at the western edge of the world, where those who
had lived virtuous or heroic lives spent eternity in picture-postcard
countryside, doing sport, listening to music and relaxing. As he lay
dying, Keats sent his companion, the artist Joseph Severn, to inspect
the informal cemetery and was, Severn later wrote, consoled by the
description he brought back of wild anemones and white and blue
violets. 'I can already feel the flowers growing over me', he remarked.

After Keats' death, Severn was to spend hours in contemplation
near his friend's grave here at the Testaccio. 'He is at peace in the quiet
grave', he wrote home. 'I walked there a few days ago, and found it
one of the most lovely retired spots in Rome. You cannot have such a
place in England. I visit it with a delicious melancholy, which relieves
my sadness'.

By the time of Keats' burial, though, there would have been other
marked graves here. It began in the 1720s, with the arrival in Rome
of the Stuart court, chased out of Britain by the Glorious Revolution
of 1688 and more recently humiliated after the failure of a rising in
1715 to install the would-be James III on the throne. The exiled royals
were allowed by the Pope to bury non-Catholic members of their
entourage on this spot. What that meant in effect was that the papal
authorities turned a blind eye. The distinction between unofficial and
official is still sometimes hard to discern in Rome. Certainly by the

1760s monuments had started to appear on graves here and no-one had ordered that they be removed. Cardinal Consalvi might therefore be more properly seen in 1821 as legalizing something that he knew had been happening for a long time anyway.

But pre- and post-1821, one rule was strictly enforced. There could be no crosses on the monuments. That symbol belonged, the papacy believed, exclusively to it. If, as is sometimes said, the presence of the cross on the human landscape is Christianity's bequest, the popes were keen to make clear that it was the trademark of a particular brand of Christianity. So the monuments today scattered around the Parte Antica strike a slightly odd note after the rows of lopsided crosses and angels that I have grown accustomed to in countless English country churchyards and their Victorian successors. It takes a while, though, to pinpoint the precise cause of the disharmony. Much is familiar – the stout, outsized lonely Grecian column on the grave of Sir William Bowles (d. 1806), for instance, or the slender pillars, cut off halfway up as a symbol of young lives lost, on the plots of Friedrich (d. 1807) and Wilhelm von Humboldt (d. 1803), young sons of a Prussian diplomat; or, again, the classical sarcophagus of Lady Elisa Temple (d. 1809), American wife of an English baronet. But it is the lonely vigil of a rough-hewn Celtic cross, added many years later by his admirers to the grave of John Bell (d. 1820), Scottish surgeon and anatomist, that finally alerts me to what is elsewhere entirely missing.

The earliest known inhabitant of this 'antica' section was an Oxford graduate called George Langton. Excavations at the foot of the pyramid found his bones along with a buried tablet bearing a text recounting his short life and death at 25 in 1738. Long before Langton had resurfaced, though, the Romans had woven another colourful legend around the cemetery's origins. A young nobleman from Germany, sometimes given the name Werpup, is said to have been visiting the city in the 1760s as part of his 'Grand Tour', bathing in classical antiquity and the Renaissance, as had many a northern European of means before him. Werpup managed somehow to arrange a private audience with the Pope in the course of which he remarked to the pontiff upon the great love he had developed for Rome during his brief acquaintance. Idly, he expressed a wish to be buried, when he died, in the shadow of the Pyramid of Gaius Cestius. It is to be presumed that he had been sampling the delights of the area.

A matter of days later young Werpup tumbled accidentally out of his horse-drawn carriage in the Via Flaminia and was killed instantly. The Pope, recalling their conversation (and possibly prompted by relatives of the deceased in the diplomatic corps), was moved to extend to this young man the exemption already granted to the Stuart court from the official Catholics-only burial policy. And so Werpup's became the first marked grave in what was to become the Cimitero Acattolico.

*

Whatever the truth of the tale – and there is indeed a tombstone here now in memory of George Antony Frederick Werpup (1740–65), son of Baron Werpup, representative of Hanover at the papal court – one element that undoubtedly has the ring of authenticity in the whole tale is the fascination caused by the juxtaposition of this site and the Pyramid of Gaius Cestius.

The surviving details of the life of Gaius Cestius, inscribed on the marble cladding of the pyramid, are brief, straightforwardly distinguished but, in the bigger plan of centuries, utterly unremarkable. He died between 18 and 12 BC, was a member of one of the ruling families of Rome, and sat on various august bodies. His enduring gift to history, however, lies in his dedication to drawing up detailed

plans for his own memorial. An act of huge egotism? Probably. It is one thing to reflect on death in the midst of life, but Gaius Cestius appeared to be narrowly obsessed over the precise manner of his burial. He had set his heart on it all being a homage to Egypt, the civilization that had flourished along the Nile and its delta from the fourth millennium BC, long before Rome even existed.

Gaius Cestius was not alone in invoking – and borrowing from – the greatness of the Egyptians. There was in Rome at the time a fad for all things Egyptian. The Circus Maximus, for example, scene of *Ben Hur*-like chariot races and roughly a contemporary of Gaius Cestius's pyramid, featured an Egyptian obelisk. Fifty years later, as we have already seen, the Emperor Caligula would bring back the real thing from Egypt and place it in the centre of another stadium on the Vatican Hill.

The pyramid, as a suitably grand tomb for those of accomplishment, has drifted in and out of fashion over the centuries. It represented at best a way of claiming immortality. The memory of the man or woman who lies encased here, a pyramid-shaped monument cries out to the world, will last as long and be as influential as the Egyptian civilization. It may sound today like a foolish conceit, but the notion was alive and well almost two millennia later, when the Victorians, confident that Britain's industrial might would dominate the world ever after, were specially drawn to commissioning pyramids as their final resting place.

Perhaps Gaius Cestius had learned about the various types of pyramid design when he fought in the military campaigns of Imperial Rome as it subsumed a weakened Egypt into its empire in the first century BC. He favoured the steep and pointy model – seen in the pyramids of Nubia, especially at Meroe, and created from 700 BC onwards – rather than the shallower, wider, often more rounded and older variety found, for example, at Giza. And he embraced another key feature of the Egyptian model: the essential disguise surrounding the entrance to the central vault in which the corpse of the pharaoh was laid.

'The Egyptians', writes architectural historian Professor James Stevens Curl in *Death and Architecture*, 'were very concerned to build imposing tombs, since they placed so much more importance on an after-life. Egyptian tombs had to be solid, secure and lasting houses for the mummified body and all its parts, for, when the spirit of the deceased finished wandering the world in animal form, it would return to the tomb and reclaim the corpse: thus life would begin anew. Loss, theft, damage or destruction of the body was a singular disaster to the Ancient Egyptian, and so the architecture of his tomb reflected the importance of the function'.

Gaius Cestius' body duly lay undisturbed in its barrel-vaulted cavity, decorated in the Egyptian style with intricate frescoes (but without the walled-in servants and relatives that the pharaohs used to insist should accompany them in death) for nigh on 1700 years because no-one could find the way in. By that stage, the pyramid, originally built outside the city, had been incorporated in the Aurelian Walls, stripped of the formal gardens and statues that once surrounded it, and become so overgrown that its dedications were lost. It was known locally as the Pyramid of Remus, one of the two mythical founders of Rome, a twin to the Pyramid of Romulus that stood near the Vatican until it was demolished in the sixteenth century. It was only in the 1660s, when someone was curious enough to tunnel in, that Gaius Cestius' name was restored.

Compare and contrast, as they used to say in my 'O'-Level papers, with the modest stone on Keats' grave? 'Who, then, was Cestius/ and what is he to me?' wrote Thomas Hardy on a visit here in 1887. 'I can recall no word/Of anything he did;/For me he is a man who died and was interred/To leave a pyramid'. At the end of the poem, entitled 'Rome: At the Pyramid of Cestius near the Graves of Shelley and Keats', Hardy concludes that, by a twist of fate, Gaius Cestius has achieved 'ample fame' by 'beckoning pilgrim feet/With marble finger high/To where, by shadowy wall and history-haunted street/Those matchless singers lie'.

*

The pyramid may dominate the Parte Antica physically, but it is Keats' grave that dominates emotionally. It sits over in the far corner as I enter, its back turned to the rest of the world, almost hiding in its corner of a foreign field. I take my lead from the handful of other pilgrims who are approaching it reverently, silently, with eyes downcast. The man before me, I notice, places a note on the grave, addressed 'To Maestro Keats'. When it is my turn, I resist the instinct to kneel down and attempt to decipher the rest of the text. It would be breaking the seal of the confessional.

When Keats was laid to rest here in February 1821, there would have been no wall enclosing the meadow, just a shallow moat between it and the pyramid. The burial ground, though still technically unofficial, had developed greatly since George Langton's time. The interment of the Von Humboldt children had apparently received the Church's imprimatur, signalled by a small enclosure around the monuments, a feature not repeated elsewhere. The high proportion of tombstones dating to the early 1800s suggests that it was by then well-established and accepted, rather as a building may in some cases today be erected and then have planning permission granted subsequently.

There was, though, a lingering element of risk before the whole site was belatedly given legal status. Reports suggest that burials here in the early decades of the nineteenth century tended to be carried out very early in the morning or late at night. This may have added to the romantic aspect, or been down to the midday heat, but it could equally have been a practical precaution to avoid inflaming local prejudices against non-Catholics. It wasn't only popes and cardinals who harboured a distrust of other faiths. Where they led, those in the pews followed. In 1821 Sir Walter Synnot, a Protestant Anglo-Irish aristocrat from Co. Armagh, now a long-time resident in Rome, decided to dispense with the cloak-and-dagger approach and bury his young daughter here in broad daylight. Yet mourners were accompanied by mounted police guard 'in case they should be insulted'. Whether or not that happened isn't recorded, but when Sir Walter himself died eight months later, his funeral arrangements reverted to the previous regime, i.e. by torchlight.

Keats is honoured with a simple, pale rounded headstone, decorated with a lyre, symbol of Apollo, god in both Roman and Greek traditions of poetry, its broken string the chosen symbol in this case for a life cut short. Because Keats had insisted that his name be left off the epitaph, early visitors coming to the site to pay homage to him struggled to find their hero's modest grave. Later, a plaque was erected to guide them to the spot, featuring both a copy of Keats' death mask and an acrostic verse, each line on top of the next, so their first letters spell out his name: 'K-eats! if thy cherished name be 'writ in water'/E-ach drop has fallen from some mourner's cheek;/A-sacred tribute; such as heroes seek,/T-hough oft in vain – for dazzling deeds of slaughter/S-leep on! Not honoured less for Epitaph so meek!'

It was no doubt well-meant but it feels a little crass, especially when compared to the poet's own lines that inevitably emerge from the recesses of my memory as I stand in this spot: 'A thing of beauty is a joy for ever:/Its loveliness increases; it will never/Pass into nothingness, but still will keep/A bower quiet for us' are the ones that I speak aloud, under my breath.

The plaque was made redundant in 1882 when the surest signpost to Keats' grave became the twin stone next to it. In the same style, size, shape and lettering, it is the final resting place of Joseph Severn. Underneath a carving of paint brushes and a palate, it spells out what its companion monument does not: 'To the Memory of Joseph Severn, Devoted friend and death-bed companion of John Keats ...'

Keats and Severn had first met around 1816. Three years later, the artist entered a portrait miniature of 'J. Keats Esq' in the Royal Academy Exhibition. Though he was not in the poet's inner circle, Severn agreed at just three days' notice to accompany him on his rest cure to Rome in late 1820 because others couldn't or wouldn't. After arranging the burial, he stayed on in Rome for much of the rest of his long life, first as a fashionable painter of Italianate landscapes and miniatures, much sought after by 'Grand Tour-ists', and later as British Consul when Rome was finally liberated from papal control in 1870 and reunited with the rest of Italy as the capital of a single kingdom.

Proximity in death appears to have a particular appeal for poets. When the Poet Laureate, C. Day-Lewis, died in 1972, he was buried, far from his London home and despite his professed 'churchy agnosticism', in the churchyard at Stinsford in Dorset, two places along from his greatest influence, Thomas Hardy.

Is this another way of seeking immortality, by proximity? That would, I think, be overstating it. Day-Lewis's place of burial was the choice of his family, trying as many do to guess what he would have wanted since he left no instructions. And even a memorial in Poets' Corner in Westminster Abbey, the national shrine to versifiers since 1733, does not come with any eternal guarantee. The company may be exalted and include names that resonate down the centuries – Spenser, Shakespeare, T. S. Eliot, Tennyson, Wordsworth, Milton – but still isn't sufficient to make us remember everyone featured there – the Victorians Adam Gordon and Henry Cary, for example, or from an earlier era Charles de St Denis and James Thomson (he wrote the lyrics of 'Rule, Britannia!') or even a very recent and obscure addition, Adam Fox.

Literary reputations are like the stock exchange, they rise and fall unaccountably and rapidly. Even a prominent, well-placed, well-maintained tomb with A-list neighbours can do little to buck an unpredictable market. Yet there remains something about poets' graves in particular, as distinct from, say, the resting places of playwrights or novelists (as a sweeping generalization we appear to prefer to remember the latter by going to visit their homes and seeing their studies). Why is this? Robert Graves – who is included in Poets' Corner as part of a group of First World War poets – had a theory: 'An aroma of holiness still clings to the title "poet" as it does to the titles "saint" and "hero", both of which are properly reserved for the dead', he once wrote. 'It is only when death releases the true poet from the embarrassing condition of being at once immortal and alive in the flesh that people are prepared to honour him; and his spirit as it passes is saluted by a spontaneous display of public emotion'.

This way, Graves suggested, a tradition with ancient roots in pre-Christian times lived on, based on the notion that a poet was not just 'a professional verse-writer', but someone with special spiritual powers, like the trees in a sacred grove. 'When he died the people felt a sudden loss of power and a sorrow stole over them all', says Graves, 'even those who were incapable of understanding the meaning of his simplest poems'.

Standing at Keats' graveside, this broader appeal suddenly seems obvious. Poets possess a greater than average willingness, especially in our death-shunning culture, to look mortality unflinchingly in the eye in their verse. And verse itself has an innate capacity to spell out in a few memorable lines something to quell our confused and fearful anxieties about death.

This connection between poets, death and cemeteries was made most forcefully by a loosely connected school of mid-eighteenth century writers, known collectively as the 'graveyard poets'. Mostly clergymen, or sons of clergymen, they were particularly given to melancholy meditations on mortality, usually written while sitting among unmarked graves. To the already mentioned name of Thomas Gray – perhaps the most enduring figure in this group with his 'Elegy Written in a Country Churchyard' – should be added those of Robert Blair and Edward Young.

The 'graveyard poets' were precursors of the Romantics. Even those in these ranks of more robust health than Keats made a virtue out of dancing with death in their writing, but for him there was a more urgent imperative. He had little choice but to muse on death since so much of his short life was overshadowed by his physical frailty.

*

Official recognition of the Cimitero Acattolico in 1821 came with strings. There were, Cardinal Consalvi decreed, to be no more burials in the meadow next to the pyramid. They would, he argued, posing as a concerned custodian of the city's ancient heritage, damage the view. Instead the Church offered a plot right next door, but it had to be enclosed, out of sight and out of mind. And, in case anyone cared to peer behind the wall, the cardinal retained the ban on crosses or any reference to eternal life, henceforth to be enforced by a papal commission to which all gravestone inscriptions had to be submitted for approval, a hurdle that endured until the defeat of the Pope by the forces of the Risorgimento in 1870.

There have been a handful of exceptions made subsequently to this closure of the Parte Antica. Joseph Severn is the most obvious. Others include William Rutherford Mead, President of the American

Academy in Rome in 1928, and the archaeologists Albert and Elizabeth Van Buren in the 1960s. Keats', though, remains one of the very last 'regular' burials in the Parte Antica – though far from regular in every other sense of the word.

It is time to return to the shade of the new section, Consalvi's gift, now confusingly called (in part) the '*Zona Vecchia*' ('Old Zone') presumably in the spirit that everything in Rome is measured in degrees of age. Two stray cats stand guard at the connecting gateway as I approach, backs arched in defiance until the very last minute when they turn tail and scarper.

The informality of the meadow gives way once more to a grid of long, leafy paths, lined with box hedging that is low enough not to obscure the vistas through the Zona Vecchia to the sections beyond, added seamlessly at the end of the nineteenth century thanks to the

German government. Pansies and roses mix with orange and lemon trees in fruit. There is even a lizard running up the old city walls.

The graves leave no space for grass or meadow here. The absence of crosses, the traditional hallmark of a Christian graveyard, is noticeable once again, though not so striking as in the Parte Antica, and indeed they grow more numerous the further I cast my eye. Time has removed most of the old restrictions. As well as traditional Latin crosses, I spot square Greek and rounded Celtic ones, plus the occasional three-barred Orthodox version, with two or even three crossbars, depending on the inclusion of a short projecting nameplate at the top, but all with a slanting bottom bar. This, by tradition, was where Jesus' feet were nailed, but it is angled upwards at one end towards Saint Dismas, the penitent thief, crucified next to Jesus, who according to the gospel accounts recognized him in the midst of their shared agony as the saviour, and was therefore granted eternal life.

A controlling eye has continued to be kept on the designs, so a benchmark of good taste is maintained, though a few flamboyant examples have crept in, notably, up at the top of the slope, the life-sized angel draped, weeping, over the tomb of its creator, the American sculptor, William Wetmore Story, and his wife, Emelyn, long-time residents of Rome who both, the inscription reads, died in 1895. (On my travels I note time and again how many couples, buried together, die separately, but within the same calendar year, the pain of loss after a shared lifetime apparently just too great.) Story's 'Angel of Grief' is a much-copied design, with numerous examples in US cemeteries, one at Stanford University in California, and regular guest appearances on the covers of rock albums which seek to convey a Gothic twist.

There are almost 4,000 graves here. Sometimes, when I'm walking the dog round our local cemetery, I find myself imaging a nocturnal assembly of all the ghostly residents. Here, in Il Cimitero Acattolico,

it would be a much more distinguished gathering, a phantom-like version of the House of Lords with experts in every field sharing their accumulated wisdom with the group. Competing for the despatch box would be ambassadors, scientists (including the distinguished physicist, Bruno Pontecorvo, who defected in the 1950s to the Soviet Union but came back to his native Italy in death), inventors (the Canadian pioneer of flash photography, Charles Smeaton), military figures (Thomas Jefferson Page, nineteenth century US Navy commander and grandson of the founding US president), and business leaders (the elegant, simple, white family grave of the Bulgari, jewellers and luxury goods manufacturers, is here).

But it is the artists and writers who could outvote all the rest in this 'new' section. Many of them are now forgotten – or at least their names mean nothing to me – but among those that ring the faintest of bells are R. M. Ballantyne, the Scottish author of the children's classic *The Coral Island*, Constance Fenimore Woolson, the American novelist, short-story writer and friend of Henry James, and the late-nineteenth century English poet, John Addington Symonds.

Symonds had died in Venice in 1893 but left instructions that he was to be buried in this cemetery. And that same request from writers has continued to be heard regularly in the twentieth and into the twenty-first century. The Beat poet, Gregory Corso, close friend of Kerouac, Ginsberg and Burroughs, best remembered for 'Marriage' (where he imagines a date with the girl next door and writes 'Don't take her to movies but to cemeteries'), came from an Italo-American background, but died in Minnesota in 2001. However, in a documentary film made shortly before his death, Corso had visited the Cimitero Acattolico. On camera, he points to a plot and says he has always liked 'good company' and so wants to be buried near to Keats.

Even though it stretched their rules, the authorities agreed. There remain three basic tests for admittance – non-Italian, non-Catholic and resident in Italy. These have been enforced since 1953 by a managing committee made up of senior diplomats from non-Catholic countries based in Rome.

*

The most celebrated grave in the 'new' section is that of Shelley. His presence is this place's other great claim to be a literary shrine. He died aged 29 in July 1822, just too late for his ashes to be allowed into the Parte Antica, as he had requested. He wanted to lie next to his young son, William, who had died in 1819 in Rome at the age of three and been buried in the meadow. But the newly-granted legal status of the cemetery was still fresh and much scrutinized, so it had little wriggle room as yet to make exceptions from the rules that Cardinal Consalvi had set out. The acting British Consul in Rome, John Freeborn, did try his best to persuade the Vatican to be generous and grant an exemption for Shelley, but it remained unmoved by special pleading on behalf of a writer who, whatever his literary merits (and they were still disputed at the time of his death though rarely subsequently), was twice-married, espoused radical political causes and had published a pamphlet entitled *The Necessity of Atheism*.

As he was going about his thankless task, Freeborn kept the casket of Shelley's ashes in his wine cellar. He even recruited Severn to his campaign, but to no avail. A compromise was finally reached whereby, in January 1823, the body of young William would be exhumed and buried with his father in the 'new' section. Severn described what happened on the appointed day. 'Our plan was frustrated, after I had got permission to disinter the bones of the child for, on opening the grave, we discovered a skeleton 5½ feet. Yet it appeared to be under the Stone. To search further we dare not, for it was in the presence of many respectful but wondering Italians: nay I thought it would have been a doubtful and horrible thing to disturb any more Stranger's Graves in a Foreign Land'.

The problem seems to have been the *ad hoc* nature of the original burial ground in the Parte Antica. Proper records had not been kept because, officially, the cemetery didn't exist. To be fair, today even graveyards run with computerized maps and military precision still suffer the same distressing problem. In September 2010, officials at Arlington Cemetery in Washington DC, America's most hallowed military burial ground, were forced to admit that dead servicemen had been buried under the wrong headstone, that some graves contained more than one set of remains, that others existed in fact but not on their plans, and that some urns had been found in what was effectively the compost heap.

Shelley's ashes were finally buried alone in the new section. Cremation remained frowned upon in Catholic Italy but his body had been burnt, in line with quarantine regulations, on the beach at Viareggio where it had washed up. A story, disputed by some, holds that his grieving wife, Mary, rescued his heart from the ashes and kept it with her for the rest of her life, finally having it buried with her. The tradition of separate fates for hearts and corpses has a long history stretching all the way back to Eleanor of Castile, Queen Consort of Edward I in the thirteenth century, whose body went to Westminster Abbey but her heart to the Dominicans' church in London.

Shelley's ashes had one more journey to make. A few weeks after their burial, his friend, the writer Edward Trelawny, arrived in Rome and visited the grave. 'When I came to examine the ground with the man who had the custody of it', he recalled in his memoir, 'I found Shelley's grave amidst a cluster of others. The old Roman wall partly enclosed the place, and there was a niche in the wall formed by two buttresses ... There were no graves near it at that time. This suited my taste, so I purchased the recess, and sufficient space for planting a row of the Italian upright cypresses. As the souls of Heretics are foredoomed by the Roman priests, they do not affect to trouble themselves about their bodies. There was no 'faculty' to apply for, nor Bishop's licence to exhume the body. The *custode* or guardian who dwelt within the enclosure and had the key of the gate, seemed to have uncontrolled power within his domain, and *scudi* impressed with the image of Saint Peter with the two keys ruled him. Without more ado, masons were hired, and two tombs built in the recess. In one of these, when completed, I deposited the box, with Shelley's ashes'.

Trelawny chose well. This section of the cemetery banks steeply up to the Aurelian Walls and Shelley is right up at the top, opposite the main entrance. The tombstone is a plain, off-white rectangular slab, laid flat to the ground. The inscription is simple: Shelley's name, dates, the words '*Cor cordium*' ('heart of all hearts') suggested by another Romantic poet, Leigh Hunt, and, from what Trelawny said was Shelley's favourite play, *The Tempest*, a few lines of 'Ariel's Song' in reference to his death at sea: 'Nothing of him that doth fade / But doth suffer a sea-change / Into something rich and strange'.

The Zona Vecchia is meticulously tended, but Shelley's grave, as befits its status, is especially pristine. Even the red rose laid on the stone by an admirer is more artfully placed than tossed. A volunteer comes regularly to give it the care that grieving relatives usually provide elsewhere and which tails off after their own deaths. For that to continue almost two centuries later is one of the blessings of literary immortality.

Another – as Keats has found – is to be surrounded in death by friends, but in Shelley's case the circle has been widened to include acquaintances and admirers he never even knew. Because of the 'no new burials' rule in the Parte Antica, only Severn could get close to Keats, but here in the Zona Vecchia Shelley presides over a *salon des morts*. In Severn's slot, alongside, Shelley has Trelawny. When he purchased Shelley's plot, Trelawny also reserved the adjacent one for himself, though it waited almost 60 years to be used.

The novelist, biographer and chronicler of the Romantic era chose for his own tombstone Shelley's lines: 'These are two friends whose lives were undivided./So let their memory be now they have glided/Under the grave: let not their bone be parted/For their two hearts in life were single-hearted'. Shelley is thought to have written them not for Trelawny but for his friend, Edward Williams, who died with him in the boating accident. It has subsequently been seen by some as an unprincipled act of appropriation, the summation of Trelawny's attempts during his lifetime to portray himself as closer to Shelley and Keats that he really was. Another example of memorial stones being used as a final act of positioning oneself in the eyes of history?

Others who have subsequently booked in nearby include Corso, Symonds, the sculptor William Story and his wife, and Belinda Lee, the English starlet of the 1950s who went on to make a name for herself as a serious actress in Italian films before her death in 1961 in a car crash. And there are others, dotted around the extended 'new' section also drawn by the presence of Shelley, directly or not. The cemetery authorities report that the third most-visited grave here – after those of Keats and Shelley – is that of Antonio Gramsci, one of the founders of Italian communism, buried here in 1937. Pilgrims are drawn not just by admiration of the ideology he espoused – he was one of the leading Marxist thinkers of the twentieth century – but also out of respect for his courage in refusing to bend in his beliefs in the face of persecution throughout the 1930s by the fascist authorities in Italy. Gramsci died after being released from prison (the Vatican claiming he had returned on his death bed to the Catholicism of his cradle, a story rejected by those close to him, who therefore buried him here). Gramsci's grave can claim an indirect link to Shelley's for it was the experience of visiting both of them that inspired the left-wing Italian poet and film-maker, Pier Paolo Pasolini (best remembered in the English-speaking world for the remarkable *Gospel According to Saint Matthew*) to pen 'The Ashes of Gramsci' which drew parallels between Shelley's Romantic radicalism and Gramsci's communism.

And Keats too casts a shadow from beyond the wall that divides this cemetery, as I discover as the afternoon sun starts to wane and the cicadas pipe up. The Swedish poet, Harald Jacobson, claims a sort of literary fellowship with Keats by omitting his own name on his iron grave marking, which features just the words 'Never misuse the name of Christ'. The same excuse probably can't be made in the case of August von Goethe, the only son of the celebrated German writer

Johann von Goethe. His monument, erected by his grieving father, likewise makes no mention of August's name. He is described only as 'the son of Goethe'. An act of fatherly devotion, wanting to wrap his dead son in the shroud of his own (hoped-for) immortality, or monumental egotism? At this distance in time it is probably best not to judge. Cemeteries are better suited to questions than answers.

7

Paddington Old Cemetery, London

The crows caw as they move noisily from tree to tree. When it opened in 1855, as part of the spectacular Victorian boom in new burial grounds, Paddington Old Cemetery was on the rural fringes of north-west London. Today it is surrounded on all sides by streets of prosperous terraced houses, and the occasional modern block, taking advantage of the views from this gently elevated site back over the saucer of central London. But it is still a world apart.

The collective nouns for different varieties of birds are often bizarre and unfathomable, as if the result of a dictionary lucky dip, but nothing better justifies that for crows – a murder – than their bitter, hard-edged chitter-chatter in this graveyard on this bright, damp November morning. They are offering their own heartless commentary on a funeral that is taking place amid the elaborate, elderly and often tilted memorials of this garden necropolis. A line of mourners shuffles along behind a coffin and its bearers towards an open grave. The black coats and suits and hats strike a discordant note in the lemony sunshine. All walk in silence, apparently oblivious to the noises off.

The scene is familiar enough to anyone old enough to have known death in their circle of family or friends. Traditional burials remain stubbornly popular in an age of disbelief. They may not be ubiquitous as when this cemetery first opened its heavy, black wrought-iron gates, flanked on either side by Gothic lodges, but an 'old-fashioned' funeral is one of the few social and religious formats to have remained for the most part insulated from the insistent contemporary demand that all public celebrations and ceremonies be restlessly updated, with 'stuffy' rule books discarded or shrunk to the size of a raffle ticket. It is, I reflect as I look on, another indication of our modern disconnection with the business of death that it, alone, has managed to stick to time-honoured patterns, even when the religious belief that underpinned elaborate rituals and incantations has long since been abandoned by most of the mourners. Religion may have no relevance to their lives, but they instinctively reach for it in death.

Though it never 'belonged' to a particular denomination, in the way that the English country churchyard was the domain of the local Anglican vicar, Paddington Old Cemetery was still self-consciously godly, as were all of Britain's Victorian cemeteries. Death then was much more explicitly bound up with belief. The key organizational difference in these 'new' cemeteries was that other beliefs were accorded similar treatment to state Anglicanism. So at the centre of the cemetery are twin, conjoined chapels, almost identical in an architectural mish-mash of rural ragstone and Gothic pointedness, one reserved for the Church of England (and hence with stained glass and a cross on the roof) and the other for the rest (more starkly unadorned).

However pious and God-fearing, though, the Victorians weren't above making a statement by their treatment of the dead. So their garden cemeteries were the source of civic pride, symbols of the progress they were making, of their essential civilizing mission. And, in the entrepreneurial spirit of the time, they were also a way of making money. The Church's monopoly on burial was privatized. Paddington Old Cemetery belongs to that nineteenth century innovation of the grand, eye-catching non-denominational burial ground, many run as commercial joint-stock companies.

This break with the past started in Liverpool in 1829, then spread to burgeoning London at Kensal Green, Highgate and Brompton, and after that did the rounds of Britain, where a carefully-planned garden cemetery became as much a landmark of the age as ornate municipal buildings, gloomy railway terminus hotels, and the gingerbread trim on the gables of suburban villas.

The mourners are now assembling around the grave, heads bowed, while the undertakers, bending stiff and low over the six-foot pit like Anglepoise lamps, lower the coffin on pulleys into the ground. A whole life, I remember thinking at the same moment in my mother's funeral, shrunk into that narrow opening. The solemnity of the moment has even stilled the crows.

I watch from a distance, shrinking back out of respect. We may no longer remove our hats or stand still when a funeral cortège passes us in the street. A 2012 survey by Co-operative Funeral Services revealed that a quarter of those questioned no longer feel the need to make any sort of gesture of respect if a funeral procession goes by them. Save, perhaps, to avert their eyes because the sight of a line of black cars following a hearse cannot but trigger thoughts of mortality, and we prefer to shut those out. But there are still other inherited codes of behaviour that survive here within the walls of a cemetery. First amongst them is do not intrude on others' grief.

I cannot look away, though. There is, I observe from my vantage point, a curious mix of military formality and uncontrolled weeping about the spectacle that carries me back. As the mourners take turns to cast a handful of dust into the grave, I remember my father, at the same moment, telling me he wanted to throw himself in with my mother. Making the funeral arrangements gave a structure in those days that followed her death, and later his. It did something to lessen the feeling of being in alien territory. I'd thought about how it might be, when they were dead, not in any spirit of wanting to hasten it, but simply trying to prepare myself for the inevitable (they had both been in their forties when I came along). Yet this was so much worse than any part of my imagining. And, when lost, the temptation is to fall back on the familiar, the way it has always been done, no matter how much later we may wish that we had been braver, more radical, tried to fashion a last goodbye that was more bespoke. In that moment of grief, it comes as a relief to have undertakers on hand with a ready-made pattern to fall in with, brochures of coffins and an easy patter. My mother, who died first, had rebuffed all attempts in what we all knew were her last weeks to talk about her funeral, much less confront her impending death – save for on the night the verdict was delivered and she lay awake in her hospital bed, telling me she was terrified. So a traditional burial was our default position. It was what we knew, what we had attended before. And then, when it came to his turn, my father's only wish, in death as in life, was to be treated exactly the same as my mother.

*

It is All Souls' Day, 2 November. On this day Christians everywhere, since the fourteenth century, have been encouraged to recall their dead, 'the souls of the faithful departed', and pray that they may find eternal rest in heaven. It has always been one of those days, in my

Catholic upbringing and fumbling attempts to keep the faith ever since, when the piece of string that is belief, that same piece of string that I somehow have managed to hold on to as it disappears into the skies, is given a sharp tug from above. Sometimes the sudden yank is almost enough to make me let go altogether as I am forced to confront my own ill-informed, confused and conflicting views on eternal fate by the fate of those that I have loved, who have died and who I try to honour on this day of remembering.

Once All Souls' Day was part of an intense prescribed period of prayerful connection with the dead that lasted for the whole month of November (the Orthodox Christians of the East still have a series of 'Soul Saturdays'). Now it has been reduced to just 24 hours and so, on this All Soul's Day, I am attempting to make the most of the invitation it offers to contemplate mortality by standing with death and decay all around me in Paddington Old Cemetery.

The autumn leaves are still thick and sloppy on the muddy ground round the tall Celtic cross next to me. It is at the bottom end of this sloping, fan-shaped 25-acre other world. The white stone of the cross is discoloured, but on the three greenish steps at its base someone has left nightlights, in red containers, their flames visible all the way up the main drag that leads down from the twin chapels. 'To the memory of those who are laid to rest in this portion of God's acre', reads the inscription at the base of the cross, 'whose names are unrecorded in stone, who have gone hence in the faith of Christ looking for the resurrection of the dead and the life of the world to come'.

This area is what is sometimes in other cemeteries called the Potters' Field. It is where the paupers' graves were located, unmarked but one step up from the common pit. Potters' fields were originally areas of heavy clay soil, used as raw material for the kiln. Matthew's gospel tells how Judas Iscariot, after he had repented of his betrayal of Jesus, returned the 30 pieces of silver that had been paid to him by the

Jewish high priests and killed himself. Since the money was 'tainted', it was then used by the clergy to buy a potters' field for use in burying 'strangers'. The term was taken up with gusto in the United States in the eighteenth century as a label for the site of paupers' graves, but was in use in Britain too, the best-known potters' field being next to Tower Bridge in London from the end of the seventeenth century until 1854.

This back-row-of-the-pews area of the Paddington Old Cemetery is as far distant from the main entrance as possible. A few small headstones, long since removed from elsewhere, presumably when they fell down, are propped up against the high brick wall that separates the cemetery from a row of fashionable studios offering Pilates, therapy and re-enamelling of your Victorian bath tubs. On one side of the wall, that nineteenth century pedigree is esteemed and preserved. On the other, it is left to rot.

Amid the leaves are a couple of larger memorials, headstone plus the marble skirting that once marked off a single plot, all still connected in a single piece. They have apparently been washed up here, at curious angles, sitting on top of the ground rather than in it, like boats beached on land after a tsunami. They give an added twist to the sense of neglect that pervades this section and carry a faint echo of the imagined cries of Thomas Hardy's poem, 'The Levelled Churchyard':

O Passenger, pray list and catch
Our sighs and piteous groans,
Half stifled in this jumbled patch
Of wretched memorial stones!

We late-lamented, resting here
Are mixed to human jam,
And each to each exclaims in fear,
'I know not which I am!'

Though Paddington Old Cemetery is still open for burials – such as the one now drawing to a close away in the distance – they are few and far between. Once the initial enthusiasm for this new generation of graveyards had all but filled the grounds with corpses stacked three and four deep, usually in brick-lined shafts, the private investors saw their dividends tail off steeply. With little coming in by way of new fees, they had only bills to pay to maintain the exacting standards that had attracted business in the first place. Since the careful Victorians had tended towards buying plots in perpetuity, the economic model of these cemeteries was quickly revealed as fatally flawed. The bubble burst within 20 years. They struggled on, but by the middle years of the twentieth century, most had passed into the hands of local authorities who seem at a loss to know quite what to do with them.

Belonging as it did to the second wave, Paddington Old Cemetery was never saddled with greedy investors to satisfy. After the initial cemetery openings of the 1830s and 1840s, another outbreak of cholera hit Britain and led to demands in Parliament for more graveyards with the same public health requirements as had been demonstrated by the pioneers. A fresh series of Burial Acts was passed, aiming to establish a national network of hygienic urban cemeteries. Public money was made available to complement private funds, and fill geographical gaps where none had been forthcoming. The result was that these later projects were placed in the hands of not-for-profit boards of upstanding citizens rather than joint-stock companies.

The final result was the same. Plots filled up, income dried up, while outgoings increased, and local authorities had to take on the burden. In the case of Paddington Old Cemetery, it is the London Borough of Brent, and it does its best (compared with neighbouring Westminster, which in the mid-1980s under the stewardship of the supermarket heiress, Shirley Porter, caused a public scandal by trying to off-load its cemeteries for 5p each to private contractors as a way of cutting costs). In 1999, this place even won a gong in the National Cemetery of the Year Awards, but its regime is best characterized as subsistence. A small and hard-working team of groundsmen labour heroically to keep it in good order, their future seemingly forever up for discussion at the town hall as it seeks to balance budgets. Its latest scheme is to sell off the gatehouses as private dwellings – no matter that they are inside the perimeter wall or that one currently houses one of the groundsmen who acts as watchman.

The maintenance team, though, can do little about the tombstones at curious angles, the mausoleums that are crumbling, their entrances secured only by corrugated iron, or the ivy that ensnares and decapitates so many angels on graves that haven't been visited for decades. And that is, to my mind, a bonus, for the slow decay above ground of this once pristine Victorian garden cemetery mirrors the physical corruption that is going on below the surface.

New plots – and hence new revenue – have been crudely created by filling in old 'B' road paths that once linked the main avenues, or by building up the ground in certain of the less prominent areas with great mounds of imported clay lumps which are flattened into another layer for graves atop hillocks that look as implausible as any landscaped slagheap in former coalmining areas. The mourners at today's funeral are now making their way down the concrete ramp from one such artificially elevated section. It is the opposite of Hardy's 'levelled churchyard'. Now we are building up, too squeamish to disturb what lies beneath.

Perhaps if Paddington Old Cemetery had a few of the famous names that draw the curious to its contemporaries, it could augment its coffers by offering walking tours. At Highgate (East and West), visitors are conducted round the graves of George Eliot, Christina Rossetti and Karl Marx. At Kensal Green, Isambard Kingdom Brunel, Wilkie Collins and Harold Pinter span the centuries and compress timescales on the itinerary. But here there is no standout reputation to tempt the crowds.

Which, again, being selfish, I can't help but see as a good thing. The drawbacks of becoming a celebrity cemetery had been all too obvious in Paris. The stories that Paddington Old Cemetery tells are all the more engaging for being so forgotten. There are within its boundaries figures who were lionized in their own time, who might even have attracted their fair share of tourists in the years after their deaths, but whose reputations are now as faded as the lettering on their tombstones. Leonard Charles Wyon (1826–91), for instance, was a noted engraver who produced coins for Queen Victoria's Golden Jubilee (1887) and medals for the Great Exhibition of 1851. Orlando Jewitt (1799–1869) won plaudits as an illustrator and wood engraver. Arthur Roberts (1852–1933) was a comedian and actor who used to top the bill in music halls. He is even credited as the originator of the word 'spoof' to describe a send-up. Captain Martin Becher (1797–1864) was the jockey after whom Becher's Brook, one of the notoriously tricky jumps on the Aintree Grand National course, is named. His party trick, it is said, was to leap up onto a mantelpiece from a standing start. All are buried here in Paddington Old Cemetery.

The most beguiling story, though, is that of Jabez Spencer Balfour. He doesn't have his own memorial, and is instead buried with his parents in their own modest plot. Though he resided in splendour in a typically vast Victorian villa in nearby Maida Hill, he funded it all with an infamous fraud that finally left him penniless, imprisoned and widely reviled. Named Jabez after his godfather, the Baptist preacher Jabez Burns – also buried here with a grand monument, topped by a bust, on the main avenue – J. Spencer Balfour, as he liked to sign himself, exploited his family connections to set up the Liberator Building Society, aimed directly at those from Nonconformist backgrounds. Thousands of small investors saw him as one of their own that they could trust with their savings, but he diverted the money into his own risky property speculations. This is the flip side of the upright Victorian piety, religiosity and respectability that this cemetery ostentatiously symbolizes.

The financial crisis of the early 1890s left Balfour exposed, as surely as the recession of 2008 caught out the American financier Bernie Madoff and his Ponzi scheme. He tried to flee to the Argentine but was brought back to face trial and sentenced to 14 years' hard labour. When he died in 1916, he was still in disgrace. His lasting memorial is not a headstone here but rather a piece of legislation, the 1894 Building Societies Act, which ensured that the tricks he used could never be played again.

*

Père-Lachaise, across the Channel, was the obvious inspiration for the movement that gathered pace in Britain in the early years of the nineteenth century to provide hygienic, dignified, non-denominational burial grounds, especially in the ever more overcrowded towns and cities of the Industrial Revolution. At the start of the nineteenth century there were no towns in England and Wales outside London with a population of more than 100,000. By the end of it, there were 23. The old churchyard system, already struggling to cope, collapsed into chaos under the strain.

The new-style cemeteries were the result of a coming together of various interest groups: Nonconformists who had long objected to being forced to submit to an Anglican funeral if they wanted to be buried in consecrated ground; an increasingly professional group of doctors and public health officials who were appalled by the unsanitary conditions in urban churchyards; and entrepreneurs who saw a chance to make money.

The number of Nonconformists who rejected the exclusive role of the Church of England in the post-Reformation settlement grew as different branches of Protestant Christianity set up on their own. Their members faced a stark choice in death: accept interment in an unmarked grave, or ignore their differences with Anglicanism, pay the burial fee to the local parish, and hope the vicar would allow their corpse into his churchyard even if, by law, he was obliged to read from the burial service in the Book of Common Prayer.

There was no single great declaration of tolerance in death but rather a slow evolution. In 1665, what was already an unofficial burial ground at Bunhill Fields, near Moorgate, in the City of London, was leased by the corporation to a Mr Tindal with the agreement that he could enclose it with a wall and use it for graves. 'Mr Tindal's Burial Ground', as it became known, operated outside the control of the Church, so it was popular with Nonconformists. Among its best-known customers were John Bunyan, author of *The Pilgrim's Progress*, the mother of John Wesley, founding father of Methodism, and William Blake, the artist, poet and visionary. But having established a precedent, it only provoked demand for similar provision elsewhere.

The public health 'lobby' – to use a word they wouldn't have employed about themselves – ran in parallel with its counterparts in France in their concerns about the illnesses and epidemics caused by badly buried corpses. One estimate suggests that, between 1600 and 1900, six million people had been buried, often badly, in the churchyards of London. But it was finally the entrepreneurs who distinguished the British cemetery reform movement from its continental counterparts. Père-Lachaise was firmly in the hands of the municipal authorities, but on the other side of La Manche a newly-prosperous middle class sought both an opportunity to build grand memorials to their own business acumen (a desire often stymied by the restrictions and social hierarchy of their local Anglican church), *and* a chance to make a profit out of death as they were out of every other aspect of human existence.

In some places, all the different interest groups joined forces. George Hadfield, who founded the Rusholme Road Cemetery in Manchester in 1820, was both a businessman and a Dissenter in religion. His key innovation was to set up a joint-stock cemetery company. Investors put up the money to acquire a few acres and landscape it as a formal garden (around £5,000), and were then paid a dividend when individuals bought plots in the new graveyard.

Hadfield's claim to be the first to follow this model is disputed. The Rosary Cemetery in Norwich, founded by Nonconformists, opened its gates a shade earlier, in 1819. Thereafter the idea spread as quickly as cotton mills, railways or canals. The Liverpool Necropolis (or Low Hill General Cemetery) opened in 1825, £8,000 having been spent on creating both 'grandeur' and 'sobriety' at its small two-hectare site. Investors were soon receiving a return of 12 per cent per annum.

Where Liverpool led (and by 1829 the Necropolis had local competition in the form of Saint James', developed in a disused sandstone quarry next to the site that was later to host the city's Anglican cathedral), others followed. Belfast, Glasgow and Exeter all opened non-denominational burial grounds. In the latter, Saint Bartholomew's took the process one stage further. It was built on the rates rather than relying on private investors.

London, too, joined the rush, prompted by a cholera epidemic in the autumn of 1831. Between 1832 and 1847, parliamentary approval was given for commercial cemeteries in the capital, beginning in 1833 with Kensal Green (second choice after a scheme at Primrose Hill had failed), soon followed by Norwood (1838), Highgate (1839), Abney Park (1840), Brompton (1840), Nunhead (1840) and Tower Hamlets (1841). Subsequently they have been dubbed 'the magnificent seven' by architectural historians. At the time success was measured in more practical terms. By 1839 shares in Kensal Green had doubled in value.

*

The Victorians are often quoted as the supreme calibrators of the symbols of mourning. It is said they were obsessed with death, but the truth is more precise. They were obsessed with piety and correct form. The outward sign of inner grief, they believed, had to be calculated and set out in a series of rules and regulations.

Many of these applied particularly to middle- and upper-class women. For men, it was often a question of simply wearing a black armband, or cravat. Widows, by contrast, followed a clear timetable and dress code. Any deviation would be taken as bad form. The focus on women of the etiquette of mourning in Victorian times may have been down to the fact that they weren't in general allowed to attend funerals (though this prohibition faded in the last years of the century). They therefore had to find alternative ways of demonstrating their grief in public.

'Deep Mourning' would last for one year and a day, during which time the widow should wear black gowns, made of lustreless silks, or their cheaper equivalent, bombazine, and trimmed with scratchy crepe. The only acceptable jewellery was black jet, often used as a stone in mourning rings. (An alternative was a clear stone covering a lock of the deceased's hair.) The widow also had to wear a cap and veil. Its presence would effectively bar her from most social gatherings. As *Harper's Bazar* instructed in April 1886, 'no one wearing a heavy crepe veil should go to a gay reception, a wedding or a theatre; the thing is incongruous'.

The connection between the colour black and mourning is of much longer standing. In Ancient Rome, the traditional garment for mourners was the *toga pulia*, a simple woollen garment in black. That custom continued into Christianity, though among the high-born in medieval France and Spain white clothing would also be worn – '*deuil blanc*'. The habit can still be seen in the Low Countries in recent years. At the funeral of King Baudouin of the Belgians in 1993, his widow, Queen Fabiola, wore white, as did the daughters of Queen Juliana of the Netherlands at her funeral in 2004.

After 12 months of 'Deep Mourning', the Victorian widow could enter 'Second Mourning', which allowed her to discard, if she wished, the veil and the crepe. And then, after another year had passed, there was 'Half Mourning', a further period of 12 months when she could wear mauve or grey as alternatives to black. Some widows, however, took their lead from Queen Victoria, who routinely wore mourning for the rest of her life after the death of her consort, Prince Albert. Those who decided instead to 'lighten' their mourning would signal its end by leaving visiting cards for friends and acquaintances.

There were also prescribed periods of mourning for other relatives. A parent would mourn their child for a year. The loss of a grand-parent or sibling would require six months, and a first cousin four weeks. Whole houses went into mourning. During the period of Deep Mourning, the servants' garb was simplified, clocks were stopped and mirrors covered, and all letters sent out on black-edged paper. The front door bell would be dressed with black ribbons and, occasionally, a bunch of violets.

*

In the same spirit of taking the externals of death with a studied seriousness, cemetery design became a flourishing area of artistic endeavour in the nineteenth century. Public competitions would be announced, usually in *The Builder* magazine. A brand new burial ground was as integral to any self-respecting city or town as that other Victorian passion, suburbs. And, indeed, the two came to mirror each other, both sharing in particular a penchant for contrived pseudo-rural layouts, where formal gardens strained to appear casual, especially via manicured greenery. In both suburban crescents and cemetery driveways, there was a premium placed on bagging the best locations in order to put on an outward show of prosperity. The ornate family vault or memorial was as envied by neighbours as the scale and embellishments of the family home.

The high priest of the Victorian cemeteries' cult was John Claudius Loudon. The appearance in 1843 of his *On the Laying Out, Planting and Managing of Cemeteries* coincided with the heyday of this boom. Loudon's first vocation had been as a garden designer, but by the early 1820s he anticipated the mood of the moment by extending his expertise and writing in the *Morning Advertiser* to suggest a ring of new cemeteries round the capital, laid out as 'botanie gardens'. He added that they should be 'sufficiently large to serve at the same time as breathing places'. The irony of using the terrain of the dead as the lungs for the living was apparently lost on him.

Loudon's interest sprang from a number of concerns. He worried, for example, about public health and in particular condemned in writing the conditions in the churchyard of Saint Bartholomew the Less in London's Smithfield, where locals would empty their chamber pots on the graves, leaving it 'so covered with the excrementious matter floated over from the cesspools of privies, that it is difficult to walk across it'.

He was also excited, in classic Victorian fashion, by the new and new-fangled, promoting in another area of his life the use of heated greenhouses to make different produce more readily available to the market. And, finally, he wanted to make money. Though his writings were popular – as were those of his wife, Jane Webb, a novelist – the couple was habitually short of funds.

Loudon made the biggest impact by offering opinions on cemetery design as editor of *The Gardener's Magazine*, the first specialist title for the green-fingered, which he established in 1825. Often he was highly critical of others' plans for graveyards, arguing passionately, for instance, against the inclusion of catacombs on public health grounds. The corpse had to be buried in the earth, he insisted, to stop the spread of disease. He condemned as 'evil' the practice of 'not sealing up coffins in catacombs but merely closing the cell with open ironwork'.

Such trenchant views led to Loudon being invited to practise what he preached. He rose to the challenge and designed two graveyards, the Cambridge General Cemetery (also known as Histon Road) and Bath's Abbey Cemetery. A third major project, in Southampton, had to be finished by others after Loudon's premature death in 1843, just after his textbook appeared.

It was the book, though, that saw him – posthumously – wield enormous influence over that bigger second wave of Victorian burial grounds, such as Paddington Old Cemetery. *On the Laying Out, Planting and Managing of Cemeteries* was not just a practical guide, it was a manifesto, the first ever in what Loudon saw as the distinctive discipline of creating a graveyard. At the heart of his programme was better design. If the new cemetery companies were going to sell their plots at a premium to the wealthy middle classes, he argued, they had to provide a fitting and well-managed backdrop against which individuals could erect their own monuments. So layout was key, getting the mix of formal and informal right, striking a balance between straight elegant carriageways and serpentine paths, gardens and the paraphernalia of death.

In Paddington, the basic grid around which the cemetery is formed is horse-shoe shaped, with the main avenues running diagonally across a series of concentric curves, and the chapels right in the centre. But there are areas, too, especially in the corners, where less formal paths meander over what would originally have been left as meadows. Planting, too, Loudon stressed, must be carefully managed to ensure not just a pleasing environment all the year round, but also to adhere to what he prescribed as a distinctive funerary aesthetic. The dominant influence on this was late eighteenth century Romanticism, borrowed directly from Père-Lachaise, and so Paddington still today has its carefully placed dark evergreens which guide the eye towards the chapels and break up what might otherwise be a sea of monuments and tombstones.

Loudon trod cautiously, though, when it came to the relative merits of different architectural styles for the buildings and memorials in graveyards. He seems to have regarded this aspect as outside his remit. Or it may simply have been that the pioneers of his age had already established the principle that the best contemporary cemeteries included a smattering of everything. The western section of Highgate, for instance, boasts an Egyptian Avenue. Exeter, too, opted for an Egyptian look, with its main gates in the style of pyramids, but Brompton took its cue from the Renaissance, with a domed central chapel, based on Saint Peter's Basilica in Rome. Meanwhile West Norwood championed Gothic, which was ultimately to become the dominant look in Victorian cemeteries by the 1870s.

Paddington, for its part, has elements of all of the above, including classical references with draped urns on the gateposts, Gothic touches on the chapels, Greek pillars on some individual graves, Romanesque sarcophagi and oversized neo-Egyptian slabs on others. If there can be said to be a predominant look, it is dictated (as in all cemeteries) by the chapels with their rural revivalist overtones, conjuring up the impression of a slice of idealized countryside next to (now in the middle of) the city. The presence of a disproportionately high number of Celtic crosses (it stands in the part of London that saw the highest levels of Irish immigration) only adds to the allusion to a village churchyard.

Loudon took a typically scientific approach to his work, in line with the spirit of the age, setting out in his textbook specifications for correct, sanitary burial. He carefully charted the speed at which bodily decay could be expected to progress. 'The face of a dead body', he wrote, 'deposited in the free soil is generally destroyed in three or four months, but the thorax and abdomen undergo very little change, except in colour, till the fourth month'. He added to his expanding list of 'evils' the practice of 'interring a number of bodies in the same grave, without leaving a sufficient depth of earth over each coffin to absorb the greater part of the gases of decomposition'. He wanted nothing more, he claimed, than to do away forever with the stench commonly associated at that time with graveyards. It could, he argued, have no place if cemeteries were ever to be regarded as places of beauty.

To the same end, he advised that cemeteries be located, if possible, on chalky or gravelly soil since both drained well. It proved an impossible request in London, built as it is mostly on clay, which retains water and so slows the process of decay in corpses. Loudon, though, even had that covered, counselling that such unpromising raw material could be improved by including as many gravel paths as possible. 'To be convinced of the bad effects of the neglect of surface drainage in a cemetery', he pointed out, 'it is only necessary to walk on the grass of that at Kensal Green during the winter or summer'. (His concern about its design shortcomings did not prevent his widow from burying him there.)

Image, though, was ultimately more important to Loudon than hard, scientific fact. He did not, for example, want poplar and willow trees in a cemetery, simply because they were usually seen on river banks and would therefore prompt visitors to imagine that the burial ground was badly-drained, even if it was not. His favourite trees were conical in shape. '[They] not only interfere less with ventilation, sunshine and the performance of funerals, but more especially when a dark colour are naturally, from their great height in proportion to their breadth, more sublime than spreading forms'.

Cypresses were a particular favourite, though pines, firs, Irish yews, Swedish junipers and hollies all received his imprimatur, and are all here in Paddington. Deciduous and flowering trees were to be eschewed since they 'lacked solemnity' and made a mess. That rule has been ignored here, but most of the offenders are youngish saplings. And flowerbeds for Loudon were always surplus to requirement. The image of bare earth, or worse, of the earth being dug, he warned, would upset mourners and deprive the whole scene of a proper sense of repose.

Pernickety he may have been, overbearing even, but he was certainly ahead of some of the private cemetery companies in planning for the day when their burial grounds would be full, income would fall and the profit and loss account would slip into the red. Loudon proposed two schemes to tackle this eventuality – one for the wealthy and one for the poor, with that unapologetic Victorian acceptance of social hierarchy. The needy, he suggested, should be buried in temporary cemeteries, located, for example, next to the network of railway lines being established at that time into the countryside. Once all the space trackside had been filled, he wrote, the ground could be covered over, ploughed and returned to agriculture as long as basic standards of hygiene had been adhered to regarding burying corpses deep in the ground.

As for the cemeteries of the wealthy, Loudon had a vision that, once full, existing and future burial grounds, so lovingly created, should be closed for a period, to observe the decencies, and then reopened as public parks, full of spiritually uplifting works of art in the form of the existing memorial stones which would remain *in situ*. He even anticipated the day when commercial owners would want to hand such 'parks' over to municipal control so they could officially become both 'a burial ground and a promenade', a mixture of pleasure gardens and graveyard, following the examples he quoted at Pera and Eyub near Constantinople, and at Hafiz in Persia.

There was a strong element of education in Loudon's vision. 'Churchyards and cemeteries are scenes not only calculated to improve the morals and the tastes', he proposed, 'and by their botanical riches to cultivate the intellect, but they serve as historical records ... The tomb has, in fact, been the great chronicler of taste throughout the world'. Walking around one of his cemetery parks would, he hoped, be a history lesson, a holiday and a religious experience rolled into one. 'A general cemetery in the neighbourhood of a town, properly designed, laid out, ornamented with tombs, planted with trees, shrubs and herbaceous plants, all named, and the whole property kept, might become a school of architecture, landscape-gardening, arboriculture, botany, and in these important parts of general gardening, neatness and high keeping'.

*

It is turning into the sort of damp November day where the mist never quite clears, and so leaves your top lip forever slightly moist. In place of the crows, I can now hear parrots – collectively a pandemonium, a more cheerful word than murder, and equally well suited to the mood they create. There may, at some stage, have been a mass escape from a local pet shop, or perhaps one by one they have slipped out of their cages and found a refuge here. However it came about, they sound delighted with the outcome.

More planned was the arrival of hives of bees in one corner. A local group, keen to promote greater self-sufficiency in food, has established a small apiary. It is a choice that gives a new twist to the

folklorish tales of 'telling the bees' about a death in the family of their keepers, or even their community. If they are not told, the legend goes, they will desert the hive. The origins are obscure: some say bees are traditional symbols of fertility, and so instinctively flee death, others that they used to have a role in some cultures in carrying souls into the afterlife, while their honey was a symbol of the divine, or even heaven. It inspired the memorable opening stanza of a lament by Irish poet, Katharine Tynan, to her friend and fellow poet, Edward Tennant, killed in the First World War:

Tell it to the bees, lest they
Umbrage take and fly away,
That the dearest boy is dead,
Who went singing, blithe and dear,
By the golden hives last year.
Curly-head, ah, curly-head!

In the opposite corner of the cemetery, where an old Victorian school building abuts the wall, a gate has been created (the only other way in save for the main entrance) so that the pupils can access a cordoned off nature garden. Children and cemeteries do not traditionally mix. Or at least living children. There is a section of smaller, scaled down grave stones, a place where the children remembered no longer make any noise, but break your heart silently.

Here, in the school nature garden, though, the shouts and screams add to a cemetery soundscape that is already curiously alive. Modern parents may talk of not wanting to 'infect' their youngsters with death by taking them to gravesides, but the playground noises bring a note of celebration to this otherwise sombre place of the dead.

Loudon didn't like laughter or running or jumping in graveyards, but I suspect he might just have liked this use of the cemetery as an outdoor classroom. He might even have tried to extend the range of subjects on offer, for there is social history aplenty in Paddington Old Cemetery, though it does require a pretty decent grasp of the basics before you can spot it. One of the more flamboyant graves, for instance, recalls one Garibaldi Stephenson. The monument is white, albeit now greening away, and features a weeping female figure, half-standing, half-leaning, over the tombstone. There is no date of birth given, but the occupant died in 1932 at the age of 67. A quick bit of mental maths brings me to 1865. Nine months earlier, London was swooning over the visit of Giuseppe Garibaldi, the dashingly romantic 'Liberator of Italy'. Crowds lined the streets to catch a glimpse of him. One biscuit manufacturer saw fit to launch a new product, a currant sandwich, named after this popular hero. And one mother-to-be, surname Stephenson, it is to be assumed, decided to name her child Garibaldi.

8

Deane Road Jewish Cemetery, Liverpool

'On the whole, in the Jewish tradition, we don't die well. We rage and storm. For us life, chayyim, is the great blessing, the toast to which we raise our glasses.'

RABBI JULIA NEUBERGER: *ON BEING JEWISH* (1995)

'Manchester's toll of antisemitism': the headline catches my eye as I scan the newspaper on my train journey northwards. There were, the article reports, 586 recorded antisemitic attacks in Manchester in 2011, more than in any other British city, including London, where the Jewish community is seven times larger. They included street attacks and threats to individuals, vandalism and desecration of Jewish property, including gravestones.

Jewish cemeteries make easy targets for antisemites. Usually they are unguarded, unlike many synagogues today, so there is little risk for the cowardly of being caught pouring out their bigotry and bile. And a desecrated tombstone carries with it a peculiar horror, piling violation upon violation, on a par with the grave-robbers of old. Even the dead are not safe, it says to grieving relatives.

That warning can be issued by intolerant individuals. And it can be issued by intolerant regimes. When Sir Reginald Wingate retook the Sudanese capital Khartoum in 1898 after its previous colonial overlord, General Gordon, had been besieged, starved into submission and then brutally killed, he made a point of destroying the tomb of the leader of the uprising, the *Mahdi*, and of flinging his bones into the Nile. That was straightforward imperial revenge. The horror went deeper, though, when Jewish cemeteries of eastern Europe were destroyed as the Nazi horror swept through before and during the Second World War. Even when it was over, and the scale of the Holocaust revealed, communist regimes behind the Iron Curtain continued pointedly to target cemeteries, Jewish and Christian alike, broadcasting their atheistic zeal by violating the last resting places of those who had believed. The Soviet regime delighted, for example, in re-using old gravestone memorials from bulldozed cemeteries to line the walls of underground stations

Such attacks are not just history. There were 41 reported attacks on Jewish cemeteries in 2011 by neo-Nazi groups in Germany, some 300 in eastern France during a spree in 2004, culminating in 60 memorials to those who died in the Second World War being daubed with swastikas and other graffiti in the city of Lyon, and in east London in 2005, 100 monuments in a Jewish graveyard were vandalised, toppled or attacked with axes in what police called 'a despicable act of racism'. The antisemitic tide in western Europe, the newspaper report goes on, is once again steadily rising.

Not in Liverpool, though. In Manchester's near neighbour (and traditional rival), and my destination today, such attacks are extremely rare, I am told when I arrive at Deane Road Jewish Cemetery. This graveyard may have suffered the sort of mindless vandalism seen everywhere, says Arnold Lewis, one of the custodians from Liverpool's Old Hebrew Congregation, protected by his fake fur hat against the biting wind blowing in from the sea on a sunny February morning, but none of it could be put down to hatred of Jews. Instead it has been Japanese knotweed and fly-tippers targetting this historic but, until recently, abandoned burial ground.

The bamboo-like perennial spread over it at an alarming rate, he reports, swallowing tombstones and using the high brick walls as a climbing frame. Beyond them, pressing in, are two-storey terraced houses some of whose residents treated the graveyard as an informal council dump, in a fashion that recalls the eighteenth century habit of emptying chamber pots each morning out of the window into the neighbouring churchyard.

Deane Road Jewish Cemetery is a five-minute taxi ride from Lime Street Station, up the hill from the Victorian grandeur of the city centre, still looking very trim after its face-lift for European Capital of Culture in 2008. The restoration money back then didn't trickle down – or up – to the run-down Kensington district, but almost half a million pounds have recently been given by the Heritage Lottery to rescue this slice of local history that many had forgotten existed. Even local Jews. When I ask a novelist friend, born and bred in Liverpool's Jewish community in the 1960s and 1970s, for her memories of Deane Road, she looks blank. She'd never even heard the name.

After 60 years of being locked away behind chained-up gates, this crumbling, neglected gem in Liverpool's extraordinary architectural treasury – the city has more listed buildings (2,600 at the last count) than any other outside London – is ... well, coming back to life. Opposite a scruffy Lidl supermarket, its trolleys littered around the car park, there are builders' hoardings cloaking the semi-circular carriageway drive that leads up to the cemetery's entrance.

The price of admission to the site is putting on a fluorescent tabard and hard hat. Reluctantly Arnold Lewis discards his warmer headgear. Once inside it is immediately clear that huge strides have

already been made in this ambitious scheme to turn a lost cemetery into a museum that celebrates both the Jewish contribution to Liverpool's history, and Jewish life and rituals. The very reasonable hope is that promoting knowledge is the best antidote to prejudice.

So the knotweed has been all but eradicated – a lengthy and painful process since it is apparently harder to kill off than a soap opera villain – and the discarded washing machines have been removed. Are the neighbours behaving better? 'So far'. Lewis smiles politely. Perhaps now that the gravestones have re-emerged from the jungle, that core instinct shared by 99.9 per cent of humanity to respect the last resting place of the dead has also resurfaced.

The grand stucco and stone front wall that separates the graveyard from Deane Road is being re-rendered. It is as perfectly proportioned as the façade of a Greek Temple. The archway at its centre is Grade II listed (along with the front railings). Through the scaffolding, I spy the

inscription across the top: 'Here the Weary Are At Rest' in both English and Hebrew, taken from the Book of Job in the Hebrew Scriptures, which Christians subsequently appropriated as the Old Testament.

It was Liverpool's reputation for tolerance that attracted Jews here to establish a community in the middle years of the eighteenth century. That, and its prosperous port, the transit point for trans-Atlantic trade, later the transport hub for the whole British Empire. Ports thrive on welcoming all-comers, being more cosmopolitan and accepting than their landlocked neighbours. Liverpool's genius was to see itself unambiguously as an international city, looking out to the world from its famous Pier Head rather than back towards its hinterland. It boasted the first resident Caribbean and Chinese communities in Britain.

In the 1770s, the fledgling Jewish community established a synagogue in a private house at 133 Upper Frederick Street. City of toleration or not, however, when it came to burials the congregation of between 50 and 80 members faced the same dilemma as others outside the religious mainstream in those times. Submit to a Church of England funeral service, or make your own *ad hoc* arrangements. It chose, like many a dissenter before and since, to bury its dead in the back yard. Subsequent excavations date the start of the practice to 1773.

City centre houses do not have much land behind them and by 1802 the plot was full, though it remained in existence until the early years of the twentieth century. A pamphlet by a local historian, published in 1899, records, 'the yard in Frederick-street is about the size of an average semi-detached villa residence. It is now in a poor condition, wedged in among back slums, with a few erect and fallen tombstones, bearing here and there the trace of Hebrew characters, almost obliterated and illegible'.

With their unofficial graveyard complete, at the start of the nineteenth century the congregation at Upper Frederick Street took advantage of evolving attitudes to what we would now call minorities to purchase land in Oakes Street from the city authorities to establish a new and more public burial ground. What they hadn't calculated for, though, was the rapid expansion of Liverpool – and of their own community, up to a peak of 10,000 – in these prosperous times. By 1835, Oakes Street was full and hemmed in on all sides by housing and factories, servicing the self-styled 'Port of Empire'. Moreover, it was regarded by many in the Jewish community as a bit down-at-heel. It had grown, by its own hard work, into an influential and respected community of silversmiths, watchmakers, shipping brokers, bullion merchants and bankers. If others among Liverpool's City Fathers were going to parade their wealth in death by erecting ever grander memorials to their own achievements in the new model cemeteries founded by joint-stock companies, why shouldn't their Jewish colleagues do so too?

There was not, it is worth noting, any suggestion that Jews might use these new non-denominational cemeteries themselves. There were limits to assimilation and Jewish attitudes to burial remained (and largely remain to this day) distinctive enough for them to require their own plot. Yet they were also sufficiently in line with those of their fellow citizens to hanker after a suitable setting for their own grand memorials. Which is why £1,000 was raised in 1833 to purchase the land in what was then called Deane Street.

At that stage, it was outside the city boundaries in open countryside. Today it is all but submerged in the grids of hastily-erected, undistinguished terraced houses that in the latter part of the nineteenth century spread up over this sandstone ridge towards Everton like an invading army. After the first burial – in September 1837 of Henry Hiams, a former warden and treasurer of the new purpose-built Seel Street synagogue – Deane Road filled up remarkably quickly, in part as a consequence of the Jewish tradition that each body be buried in a separate plot. Husbands and wives lie side by side, but never share a grave. The only exception made for multiple occupancy is in the case of stillborn children or those who die within 30 days of birth. They can be buried with their parent, though by tradition they are not mentioned on the stone. (So in Deane Road, for instance, there are 900 marked graves, but also another 900 unrecorded burials.)

This custom cuts across an urban myth still occasionally heard that Jews are buried standing up, with one embellishment suggesting that those who have led wayward lives are put in the ground head down. It is tempting to attribute its continuing circulation to the residue of antisemitism, but a more benign source may just be the practice, seen most strikingly in the much-visited ancient Jewish cemetery in Prague, of layering graves one on top of the other. There were in the fifteenth and sixteenth centuries restrictions on Jews purchasing additional land in Prague, and a ban in holy law on disturbing existing graves in all but exceptional circumstances, in contrast to the standard procedure in Christian churchyards at the time. Once all the plots were full, Prague's Jewish community resorted to adding a new layer of earth, raising the ground level, and then filling it with fresh graves. But since there is also a prohibition on tombstones being wilfully discarded, existing memorials had to be put back onto the newly-elevated surface. This is thought to have happened as many as 12 times, and so the tombstones seen today in Prague stand shoulder to shoulder in some places, giving the impression that those they recall may indeed have been buried standing up.

In Liverpool, the affluent and accepted Jewish community had no need to fall back on such desperate remedies. Once Deane Road was full in 1904, a larger site was purchased, further out of the city again, this time at Broad Green. Some of the remains from the original Frederick Street informal graveyard were taken there, along with those from Oakes Street.

Those who already reserved plots in Deane Road continued to be buried here, but by 1929 it had reached the end of its working life. For some years a resident caretaker remained, but since the 1950s, when the *ohel* (or prayer hall) that stood inside the gates was demolished, along with the custodian's cottage, the whole place was left to the knotweed. Such neglect may be judged to show insufficient respect for the dead, but highlights a common problem where small and dwindling communities struggle to maintain graveyards from an earlier more expansionist age. After the Second World War Liverpool's Jews – today numbering only a couple of thousand – weren't able to meet the costs of keeping the site secure and in good order as the number of family visitors to the graves inevitably fell off. Synagogue-goers were, like everyone else in the city, suffering from one economic reverse after another, as staple industries closed or moved away, sea traffic switched to other ports closer to the expanding markets of Europe, unemployment soared and depopulation occurred on a major scale. Even the city's crown jewels were left to go to wrack and ruin. Deane Road's near contemporary Saint George's Hall (the concert hall and law courts described by architectural historians as the finest neoclassical building in Europe) was in a shocking state of disrepair at this time.

The synagogue authorities were clearly troubled by the state of affairs at Deane Road. On several occasions, they came close to securing funding from outside sources for restoration work, but were always let down at the last minute. One partnership with the city council in the late 1970s aimed at transforming it into a park. On that occasion special permission was sought and obtained from the Beth Din (or rabbinical court) in London to allow tombstones to be uprooted. But finally it all came to naught. Until now.

As we walk through the archway, Arnold Lewis points out on our left the foundations of the old custodian's cottage, and on our right those of the prayer hall. This is to be rebuilt as a small visitors' centre. In the past, he explains, the *ohel* was where some bodies would have been prepared for burial. Some, but not many. It was much more usual for such rituals to be performed at home.

Lewis speaks as an expert. He heads the Liverpool *chevra kadisha* ('holy' or 'burial' society), a group of volunteers who oversee all aspects of burials of their fellow Jews as a *mitzvah* or religious duty on behalf of the community. Some Orthodox Jews go so far as to forbid non-Jews to lay out the bodies of their co-believers.

Jews are usually buried within 24 hours in the town where they die, though not on the Sabbath or religious festival days. The origin of this custom of rapid burial probably lies back in the Middle East, in the days before refrigeration (embalming continues to be forbidden) when bodies would decompose quickly and pose a health risk if not consigned to the earth. There is also a sense in Judaism that to delay a burial is a form of posthumous punishment for the individual concerned, though in exceptional circumstances (to allow close relatives who live far away to get there), a stay can be granted by rabbis, seldom of more than three days.

The *taharah* (preparation of the dead) has three stages, bathing the corpse, ritually purifying it (pouring water then drying), and finally dressing it in a simple white linen shroud, often made up of five separate pieces and usually (for men) including a *kittel*, a smock-like garment. Different traditions within Judaism have their own variations on these practices. Orthodox Jews, for example, do not permit cremation, but some Liberals do, believing that the life of the soul after death is independent of the body.

The twin key concepts shared throughout Judaism, however, are equality and simplicity. So an unadorned coffin is used by all, save in Israel where bodies tend to be buried wrapped only in a shroud before being placed directly in the ground, on the principle that it is their ancestral homeland. Elsewhere, inside each coffin a handful of earth from the Holy Land is placed, plus the individual's prayer shawl, with one of the fringes removed. The coffin is then closed but not sealed. All of this is done by the community, members of which then keep watch until the burial. If undertakers are used at all, it is only for transport.

After the burial service, close family of the deceased begin a period of deep mourning, known as *shiva* or 'seven', because it lasts for seven days. During this time, daily prayer services are conducted in the home where the family confines itself. When visitors call to pay their respects, they will find the mourners sitting on low stools, wearing non-leather footwear (as a sign of eschewing luxury) and avoiding performing even basic household tasks. Washing is kept to a minimum and the men often do not shave. Neighbours will bring 'meals of consolation', including lentils, eggs or bagels, whose round shape signifies the seamless continuity between life and death.

Wearing black is not customary, but clothing must be plain. The *keriah* – or rending of garments – is a traditional practice where a cut is made in the principal mourners' clothing as a symbolic release of emotion, as in the Hebrew Scriptures where Jacob tears his own jacket ('rends his garment') when he is presented with his son Joseph's blood-splattered coat of many colours.

The *shiva* is followed by the *shloshim*, or 30 days of lesser mourning, and then 11 months later by the unveiling of a memorial stone. Those who were buried at Deane Road, Lewis explains as we walk among the memorials, tended to be wealthy, upper-class Jews, hence the scale and decoration on some of the monuments. The principle of equality in death was being stretched, in contrast with the more modest resting places located in other parts of Liverpool used by the less prosperous, recent immigrant Jews.

That may simply have been another feature of assimilation. One of the peculiarities of Liverpool's spectacular economic boom and bust was that its rise was based on a society of extreme highs and lows, very rich and very poor, with little of the layer of bourgeoisie found in other thriving Victorian towns such as neighbouring Manchester. Many argue that it was the absence of a sizeable middle class that caused Liverpool's subsequent rapid decline, but the point here is that this exclusive cemetery simply followed the pattern of civic life around it, with residential areas of grand houses for the prosperous, such as Princes Park, an open green space shut off to the public and lined with mansions, and then the insanitary closed courts, tenements and terraces spreading out from the Dock Road for those who provided the brawn that drove economic growth.

Evidence of this assimilation is immediately apparent once we start looking at individual gravestones, some of them newly righted and restored (with the blessing of any existing relatives who have been traced). Most of the memorials combine both the traditional

features demanded by Judaism with the trappings and embellishments favoured by the rich in the Victorian age. So, on the very first
tombstone that greets us, English and Hebrew scripts sit side by
side in what would otherwise be a typical monument of the time.
'In Loving Memory of Julia Coppel', it begins. 'And above it', Lewis
points out, 'the Hebrew letters "pe" and "nun", an acronym for "here
lies". Jews in Liverpool have never been particularly devout. That was
more a feature of Manchester. And so many of them would only have
had a limited Hebrew vocabulary. Their ancestors would have spoken
Yiddish, but again because they set a high store by adapting, they
educated their children in English and English customs'.

Such a high store, indeed, that the epitaph on the next grave along
– of Simon Eschwege, 'a devoted husband' who died in September
1902 – contains only English. His relatives did not even bother with
including the equivalent from the Hebrew calendar next to his date
of death on the standard western Gregorian calendar, a concession
accommodated elsewhere on otherwise 'all-English' stones.

One reason for this wholesale blurring of boundaries was, Lewis
explains, that most Liverpool Jews were Ashkenazi – the majority
(today 80 per cent) group in this country with their roots in
medieval Germany and later eastern Europe, who migrated en masse
westwards to escape the pogroms – as opposed to the Sephardi,
drawn originally from Spain, Portugal and France. Ashkenazi were
more willing, by repute, to adapt to local customs wherever they
found themselves.

Almost half the memorials have already been righted. Some are
still in a poor state of repair, but it is intended that all will be restored.
Those now in pieces, or wiped of their lettering by neglect and the
tentacles of creepers, will present an even bigger challenge.

The current task for the workmen on site is to finish cleaning and
repointing with lime mortar the high brick walls that enclose the

cemetery on three sides. There had originally been some suggestion, in the minutes of the committee that oversaw the building of Deane Road in the 1830s, that the walls should be of grander stone, more in keeping with the architectural pretensions of the rest of the city. But marble was rejected on the grounds that such ornament would take longer to complete and time was pressing. Oakes Street was full. I'm rather glad they stuck to brick. There is something about its reddy-orangey mellowness, even on such a stark day, that chimes with the quiet respect for all the dead that should lie at the very heart of any cemetery. And because the space here between such high walls is relatively small – the whole cemetery is no bigger than a large suburban garden – there is also a curious and curiously reverent sense of being inside a church or synagogue or temple (any place of worship indeed) that has had its roof peeled off to the elements so heaven and earth are joined. In earlier times, the two most commonly used words in Latin for a graveyard were *cemeterium* (with its connotations of sleep) and *atrium*, originally a reception room in a house, open to the sky, in the context of burying the dead embracing the concept that the dead would rise up to the skies unimpeded.

Only one wall plaque breaks up the parallel lines of the brickwork. The custom was for graves and memorial stones to be in the ground, but at the far end of the cemetery an exception was made for the simple carved tablet that recalls one Dr Joshua van Oven, a pioneering surgeon, writer, educationalist and Hebrew scholar, originally from London, where he founded schools and hospitals for his community, but latterly part of the congregation here until his death in 1838.

Spread out in front of this single wall plaque, the details of the other memorials add an opulent edge, tastefully in some cases, more loudly in others. The grandest of the gravestones are grouped just off centre, halfway down the left-hand side of the cemetery. David Lewis ('no relation', remarks Arnold) was the founder of Lewis's stores, with branches around the country, but a flagship shop that was a feature of Liverpool at the junction of Ranelagh and Renshaw Streets right through my childhood here until its eventual closure in 2010. Above the main door was another Epstein statue, again controversial, this time of a naked man.

Lewis and his wife, Bertha, are recalled by sober, twin, tall, grey marble monuments. At the time of his death in 1885, it is said that the people of Liverpool lined the streets to bid farewell to this philanthropist, but his memorial stands in the shadow of another, the cemetery's largest and most imposing, recalling local girl Miriam Gollin, who married into the titled de Menasce family of Egyptian financiers. She was widowed young and died herself in Paris in 1890, aged just 39, but requested that she be buried in her hometown. Her monument – with her parents alongside – is a vast, domed, granite structure, richly decorated with Egyptian motifs.

As with other graveyards I've visited, it takes a while to adjust to what is before me and spot its unique characteristics. Deane Road has an artificial bareness because the builders are still engaged in stripping back the debris of decades of neglect, but even in its heyday there would have been no trees or plants here to disturb the dead, or to distract from the message in the Book of Genesis, 'For dust you are, and to dust you shall return'. Neither would flowers have been laid on graves. The Jewish way is rather to place a small stone or pebble on the grave itself or on the memorial tablet, as has been done on some of those freshly restored here, by distant relatives who have already travelled from all corners of the world in search of their ancestors.

The origin of this practice of placing stones is obscure. One straightforward explanation says that they were favoured because they last while flowers quickly die, and so are a symbol of eternal life while withered blooms spell out instead the fragility of earthly life.

It is a more comforting thought, even if the overall visual effect is harsher. Another theory looks back millennia to an earlier age when very few indeed were accorded any sort of grave monument, and the Jews therefore routinely marked the place where they had buried their loved ones with stones, initially as part of the burial ritual and then, as time passed and the pile was eroded, by each new visitor placing a fresh stone so as to show that the grave was tended and that the memorial would be maintained permanently.

The Talmud, Judaism's holiest book of teachings, suggests in several passages that the souls of the dead carry on living in the grave, for at least a period after burial, and this became the basis for a folklorish tradition, seen to best effect in the stories of Isaac Bashevis Singer, Nobel Laureate in 1978, that stones had to be placed to stop the recently departed rising from the ground and haunting the living.

And, in a different vein, there are those who argue that another ancient Jewish custom of leaving notes on graves – still seen at the Western (or 'Wailing') Wall in Jerusalem – also explains the placing of stones. In the Western Wall there are niches for notes containing prayers to the Almighty, but on flat graves they would blow away in the wind. So they were anchored by stones. Slowly the custom evolved until there were no notes but only stones.

Other ritual laws, Lewis points out as we move round, are carefully observed in the layout of the plots at Deane Road. The class system, with its roots in the Hebrew Scriptures, gives precedence to the descendants of the priestly caste, the *kohanim*, once keepers of the Temple in Jerusalem. Their Anglicised surnames are usually, he says, a variation on Cohen. Avoiding ritual impurity (as contracted, for instance, by proximity to a dead body) was, and still is, important to this group. As a consequence *kohanim* are buried next to the pathways, to limit the exposure of visiting relatives to other graves in the vicinity. (This principle can be taken to extreme lengths. In his book *Jacob's*

Gift, the writer and broadcaster Jonathan Freedland tells of the British member of the priestly caste, who insisted on wrapping himself in a black plastic bin liner whenever he flew over Israel lest he made contact with particles of air emanating from the cemeteries below.)

'Here's one', Lewis indicates. It is the grave of Isaac Cohen, who died in 1890. On the headstone, as well as the words in English and Hebrew, is the traditional symbol of the *kohanim*, two hands outstretched in blessing, thumb to thumb, palms facing down, with first and second fingers pressed together and third and fourth likewise, leaving a V-shape between them, representing the letter 'Shin', for *Shaddai* ('Almighty God'). It is a symbol equally well-known now amongst a group of sci-fi obsessives, as the 'Vulcan Salute', after being borrowed by Jewish actor, Leonard Nimoy, when he played the half-Vulcan Mr Spock in the TV series, *Star Trek*.

It is the individual stories that have re-emerged into the public domain with the clearing and re-opening of this cemetery that are most poignant. The tombstone of Eliza Meyer, for example, who departed this life in 1892 (5652 in the Hebrew calendar), contains no mention of relatives. 'My life was a chain of troubles', it begins, 'wanderer envy not my rest'. There are, on others, a word or phrase that now rings hollow in modern ears, with widows, for example, described as 'relicts' of their dead husbands. A word in widespread use in Victorian times, it conveys an impression in the twenty-first century of submission, that a wife is part of a man's goods and chattels.

There is, I notice, not a single Star of David on any tomb. Another sign of assimilation? 'Not really', Arnold Lewis explains, 'It wasn't always the traditional symbol for Jews or Judaism that it has become, but was historically associated with mysticism and magic'. Nowadays, however, the interlocking equilateral triangles have been adopted as the key sign of Jewish identity, and are commonly used in modern Jewish cemeteries. The symbol is even incorporated as part of the flag of the State of Israel.

The high walls are casting long shadows and, out of direct sunlight, my fingers are too cold to note down any more pearls of wisdom from Lewis's lips. We repair instead to an old-fashioned Italian café just round the corner to warm up, and to disentangle the various threads of the story that will emerge once the builders have finished, the hoardings come down, and Deane Road Cemetery is open again to the public. Since it is extremely rare for Lottery or other public funds to be given to restore a disused cemetery, when so many other Victorian graveyards are struggling to keep up even minimum standards of maintenance, how, I wonder, will Deane Road justify the investment?

Graveyards can, as Père-Lachaise shows, attract crowds because of who is buried there, but that's not an option here. Lewis's may remain a Liverpool institution, even though the department store is now closed. Indeed it's referenced in the still popular song, 'In My Liverpool Home' ('We speak with an accent exceedingly rare/ Meet under a statue [Epstein's] exceedingly bare'). But Liverpool isn't short of characters and David Lewis's own reputation, however exalted in life and at the time of his death, is no longer going to draw more than a trickle of the curious.

What is more likely to exert a pull is the opportunity this graveyard offers to be immersed in Liverpool's 'golden age' – the architecture, the ambition (when there was a problem with drainage at the site during its original construction, the congregation thought nothing of calling in for a second opinion Jesse Hartley, the engineer then busy building the Albert Dock), and the belief that the monuments speak powerfully of the city's then assumption of eternal prosperity. It is of a piece with so many other buildings here that has proved so much of a magnet for visitors in recent years.

The educational aspect, too, will be very important. The cemetery and its visitor centre will play host to school groups who will learn history – of the contribution made by the Jewish community to Liverpool – and about other religious traditions. But perhaps the most affecting aspect, demonstrated already by those distant relatives who have been traced and who have come here to right and tend the graves of their ancestors, is the role that this cemetery (and indeed all cemeteries) can play in nurturing a sense of identity by offering context and continuity. We all come from somewhere, are part of a family and of a human chain that links us back to previous genera-tions, but too often in an increasingly socially and geographically mobile world that connection is discarded in favour of a concen-tration on the here and now. In a cemetery, the thrill of the moment pales and our place in a family line is given due consideration.

Now the knotweed that obscures the past has been stripped away in Deane Road, individuals and communities are to be offered the chance to find out where they come from. You can get something similar in other places – museums, galleries, old houses, old churches, landscapes even. All of them remind us of our roots. But in a cemetery, it's more human, and potentially more immediate, especially when, as is the case with Deane Road, the graves refer to a small and distinctive group in the midst of something bigger.

9

The Commonwealth War Graves, northern France

If I should die, think only this of me:
That there's some corner of a foreign field
That is for ever England. There shall be
In that rich earth a richer dust concealed;
A dust whom England bore, shaped, made aware,
Gave, once, her flowers to love, her ways to roam,
A body of England's, breathing English air,
Washed by the rivers, blest by suns of home.

'THE SOLDIER' BY RUPERT BROOKE (1914)

The poppies are in bloom on the grass verges of the stringy roads that join the stringy villages of the Somme *département* in northern France. Long, thin, intensively-farmed fields, hardly a hedgerow or tree in sight, sweep away from the road into ridges and then gently subside into hollows like one great undulating carpet runner. But beneath the thick pile of ripening crops and lettuce-green pasture, the rich, muddy soil holds a memory of a different, darker time, far removed from this sunny early summer morning and now invisible to the human eye. Were it not for the poppies.

They are standing witness today, just as they did almost 100 years ago, when this land was used not to fill breadbaskets but to house trenches where men fought, died and were buried in numbers that still beggar belief. Then, as now, the poppies took on a broader significance. Simultaneously fragile and strong, they could survive the bombardment and the barbarity just as today they can survive on these exhaust-soaked scraps of roadside land. Yet they could also be crushed casually by a soldier's foot in the bloodbath of battle, where human lives were similarly being extinguished in their tens of thousands. And today, as anyone tempted by their red blooms to pick them will know, they wilt and die in minutes when put in a vase.

Almost a century on from the First World War, the poppy remains our symbol of remembrance, of this slaughter and of the slaughters that have followed 'the war to end all wars'. Today, as we drive across the Somme, they flag up a different story from crops and harvests and agricultural plenty. In the villages, the concerns of the present are paramount in the tractor shops, boulangeries and charcuteries. On the top of the lonely ridges, wind turbines keep the lights on. But the poppies guide thoughts back into the past.

To be fair, in this place, despite its outward show of robust, rural normality, it doesn't require much more than a nudge in that direction. The Somme is, properly, an administrative region of France, named after the river that runs through it. The brown road signs show symbols of ripening corn, the main export, but other associations with the name are so much more powerful. 'The Somme' has forever been appropriated by the series of battles that took place here during the First World War, between July and November 1916, when the British, French and Allied forces engaged the occupying

German army. It resulted in one million casualties, 60,000 on the first day of hostilities alone, a scale of carnage unprecedented in military history. Over 300,000 died in the battles of the Somme in order to seize six miles of territory from German control, a distance that our German car with its English passengers covers today in six minutes.

My children, 14 and 11, sit silent but alert in the back, their habitual bickering and banter quelled by the weight of history that hangs heavy here. They need no words of explanation from their parents because they know the story already. Both have come under the influence at their primary school of the remarkable Ann Sander, one of those teachers that pupils always remember. In a 30-year stint in the Year Six classroom, she instilled in successive generations of 10- and 11-year-olds a deep and enduring reverence for the human sacrifice of the First World War, and a love of the poets who articulated it. She has also taught them – almost unheard of in primary schools today – how to recite aloud from memory Wilfred Owen's 'Dulce et Decorum Est' and John McCrae's 'In Flanders Field'. 'In Flanders fields the poppies blow', my daughter begins softly, right on cue, staring out of the window across the fields. 'Between the crosses, row on row,/That mark our place', my son joins in.

We are on what he insists on calling 'the graveyard tour'. Already they both have grown adept at spotting the other give-away feature of this vast, empty, wind-swept farmscape, the small green Commonwealth War Graves Commission road signs that point down apparently blank byways towards the cemeteries that contain the war dead. And as we slow down and turn off the main road, it is one of these signs that guides us.

*

The Imperial (since 1960, Commonwealth) War Graves Commission was the brainchild of Sir Fabian Ware. Judged too old (at 45) to fight at the outbreak of hostilities, he came here to northern France in 1914 as part of the British Red Cross and was quickly struck, as the death toll soared, by the absence of any way of marking and recording the graves of fallen soldiers.

Once this wouldn't have caused anyone to blink. War was war and death was a part of it. The niceties extended no further than dumping foot soldiers who had perished into mass graves. These were the tumuli of the ancient world, earth and stones heaped directly onto the bodies of the dead, or occasionally covering chambers dug into the ground to warehouse them. If it was a famous victory, or the winning general was included among the fatalities, there might also be an inscription carved on stone. On the site of the Battle of Marathon, for example, where in 490 BC the Athenian forces repelled the Persian invasion of Greece, is found a basin-shaped hill where the dead from the winning side were accorded a memorial. The mound has survived but the inscription is long since lost. Next to it is another bump, containing the defeated Persians, and a third, for the slaves who fought alongside their masters but were considered a race apart even in death. Neither justified any sort of plaque.

Often victory mounds and their monuments were swept away when the next army rolled through the landscape to extract its revenge. Only the wealthy and well-connected had any hope of repatriation in death, and of a grave or memorial near their home where their relatives could come to grieve.

The first conflict of modern times in which there was some effort made to record and recognize the sacrifice of those who had been killed was the American Civil War. It saw the establishment of first Gettysberg in 1863, and then Arlington in 1864 as National Cemeteries. There was initially an element of triumphalism in the choice of the latter, since it was located on land confiscated from the family of the wife of General Robert E. Lee, leader of the defeated

Confederate army. And, in its early days, there was some suggestion that Confederate dead should be excluded, but soon a more radical principle took hold. Some of those who had been killed on both sides in the conflict were accommodated and honoured. Arlington has been used to honour the US casualties in every war since.

In France, Ware's unit began to register the details of the dead on card indexes (which quickly filled 3,000 drawers) and also to tend as best they could all the graves they could identify. By 1915, the War Office had recognized the importance of this work. Grieving relatives, having received the briefest details of the loss of loved ones in battle, and in many cases simply unable to take in the news without the irrefutable evidence of a corpse, started writing to Ware for more information on the final resting place of their sons, brothers, husbands and fiancés.

The project advanced a step in May 1917 with the establishment of the Commission, thanks largely to Ware's lobbying and shining example. He argued that being seen to take better care of the fallen would both boost the morale of serving soldiers, as they continued to risk their lives in a conflict that was bogged down in stalemate, and also comfort bereft families back at home. 'Common remembrance of the dead', he explained, 'is the one thing, sometimes the only thing, that never fails to bring our people together'. There is, in his words, a hint of a bigger agenda. To be forced to confront the terrible cost of war, life by truncated life, might also discredit warfare as a way of sorting out disputes between nations. Might, but so far hasn't.

Ware's quiet revolution then ran into controversy. His new commission was based on the twin principles of the equality of treatment of the dead, and the permanence of graves and memorials. No corpses of either officers or soldiers would be brought home from the front. In part it was a practical decision. There were simply too many, including those so badly mutilated as to be unidentifiable. It also went deeper. Ware was uneasy with the distinction that had been made in past conflicts between rich and poor, officers whose families could afford the cost of transporting their bodies home, and foot soldiers left behind in mass graves and soon forgotten by all but their stricken families who had no tombstone to visit. He believed that his 'one-size-fits-all' approach was a more appropriate reflection of the 'brotherhood' between all ranks and all backgrounds that had grown up in the nightmare of the trenches, capturing the 'new' spirit abroad in British society, before the outbreak of war, of the crumbling of class barriers. Moreover, he suggested, his way of doing things matched the essential democracy of death which had been thrown into sharp relief by the sheer numbers being killed.

There were protests – largely from those who had the means to bring their lost loved ones home – that the plans were an infringement on individual rights and family traditions, a covert form of socialism, and that they heaped insult on injury for those parents who had already sacrificed sons and now simply wanted to be allowed to bury them close at hand. With the outspoken support of Winston Churchill, though, the proposals were approved by the House of Commons in 1920.

It was more than a humanitarian gesture, or a simple mark of respect. It was also enlightened self-interest by the ruling elite. The end of the conflict saw social unrest sweep across Europe, with the working classes everywhere unhappy that the price they had paid in blood in battle seemed to have resulted only in a return in peacetime to the same miserable living conditions and unequal distribution of wealth. The new Imperial War Graves Commission was to be a potent symbol that the sacrifice of all sections of the community was properly appreciated by the government.

By 1923, 4,000 headstones, identical in size whatever the dead soldier's rank, religion, and family background, were being sent each week to France. By 1927, the Commission had completed 500 cemeteries. By 1938, the work of locating and burying those among the dead who could be identified, and building memorials to those who couldn't, was more or less complete. Then a second global conflict broke out. Despite fears to the contrary, the graveyards were left largely undisturbed, even when they became once again part of the theatre of war, an early indication of their moral authority at a time when the normal rules of decent human behaviour had everywhere else been abandoned.

By 1948, the Commission was able to report that the pre-war cemeteries had been restored to their former good order and that the task of burying the 600,000 dead from the latest conflict was well under way. That required 559 new cemeteries, some of them on the other side of the world where British and Commonwealth troops had confronted the Japanese. Today the Commission tends 1,700,000 graves in 134 countries.

*

The cars in the lay-by where we pull over all have British number plates. Etaples War Cemetery, first stop on our 'graveyard tour', is beside the main road out of the port of Boulogne. A thin fence and scattered pine trees are all that divide it from the traffic, rather than the high walls that elsewhere are still erected to separate out the living and the dead. This living memorial was designed to be just that – side by side with the everyday life that was snatched away so early from those who lie here, and a potent reminder of the price of our normality. It is there, in clear view, as locals set out on the school run or for work, and as tourists head to and from the Channel ports. Its sheer scale makes it unmissable. This is the largest Commonwealth war grave in France, with 12,000 servicemen and women from the First World War buried here.

Stopping and coming in to pay tribute, the visitors' book suggests, is largely left to the British. Two simple white stone posts flank the entrance to a short path that leads through pine trees. Suddenly, sweeping down the hillside before us to a far perimeter, are row after row of graves. It requires more than a moment to take it all in. As I do, slowly, a sobering line plays in my head, Kipling's description, written in his diary during his own 'graveyard tour' (he had lost a son in the conflict) about a 'Dead Sea of arrested lives'.

The graves are laid out as if an amphitheatre of seats, albeit facing up, rather than down, to the stage, here a long podium on the terraced high ground nearest the road, sheltered by a screen wall to its rear. In its centre are the constants of every Commonwealth War Graves Commission cemetery – Edwin Lutyens' Stone of Remembrance and Reginald Blomfield's Sword of Sacrifice.

The drive to uniformity of the War Graves Commission extended not only to the tombstones and the manner of burial, but also to the design of each cemetery. None was more important than another. All would contain, it was decided, the same essential architectural components. In the language of modern business, these would be their branding, unmistakeable and unique, but such connections, I realize as I stand on the podium looking out, sound hollow when confronted with reminders of so many lives lost.

Three principal architects were employed – Lutyens, Blomfield and Herbert Baker – as well as a team of many juniors. The material of choice was a plain slightly yellowy Portland stone, and the style a stripped-back classicism. Lutyens and Blomfield had both been involved, pre-war, with building and refurbishing country houses and had toyed with then fashionable Arts and Crafts flourishes, but both

had already been moving back towards a more classical approach. Their work for the commission accelerated that.

There is something about the simplicity of classical language, its lack of distracting ornament, which enables it to rise to the challenge of commemorating in a dignified manner such human horror. Its ageless clear lines and austerity feel, almost 100 years after the conflict ended, like a point fixed in time, then, now and forever. The sense conveyed is of being rooted in something unchanging, immune to the fluctuating architectural fashions that today make, for example, Sir George Gilbert Scott's Albert Memorial in London's Kensington Gardens noted more for the extraordinary detail of its Gothic Revival style than for the life it was meant to recall.

Classicism, as readily understandable as the black clothes of mourning, stretches back beyond the lifespan of any generation or era or war. Here, as pared-down as can be, it also manages to be without obvious sentimentality. There need be, after all, no additional invitation to weep than the sight of so many graves. If there were, the river of tears might wash everything away.

Both Lutyens' Stone of Remembrance and Blomfield's Sword of Remembrance studiedly avoid any sense of triumphalism in victory, or any note that might be misconstrued as a justification of war. They feature no national symbols, no talk of 'king and country', no religious imagery, angels, biblical scenes, or uplifting words. They even treat with caution any assumption of faith, the traditional fall-back in the face of such incomprehensible human tragedy. So while engaging with what cannot but remind Christians of an altar and a crucifix, Lutyens and Blomfield (the son of a vicar) came up with something that manages to carry those echoes but also transcends them.

Lutyens' Stone features a line from the Book of Ecclesiasticus, 'their name liveth for ever more'. Blomfield replaces the Jesus figure on the cross with a bronze sword, blade down, as if it has been put away,

ultimately impotent in the face of so much suffering. The balance in both between religion and something other is a delicate one, and is even harder to judge now because of the passage of time. To today's sceptical and secular western society, it may be felt that anything that quotes the Bible and looks like a cross is an imposition too far when it comes to religion. Yet in the 1920s, some critics lamented what they perceived as paganism in the design and demanded more overt references to God.

At either end of the podium are twin, tall, arched pavilions, again severe in their simplicity. Their only adornments are banners at each corner, delicately carved into the stone to suggest they are rippling in the wind, but as we linger awhile here there is no wind, only stillness, and these are not flags, rather the drapes of mourning.

The classical language continues as I walk down among the graves themselves. Each stele of Portland stone is 2 feet 8 inches high, 1 foot 3 inches wide. Arranged in ordered rows, every one is a memorial to an individual, even if that individual's name is lost. 'Known Unto God' is the only detail over unidentified corpses.

The military camp in the small town of Etaples was well-known to the Tommies. It was often the first stop for those who had landed at Le Havre and Boulogne en route for the trenches. It could house up to 100,000 at any time in rudimentary conditions. They struggled with the French pronunciation and so renamed it 'Eat Apples'. The new arrivals were given the briefest of trainings in bayonet fighting and formation drill. More useful, potentially, though they weren't to know it then, were lectures on how to cope with lice, trench foot, and poison gas attacks. So much activity, so much expectation, and, with hindsight, so much horror ahead of them.

It was said during the conflict that, once they reached the Front, men prayed either to be spared entirely, or for their death to be swift. Those whose fate lay somewhere in between would return here to Etaples as casualties. It had 22,000 hospital beds, but facilities were basic and many died of their injuries. They lie buried here, away from the frontline, but still far from home.

In the beginning each stone, tall, thin and slightly elongated, was individually engraved, a labour-intensive undertaking but no more, the pioneers believed, than was owed to those who had sacrificed their lives. Later, however, when demand outstripped supply, such idealism gave way to modest mechanisation. The principle remained, however, that everyone remembered here was unique but also the same. So each stone features a regimental badge at top, a number and a rank and then a name, followed by regiment, and the date of death. Most also feature an engraving of a Christian cross, but it is not universal. Jewish graves have the Star of David and some – presumably atheists – no religious symbol at all. Again some conclude with an individual message, the simpler the more heart-rending – 'So Sadly Missed by Mother'. Others end instead with something more general – 'Dearly Loved' or 'Death divides but memory clings forever' – while some have nothing at all, part of that same careful balance that was struck between the individual and the collective.

I walk along one of the rows, chosen at random. Everyone here, all 20 or so graves, comes from the King's Liverpool Regiment. Liverpool, my home town, is a big city. The loss of 20 young men would devastate individual families but not the place. But what of smaller communities? There is a war memorial that stands outside the redundant schoolhouse in our tiny Norfolk village. The local young men lost in the First World War are listed there. There are two Shackcloths – Jonathan and Edward – and four Georges – Herbert, Fred, Arnold and Albert (plus an Alfred in the list from the Second World War). The total comes to around 25, enough to fill a row here, but for South Creake that represented an entire generation wiped out, breaking a human chain that had sustained

the place for centuries, a blow from which it has arguably never recovered.

There must have been members of my own family who died in the Great War. I know of an uncle, my mother's favourite brother, Teddy, lost at sea in the Second World War, but before that, no collective memory was passed down to my generation. Perhaps that is why, in my twenties, the eleventh hour of the eleventh day of the eleventh month, marking the end of the First War and recalling those who died in battle, used largely to pass me by. I needed an Ann Sander, but in her absence was in a hurry to move forward from something so long ago in the past. I have found as I grow older, though, that the sacrifice of so many has gained a significance for me that is both awe-inspiring and moving, especially now I am here. Perhaps it is to do with the ageing process, realising my own mortality, experiencing the loss of the generation above me. Or with the opening of new theatres of war around the globe in Iraq and Afghanistan that have made military deaths in service once more a terrible reality. But it is also about the power of this place. Tears are welling as I move between the gravestones.

They give no details of how each individual died, but the information they do provide allows other insights into the conflict. I count up those in a row who have died on the same day, 3 May 1917, chosen at will, not a particularly significant date in the history of the battles as far as I know, but significant for these men and their families and their futures. Number one is Private Charles Howard of the King's Liverpool Regiment. By the time I am up to number twelve – Private Walter Frederick Parker of the King's Shropshire Regiment – I am convinced that date is about to click forward by one day, but it doesn't. It is stuck fast again and again and again on gravestone after gravestone until it feels futile to continue with the tally.

All that softens the dreadful sorrow that rises from this ground and grips me by the throat are the roses and irises that have been planted between the graves. They are as delicate as the poppies on the battlegrounds, nothing next to the death that lies all about, but without them, this place would be remorselessly bleak indeed, as Fabian Ware realized. As early as 1916, he was consulting horticulturalists at Kew Gardens. In his 1918 report for the War Graves Commission on the design, Sir Frederic Kenyon, director of the British Museum, wrote: 'There is no reason why cemeteries should be places of gloom: but the restfulness of grass and the brightness of flowers in fitting combinations would appear to strike the proper note of brightness and life'.

Visiting the war cemeteries first became popular in the 1920s. This was a time before foreign travel became commonplace, and many of the relatives of the dead soldiers would hardly have set foot outside their home county, let alone cross the Channel to France. The Commission encouraged such trips as a chance to reassure the bereaved that their loved ones were properly cared for, and to provide a practical argument against those who still resented the bar on repatriation of the dead. Commerce also spotted an opportunity. First newspaper personal columns started running advertisements offering photographs of individual war graves in France, which could be sent home to grieving families and put in the place of honour above the mantelpiece. Then some enterprising companies began to accept commissions for placing flowers on graves on particular anniversaries. And finally package tours were offered to the 'Devastated Areas', just as pre-war there had been organized day trips to the seaside.

It is in the footsteps of these mourners that we are walking today. The practical challenge of delivering equality in death is not always perfectly met, at least to modern eyes. My son baulks, for instance, at the rather more spaced out rows of stones, divided by proud purple alliums, which contain only officers. There is a mix of British and

Commonwealth majors, lieutenants and captains, but no-one from the ranks.

There are also other gradations. My daughter discovers the 'German section', tucked away on the far side. Eagle-eyed, she has been drawn over because the gravestones have a slightly pointy top, rather than the smooth curve of all the others. It is the German Christian names that give away where she is: Max, Ernst, Heinrich, and plenty of Wilhelms, after the Kaiser.

Another distinction is made between the South Africans, Australians, New Zealanders and Canadians – who are buried with the British – and soldiers from the Indian sub-continent and the West Indies, who are located in their own areas. The one that captures me most, though, is up near the road. Here is a row of gravestones, resting under pine trees and arguably with the best view in the house, that read simply 'Known to Be Buried in This Cemetery" with the footnote, 'Their Glory Shall Not Be Blotted Out'. These are not the unidentified remains – I have spotted them elsewhere. They are memorials to those known to have died here at 'Eat Apples', but whose bodies have never been found, misplaced in the chaos and carnage of war, literally swallowed up in the mud. That is what Ware fought to stop.

A rough parallel, in modern times, occurs to me. The memorial museum at Ground Zero in New York commemorates the almost 3,000 people murdered in the terrorist attack on the twin towers of the World Trade Center on 11 September 2001. Of them, there are 1,100 whose bodies have never been found. After ten years of trying and failing to identify fragments of human remains found at the site after the attack, they have all been placed in a separate room in the museum. Though it is closed to the public, and access is strictly controlled, some relatives felt it is disrespectful, but it is hard to know what else those responsible could have done.

The challenge of communicating loss with new generations who have no memory of war, and carnage on such a scale, also remains with us. To judge from the effect of Etaples on my own next generation, the War Graves Commission have got it right. Graveyards are our way of making these deaths worth something. Because they were worth nothing else in conventional terms. They didn't stop another war, another slaughter, 20 years later.

*

That, though, is to reach a verdict without trying out alternative approaches. Notre Dame de Lorette, the French National Memorial to those killed in the First World War (and subsequent conflicts), is an hour's drive south-east of Etaples. Once again the distances betray how small was the theatre of the battle that swallowed up so many lives over those four years. Perched on the crest of a 185-metre-high ridge north of Arras, Notre Dame de Lorette affords views over much of it.

One of six Nécropoles Nationale run by the Ministry of Defence – rather than at arm's length from the state, as in the case of the Commonwealth War Graves Commission – this vast 13-hectare site stands where tens of thousands of lives were snuffed out in the 12 months up to October 1915 as the Allied forces crawled, inch by deadly inch, up its muddy slopes and the Germans troops at the top pushed them back down. The ridge, shaped like a whale's hump, tailing off gently to the north and east, but fronted by a steep escarpment, saw some of the fiercest fighting of the war. Once it was over, it was left as a devastated mass of wires, spent munitions, collapsed and water-filled trenches and bodies. Pictures in the small museum at the site show a quagmire where even the contours of the hill have been shattered.

Today, though, it is a slash of elegantly cultivated countryside that rises above and apart from all that surrounds it, the grass carefully clipped, the trees arranged with a neat symmetry and the vast 13-hectare cemetery itself, last resting place of over 40,000, solemn and dignified. At its centre is an ornate neo-Byzantine church, designed by Louis-Marie Cordonnier, better known for his Peace Palace in The Hague, now the seat of the International Court of Justice. It was a different sort of justice he was striving to invoke here: God's, not man's.

Large churches are time-honoured landmarks everywhere and, though still in the early stages of our graveyard tour, the rows of graves have already taken on a familiar quality, the initial shock caused by their sheer numbers, I realize shame-facedly, somehow subsiding. What stands out here instead is the 52-metre-high lighthouse, constructed in the same pale, almost death-like stone as the basilica, a green lightning conductor running up its side to the lantern that tops it, with a revolving beam that can be seen from 70 kilometres away. The practice of leaving a light on graves is an ancient one, to ward off the dark, evil spirits, or to light a path to the next life, but this tower goes further – in more than one way. This cemetery is not content just to be, to sit amid the landscape of life. It wants to draw people to it, to remind them as they close their curtains and blinds at night, or drive along the network of local roads, that it is here. And lighthouse beams, of course, also convey a warning, not in this case to steer clear, but rather to navigate away from the carnage of war.

Where the Commonwealth graveyards have no custodians permanently on site, here we are greeted by two *hommes en béret*, their distinctive headgear complemented by smart blazers, shiny shoes and armbands that feature the French tricolour. They are part of a corps of volunteers who all commit to come at least one day each year to guard the fallen. They combine a certain military stiffness, shoulders back, chests pushed out, with a twinkle in their eyes as they try

– unsuccessfully – to coax the children to practise their schoolroom French.

That permanent presence is not the only difference in approach here from the Commonwealth graveyards. In line with the tripartite French revolutionary slogan of 'liberté, égalité, fraternité', there is no distinction made between officers and the ranks. All are treated the same, their graves side by side.

Where there is no Union Jack in the Commonwealth War Graves, the French tricolour is much in evidence – and not just on the honour guards' armbands – and each gravestone includes the words *'mort pour la patrie'* – 'died for the homeland'. It is one small step from *'patrie'* to patriotism and another uneasy few to nationalism, the cause of many a conflict, but perhaps that is too harsh, or to lose something in translation. Pride in country can be a harmless and instinctive thing. I still feel the hairs go up on the back of my neck, for example, as the Union Jack is raised and the National Anthem played when a Brit wins gold at the Olympics. But, as the history of the First World War shows, patriotism can also lead politicians into dangerous waters, where the sense of the nation overwhelms the good of the individuals who make it up. It is, as ever, a question of balance.

The French have here chosen a slightly different balance in the conflicting claims of how to remember, but they have their reasons. This is, after all, their own soil, not a corner of a foreign field. And they did not adopt the uniform approach of Fabian Ware. Some 12,000 of those killed here in that battle for this strategic ridge were returned to their families and buried locally.

Still, those subtle differences are worth reflecting on for a moment. The gravestones – save for in the separate Jewish and Muslim sections on the periphery – are all mass-produced crude stone crosses with a laminated plaque screwed on to include individual details: surname, Christian name, date of death, regiment. In a corner, my son, ever the explorer, finds a pile of blank ones, waiting for details to be attached. The scales are weighed here more towards the collective.

And the use of crosses rather than non-denominational rectangles makes plain the unabashed Christianity of this place. Before the battle, a church had stood here for almost 200 years, in various forms. Nicolas Florent Guilbert, a local painter, went on a visit in the 1720s to the Holy House at Loreto, said by Catholic folklore to be the original home in Nazareth of Joseph, Mary and their child Jesus, subsequently transported to Italy by broad-shouldered angels. Guilbert was ailing and believed that he had been cured by his pilgrimage to Loreto so, when he returned home with a statue of the Virgin Mary, he built a chapel here on the ridge to house it. In some of the pictures of the 1914–15 battles, its shattered shell survives amid the debris, rather like the 'A-Bomb Dome', the skeleton of the building that was the only thing left standing after an atom bomb was dropped on the Japanese city of Hiroshima in August 1945. That attack cost 70,000 lives immediately, and left 70,000 with critical injuries. The ruins were preserved as a memorial to them, and as a way of promoting peace thereafter.

The ruined chapel here did not remain, but its place was taken, symbolically if not literally, by the basilica, placing the whole effort to commemorate the dead within a Christian context, as opposed to the more nuanced approach of Lutyens and Blomfield. Odd, I can't help thinking as I walk round the densely-coloured interior of the basilica, decorated with mosaics that Britain, with an Established Christian Church, eschewed straightforward Christian symbols in its graveyards, while France, which insists on a clear separation of Church and state, remembers its war dead in a cemetery dominated by a church and filled with crosses.

If there is an effort to embrace something wider, it comes with the extraordinary lighthouse. In its crypt, again watched over by the *hommes en bérets*, is an ossuary, containing bones that, as at Ground Zero, couldn't be identified. What is on public display is a row of tombs of unknown soldiers, from the Second World War, from French colonial wars in North Africa and Indo-China, and from the Nazi concentration camps. In the 1939-45 war, the German invaders swept back over this battleground but met little outright resistance. They allowed the puppet Vichy regime to make a show of running France, but it did as it was told, and that included allowing almost 75,000 French citizens, including many Jews, to be deported to the death camps.

Outside again, we wander along the rows of white crosses. Almost immediately we come across a double grave, Anatole and Edmond De Sars, father and son, both *mort pour la patrie*, one in 1914 and the other in 1940. That the first sacrifice was not enough, that it required the next generation to repeat it, adds to the chilling effect of reading the inscriptions.

The Muslim section – containing the graves of soldiers from the French colonial empire in North Africa and the Middle East – uses tombstones more like Lutyens' design, though still with the sign-off about dying for the homeland. These are lined up, as Islam requires, facing north-east, so that Mecca, the birth place of the Prophet Muhammad in the Sirat Mountains of Saudi Arabia, is on their right to the south-east. Despite the presence of the honour guard, this area – and some adjoining Jewish graves – has in recent years suffered repeated attacks from far-right groups. In April 2007, 52 gravestones were daubed with swastikas and taunts about the 'unwanted' presence of *Maghrebins*, those from French North Africa. The number 18 was also used, the 1 for the first letter of the alphabet, A, and the 8 for H – i.e. Adolf Hitler.

Despite increased security, the raiders returned in April and December 2008 to reapply their messages of hatred. The response of

the authorities was to organize a well-attended service of reconcili-
ation, but the attacks highlight once again that essential vulnerability
of cemeteries. They have to operate on the basis that society gives
some sort of special protection to graveyards, especially, as in this
case, to those that contain the tombs of people who have given their
lives in defence of freedom and others' rights of self-expression.

*

'The soldiers' graves', reads an engraving at the entrance to Neuville-St
Vaast War Cemetery, a few miles south of Notre Dame de Lorette, 'are
the greatest preachers of peace'. It is saying much the same as Fabian
Ware's words about the effect of 'common remembrance' of the dead
bringing peoples together, but this line is from Albert Schweitzer,
a German-born Nobel laureate who also held French citizenship.
Schweitzer, a doctor, a missionary and an ethicist, won his Nobel
Prize in 1952 for his efforts to set out and define a philosophy which
is best remembered by the phrase 'reverence for life' but which – in
the context of graveyards recalling the human toll of the two wars
through which he lived – is better summed up as highlighting the
determination to survive as the human instinct that unites us above
any other. It led Schweitzer to lecture extensively on 'the problem of
peace', and also to his connection with this cemetery.

Unlike Notre Dame de Lorette, with its beam playing over this
once war-torn landscape, or even Etaples, open to the road and in
full public view, Neuville St Vaast hides its light under a bushel. It is
the largest German war cemetery in France. Here are buried 44,833
of the vanquished. Though first established in 1919 by the French
authorities as a 'collection site', to use the victors' language, it was
later passed to a private German charity which in 1979 arranged for
it to be landscaped and in 1983 finally opened to the public – almost
70 years after the first soldier it contains was killed. Until then, it was

considered too sensitive, as if the German war dead must simply be forgotten.

There is a simple brick building at the entrance. 'Peace to men of good will', reads the inscription on a pink-coloured cross. The architecture is as functional and stark as the crosses that stretch out, in rows, under pine trees and up a gentle slope as far as I can see. Each one is made of greyish-black metal, the colour of mourning rather than the white of hope in the other graveyards, and each contains four names, two on either arm.

How should the Germans remember their dead? Indeed, how should any vanquished nation recall those who fought and died in vain? Since the Second World War, a modern Germany has emerged, which for many years concentrated only on looking forward rather than back: no Remembrance Day parades, no communal expressions of gratitude for the lives lost in two wars, and an eagerness to demonstrate (through playing a major role in the founding of the Common Market, for instance) that it wanted to build structures that would rein it in forever. Yet, there were still grieving German families. Their dead sons and brothers and husbands may have volunteered, or they may have been conscripted. They may have agreed with the Kaiser or National Socialism, but equally they may have disagreed but still felt they had no option other than to fight. A handful of German graves in Commonwealth cemeteries, and a few more in corners of churchyards didn't seem quite adequate, when so many had gone unrecorded, unmarked but, somewhere, not forgotten.

There are, the experts tell us, stages to our grieving. And there are, as the world seeks to rebuild itself after war, stages to the re-establishment of trust and mutual co-operation between nations. I suspect, walking along between these iron crosses, the rows without even the balm of flowers and bushes, that the two processes did not run in tandem here. German families yearned for a spot to mourn their dead long before governments in the countries that had defeated the Kaiser and Hitler felt able to grant it. There remains a deep-rooted antipathy in Britain, for instance, to Germans. Scratch the surface and it still has the power to flare up.

Which means it is a different experience being British and being in this graveyard. There is still the sense of the scale of the sacrifice, the decimation of a whole generation of young men, the effort to try and imagine lives and hopes and expectations all obliterated. If every man buried here suddenly rose from the dead, they would fill a football stadium. But here in particular there can be none of the mitigation to be found elsewhere on my travels in the thought that their lives defeated something that needed defeating, that they won for those who came after them a liberty, a freedom, a choice. This is a cemetery with a plain, uncomplicated message about the wastage caused by war, a rebuke to the idea that any philosophy, any leader, can think his or her views and plans so powerful, so right, that they have to be imposed on others by conquest.

But then if war didn't exist – and it feels sacrilege even to think it here of all places – humankind would surely invent it. That is the lesson of history. The sobering sight of all these crosses, littered across the landscape of northern France, visited regularly by statesmen and women, politicians and princes, has not stopped them engaging in new conflicts in pursuit of causes which they believe, and occasionally convince us, are just. The sermon, in Schweitzer's phrase, for all the emotional power it undoubtedly carries here, has fallen on deaf ears.

*

The clouds arrive on our way into Arras, to match our mood. Perhaps a 'graveyard tour' is not the right place to take children. Cemeteries inevitably confront us with our own mortality, and at 11 and 14 such thoughts are premature, death unthinkable, the future is all. In my own defence, it occurs to me that some of those whose lasting resting places we have just visited were little older than my son is now. What plans for the future did they have? Did they enter the trenches regarding death as unthinkable, in spite of the evidence around them?

Arras provides little by way of light relief. Its two landmark squares – Grande Place and Place des Héros, lined by pedestrian arcades running in front of pretty, high-gabled seventeenth and eighteenth century Flemish merchant houses – have been turned into temporary car parks. A visit to the birthplace of Maximilien Robespierre, the French Revolution's 'sea-green incorruptible', is a history lesson too far for the children. And even the 'It's a Knockout'-style festival giants who hover in the foyer of the Gothic town hall fail to raise a smile or our spirits.

Is it just us, or is this city somehow blighted by its location in the midst of a valley of death? Just us, the friendly waiter in the pizzeria (the children's choice) reassures me, though he then begins on a long list of industrial closures and economic reverses suffered by the whole region along the French-Belgian border. Those, he corrects me, are the real shadows.

Thankfully the next day dawns blue and bright. The temperature is a record for June, the local news reports, and the air-conditioning in the car is broken. The heat quickly skews our map-reading and we find ourselves in a maze of country lanes around Beaumetz. Road signs appear and then disappear in what to locals is doubtless a perfectly logical pattern, but which to visitors off the beaten track puts me in mind of that scene in *Dad's Army* where Captain Mainwaring's platoon go round switching pointers at local crossroads so as to confuse the invading German army. It is, I comfort myself, a warmer wartime image than those that concluded yesterday.

As we pick at random a road on which to leave another unremarkable, and remarkably familiar, village called Ayette, my eagle-eyed son spots a green Commonwealth War Graves sign, pointing down a farm track into some woods towards what it says is an Indian and Chinese cemetery. 'Was China part of the British Empire?' he puzzles. I embark on a whirlwind tour of Hong Kong's history but he's not listening. He wants to explore.

The potholes aren't as tough on the suspension as they first appear. We progress slowly in first gear through a tunnel of trees. The shade is welcome but I am beginning to suspect we have been sidetracked by a rogue sign, spun round by rural vandals, when suddenly we slip out into a clearing and find ourselves alongside a lazy rectangle of graves, fronted by a bed of brilliant white roses.

It is a war cemetery in miniature, hidden away in this well-upholstered fold of land and apparently forgotten by all except the gardeners who tend it. The Stone of Remembrance is here, in pride of place, and the gravestones are of standard design, but otherwise the blueprint has been adapted. The flint and rubble wall, running along three sides, gives a homely feel rather than the classical austerity of Portland stone. And there is no Cross of Sacrifice, while the small shelters at either end of the main podium have gables that turn upwards at their ends, like a pagoda. That is a nod towards the nationality of those being remembered here, Indian and Chinese civilian labourers.

The 80 men who lie buried here in a backwater of the Somme were recruited as the war progressed to maintain the trenches and carry supplies to the front. Around 100,000 'coolies' were brought from Shantung Province in southern China, encouraged to sign up by Christian missionaries there who acted as interpreters. Once in France, though, they were on their own. They worked seven days a week, ten hours a day, and lived in separate camps from the troops, were sent to separate hospitals when they were wounded, and – on the evidence of what lies before me – were buried separately too.

Yet, in death, Lutyens' design manages to integrate them into the wider sacrifice. 'A good reputation endures for ever', reads one of the 80 individual tombstones. 'A noble duty bravely done', concludes another. There is no visitors' book. The chances of relatives making the long trip in the aftermath of war were nil. Their sons and husbands had gone to the other side of the globe to fight in a remote conflict, died but were not forgotten, or consigned to a mass grave.

The care that has been, and is, lavished on this small plot is another side of our colonial history, often seen through modern eyes as uniformly inglorious and self-serving. Indeed, there is something about this hidden place that I know will stay with me. This sacred grove, at once as elemental and eternal as any Neolithic barrow, has a special calm, adds an extra dimension to the twin themes

of remembering and forgiving. Anyone who doubts the power of landscape will find here, where the private and the public intertwine, proof of its ability to console.

We make our retreat by backing all the way up the lane. As soon as we are on the tarmac-ed road, the little cemetery seems like a dream. Did we just imagine it? Could we find it again? But there are more pressing questions to answer. How to find our way to Thiepval and its Memorial to the Missing, final stop on the tour?

*

The Western Front stretched from the English Channel coast to Switzerland, but the Somme saw some of the worst fighting – the thrust, containment, static trench warfare, and the pushing back that characterized this conflict. Overall some 750,000 Commonwealth soldiers died on the Western Front, 300,000 of whom have no individual grave. At Thiepval, the War Graves Commission built a monument that records on its walls the names of 72,000 lost without trace in the Battle of the Somme.

In the end it isn't hard to find because, like Notre Dame de Lorette, it sits on another ridge. On a clear day, we are told, you can see one from the other, but we are greeted by a heat haze. Here on 1 July 1916, the British forces suffered 57,470 casualties with 19,240 killed, the worst ever battlefield losses in a single day. Beyond the bunker-like visitor centre is the graveyard and in its centre is a vast square arch, designed by Lutyens. Most of it is red brick, with only occasional trimming with Portland stone. This is, appropriately enough, yet more classicism, stripped back to the basics. Triumphal arches, celebrating battlefield victories or great military leaders, have a long history. Ancient Rome has examples dedicated to – among others – the Emperor Commanders Titus, Septimus Severus and Constantine, but here Lutyens was adapting the tradition to fashion an appropriate way of remembering not the victory, but only those who had died in such great numbers to achieve it. Again he was walking a line. So there are victory laurels carved on to the Monument to the Missing, but surely that is something the relatives of the dead would have expected to see, the bare minimum by way of symbolism that their sons and husbands did not die in vain.

Thiepval is a favourite for school parties 'doing' the First World War and today is no exception. Brightly coloured caps bob around incongruously on the steps up to the arch as we approach. I end up in the central chamber created by the main span, but crossed by a narrower one from side to side in a not entirely successful effort by Lutyens to avoid the essentially two-dimensional quality of any archway. A middle-aged American man who doesn't seem to realize the volume of his voice is lecturing the young girl who is next to him. 'If you are warehousing the dead', he says scornfully, 'this is not a monument, but a vanity project by the architect. Does it need to be so big?' She is silent, her eyes reading down the lists of officers and

foot soldiers (all mixed together here). I am tempted to engage with him in her place, but this doesn't seem to be the moment. No more conflict. Instead I follow her example.

Does the size of Thiepval matter? Was Lutyens equating the size of his arch with the size of the Allied success on the battlefield? I doubt it. Even in the aftermath of the battle for the Somme, when it was opened by the Prince of Wales in 1932, few would have seen it as a statement of triumph. Surely Lutyens was trying only to convey the scale of the price paid, to leave behind a monument that could neither be forgotten nor ignored. Hence his reference to an architectural style that has stood the test of time.

On the far side of the arch is a small graveyard, containing equal numbers of Commonwealth and French graves, their two distinctive types of tombstone mixing seamlessly. The emphasis here is much more on the collective loss than individuals, but still these plots form part of the picture. A lone gardener is hoeing around the roots of a rose, uncovering the darker, muddy soil that lies beneath the sun-dried surface. I watch him for a moment. An interview I once did, with a memoir writer called Barney Bardsley, comes to mind. She had coped with her husband's long, slow drawn-out death from cancer in his forties by discovering gardening, first planting sunflowers in the window boxes of her south London flat and then getting herself an allotment. In the face of death, I remember her saying, the experience of plunging her hands into the wet earth was an act of hope, its power to give new life somehow being transferred to her and providing her with a reason to keep living. There is something of that here in these war cemeteries. The earth may have swallowed and encased so many young men, but it does also give something back, in the fields that now grow over the battlefields that feed us, and in the arresting sorrow of these graveyards, which demand a determined response of 'never again' from all who visit.

10

Chiltern Woodland Burial Park, Buckinghamshire

'A coffin is not a box. One calls it a coffin and once you've called it a coffin it immediately has all sorts of associations.'

JOE ORTON: INTERVIEWED IN 1967

The approach road reminds me of arriving at a country park, the sort where townies go, shrug off their cars and cares, and set off on bikes or on foot, picnics in their rucksacks, to explore a lightly landscaped piece of countryside, several reassuring steps short of wilderness, with trails, information boards and wooden signposts. And that, in one sense, is precisely what Chiltern Woodland Burial Park is. It is open to the public, 365 days a year, so that they can roam freely over these 72 acres of former Forestry Commission land that cover a chalk escarpment on the outskirts of the commuter-belt Buckinghamshire town of Beaconsfield.

But – and here John Claudius Loudon, guru of the Victorian cemetery movement will be applauding from his celestial perch

– this park is simultaneously a burial ground, not in the informal way of the meadows that became Keats' graveyard in Rome, nor on the formal garden model of the nineteenth century, but designed to accommodate the laying to rest of the dead in a natural environment. The eco-cemetery, to use a generic term, is the twenty-first century's contribution to this story of how to read a graveyard. The big context is the pressure on space in an overcrowded planet, the acute and contemporary need to counter climate change, and a widespread desire to do things more simply, go back to nature, a phrase with a particular resonance in the matter of the disposal of the dead.

In the Chilterns the response is a new take on the theme of life after death, where each individual burial does not use up or deplete the earth's resources further, and, in the best case scenario, tries to do the opposite by replenishing them. As with most innovations seen on this journey, it is more properly a reconfiguration of several time-honoured parts, with contemporary elements thrown in to address present needs. So the natural burial movement – to use the name it currently most favours – draws heavily on the past: on the belief in the essential sacredness of natural landscape, which dates back to earliest times; on the later habit of burying corpses (or ashes) in the ground; on the erection of individual memorial stones (though here kept so small and bio-degradable that they are slowly fading footnotes on the various natural vistas rather than the framing feature); on the weaving of the cemetery into the natural world seen at Burnham Norton churchyard; on the element of choice, free from religious constraints and shackles pioneered in Père-Lachaise; and on the commercial *modus operandi* of the pioneering Victorian graveyards. The result is something that, in a secular, sceptical age, counts as what earlier generations would have thought of as a thoroughly decent burial.

That, at least, seems to be the popular verdict. The first British 'woodland section' added to a conventional un-eco cemetery was opened in Carlisle in 1990. The mowers from the Victorian graveyard next door were banned so that, amid the long grass, wildlife could thrive on land where the dead could be buried as they chose – wrapped in a winding sheet, in a paper coffin or a wicker basket. In 1994, the first freestanding woodland burial ground followed, at Greenhaven, in 14 acres of countryside outside Rugby in the heart of England. For each burial a tree was planted, replenishing depleted stocks of native species and leaving a lasting memorial in the form of a new area of woodland to replace all those that have been destroyed over the centuries by population growth, intense farming and industrialization.

By 1999, there were five other natural burial grounds. Ten years later, that number had grown to 255 and the 'green burial movement' (another tag) is currently spreading just as quickly as it can find new

sites – and, in some places, reassure local fears about having dead bodies on the other side of the garden fence. They had that problem here, but concerns that the local woodland would become a place where walkers would trip over corpses, or have to turn away at the sight of limbs poking out of the earth, have quickly been assuaged.

Arriving at the Chiltern Woodland Burial Park is, though, a curious experience. In almost every other cemetery I have visited on these journeys in the company of the dead, the first impression has included at least a glimpse, if not a full frontal view, of the memorials to those buried there. They all shout death – which is one of the reasons I am drawn to such places in this death-denying culture of ours. But here, that visceral encounter is absent. As I drive up the short approach road to the car park on a crisp, clear March morning, there is just undergrowth and trees, some spruce and pine, mixed with deciduous British varieties. Shafts of light filter through the foliage to create a picture that persuades you all is well with the world.

The only clues I can spot to this park's dual purposes – save, of course, for the nameplate on the wooden gates – are the freshly-laid, narrow wood chip paths leading off in various places into the trees. And even these are more of a conundrum than an indication of something else going on. At first they strike me simply as pointless. In other bits of the countryside open to the public, they would be the start of adventure trails for children, with a zip wire or similar at the end, but here they all seem to come to an abrupt halt after five or six feet with nothing beyond. It puts me in mind of those ghostly development sites where builders lay out the roads and pavements but then leave a long gap before starting to put up the houses.

The likeness is, I suppose, just about appropriate, since later I discover that these are the access paths to the rings of graves that will one day surround many of the larger trees, bigger plots for deeper coffin burials in a circle on the outside, and then closer in to the trunk and nearer to the surface, a tighter ring of places where urns can be laid to rest. Since this eco-cemetery was only opened three years ago, many of the designated burial sites remain virgin and so these paths are not yet in use. The prime locations – to use the language of the Victorian cemetery builders – that have appealed most to the first wave of buyers lie deeper into the woods.

*

The work of the Commonwealth War Graves Commission to one side, the twentieth century's distinctive contribution to the way we deal with death was cremation. By the turn of the millennium, cremations were outflanking traditional burials of corpses by getting on for four to one.

There is an element of 'back to the future' about all this, for archaeological evidence abounds that cremation was humankind's default position from the start when it came to disposing of the dead. 'The Mungo Lady', the remains of a partially cremated body, found in 1969 in the Willandra Lakes region of Australia, is thought to be between 20,000 and 26,000 years old. Archaeologists have suggested that markings on the remains point to an elaborate burial ritual that included burning the body.

Though some societies and civilizations developed specific religious reasons thereafter for shunning cremation – the Egyptians, for instance, had an elaborate 'soul theology' that required an intact corpse, and the Babylonians favoured embalming with honey and wax – cremation remained commonplace in ancient Rome and Greece. In the East, Hindus, Sikhs, Jains and Buddhists continue to insist on cremation as the best way of freeing the eternal spirit from its earthly container. And even in the Book of Genesis, in one of the central passages of the Old Testament, Abraham builds a funeral pyre to cremate his son, Isaac, whom God has told him to murder.

Yet Judaism still overwhelmingly rejects cremation. Islam regards it as a dishonour to the dead. And in the West from the fifth century onwards Christianity's promise of spiritual *and* bodily resurrection on a final Day of Judgement caused cremation to fall out of favour for almost 1,400 years. However, most Christians (save the Orthodox) dropped their objections, actual or instinctive, in the twentieth century. Catholicism was slowest, embracing it reluctantly only in 1963.

On a practical level, cremation began to be discussed again as an option for dealing with dead bodies in the seventeenth century as part of the Scientific Enlightenment, and finally made a comeback in Europe in the late nineteenth century 'in the name of public health and civilization'. As religion's hold over society was breaking down, the pressure on space in cemeteries and the spiralling cost of burial caused many to consider alternatives. In 1873, capturing the spirit of this age of industrial invention, Professor Brunetti of Padua came up with a design for an efficient cremation furnace, which he displayed at the Vienna Exposition. It drew admiring glances from many as pointing a way forward, including Sir Henry Thompson, surgeon to Queen Victoria. The following year Sir Henry founded the Cremation Society in Britain to urge what he insisted 'was becoming a necessary sanitary precaution against the propagation of disease among a population daily growing larger in relation to the area it occupied'. He attracted distinguished supporters: the Pre-Raphaelite artist John Everett Millais, the novelist Anthony Trollope, and George Bernard Shaw, who warned that without cremation 'the dead will soon crowd the living off the earth'.

It took just over a decade for the Cremation Society to win the argument in the face of staunch opposition from the churches. The first public cremations in Europe were carried out in Breslau (now Wroclaw) in 1874, and in Dresden and Milan in 1876. One of the pioneers in Britain was a Captain Hanham of Blandford who, in 1882, erected a new-style furnace in his Dorset orchard to cremate his wife and mother. Colonial service in India and observing Hindu burial practices there may have shaped his attitudes to the disposal of the dead. Despite pressure on the Home Secretary, the captain wasn't prosecuted, but two years later Dr William Price of Glamorgan, a more controversial character who had spent his adult life publicly challenging convention, did face a court after cremating his son in line with his Druid beliefs. Price's acquittal, on the grounds that there were no existing laws on the statute book that specifically prohibited a well-organized cremation, removed the final obstacle.

In 1885 the first public crematorium in Britain opened in Woking. By the turn of the century new legislation had given the green light to the widescale public provision of crematoria around the country by local authorities. They took their time, though, to take up this challenge. Hull was one of the first in 1901, followed by Golders Green in north London in 1902, but numbers grew slowly with burial still the choice of the vast majority until after the Second World War. The experience of seeing so many die in a second international conflict seems to have changed attitudes. Cremation rates were up to 35 per cent in 1960, and have levelled out at roughly three-quarters of funerals today.

Around the same time that Sir Henry Thompson was establishing the Cremation Society, another noted London surgeon, Sir Francis Seymour Haden, published a pamphlet entitled on *The Disposal of the Dead*. It also advocated cremation but then went a good deal further. Sir Francis's essential complaint was against what he saw as the waste of good fertile land on building cemeteries of any kind. He advocated the use of wicker or paper coffins in *ad hoc* natural burial grounds for those with sufficiently big gardens to make it possible, and for the rest the placing of corpses in a communal crypt filled with charcoal so that, at regular intervals, they could be burned. In this way, he suggested, the disposal of the dead could be confined nationwide to no more than 800 hectares of land in perpetuity.

He did find some takers for parts of his programme. At one London cemetery, 'earth-to-earth' coffins were offered, but for many cremation was revolution enough. It was only a century later, when concerns began to be raised about the harm done to the environment by the emissions from coal-, oil- or gas-fired crematoria furnaces (at roughly 950 degrees centigrade, it takes an hour to reduce each 100 pounds of body weight to the dry bone fragments that are slightly erroneously called ashes or 'cremains'), that Sir Francis's ideas finally found an audience. The whole question of natural burials began to be discussed once again, by free-thinking individuals such as Penny Auty.

I met Penny in the late 1980s when I was editing the *Catholic Herald* and she was working at the Catholic aid agency, Cafod. Elegant, witty and slightly out of place at those bridge-roll-and-plonk receptions that seem to go hand in hand with Church organizations, she was always challenging company. Somehow at one such bash we got on to the subject of death. Penny led the way. Though only just 50, she told me she had decided how she wanted to be buried: naturally, in a sack, with no fuss, and none of the gloomy paraphernalia of funerals.

It was the first time anyone had ever made me consider an alternative to the ceremonies that have remained essentially unchanged since Victorian times. I asked her to write an article about it, which she did in typically forthright and iconoclastic terms. There were plenty of letters, most (to my surprise since our readers tended to be conservative in matters of ritual) supporting her plea for a new approach. And then a few weeks later, out of the blue, I received a phone call from one of Penny's two daughters. Her mother, she said, had been sitting reading a book when she had suffered a fatal brain haemorrhage.

Penny's daughter was ringing about the article her mother had written. Could I help them find a funeral director who would follow her stated wishes? And so we tried and we tried and were met by every funeral director we contacted with blank incomprehension, inflexibility and, on occasion, shock. All refused. The best that could be managed – and this was 1989 – was a little more informality than usual. I felt, as I sat in congregation, that Penny would have been disappointed but not surprised.

*

Penny is in my shadow as I head into the reception at Chiltern Woodland Burial Park. Had she lived longer, even just the average lifecycle, this might have been the place to accommodate her requests. It is a measure of how quickly conventions have changed surrounding funerals in the past two decades.

Chiltern is at the top end of the new cemetery market, part of a chain of three, with more planned, all boasting a custom-built meeting room ('gathering hall') and ceremonial room ('the woodland hall') in sustainable cedar, and flexible enough to host whatever style of ceremony relatives want, from the conventionally religious to more free-flowing parties in the spirit of the dying Nana in Caroline Aherne's multi-award-winning TV series, *The Royle Family*, who asks her granddaughter, Denise, to spell the word 'funeral', stops her after the first three letters, and insists 'I want my funeral to be fun'.

What you get here, too, is a copper-bottomed commitment that the woodlands will be maintained in their present environmentally sensitive state in perpetuity. The owners have learned from the mistakes of entrepreneurs in previous ages. They take a percentage of the fees they generate and invest them in a trust fund which, it is intended, will guarantee sufficient income to look after the site even when its plots are full up and the revenue stream has dried up.

Elsewhere others offer something less structured. At its simplest, there are farmers and landowners charging a fee for either burial of bodies in shrouds and biodegradable boxes, or the scattering of cremains, in their fields and daisy-strewn meadows, where every-thing is simply and straightforwardly recycled by nature. It disappears into the earth and, as it decomposes, leaves its mark in additional phosphorous and calcium in the soil. That is the most some people want from a physical resting space. And the need felt for a permanent memorial in the form of a gravestone is, research suggests, more emotional than practical. It is down again to that calculation that the average period that most graves are visited is just 15 years. Why, then, leave a stone on the landscape forever?

For those not convinced by this argument and wanting to bequeath a modest memorial to show that a life has been of consequence, even if it is nothing in the greater story of our planet and species, other providers offer a specially designated site, again usually in a rural setting or woodland. Here wooden plaques or posts can be placed on graves, but again there is an understanding that the land in question, even if temporarily protected and maintained, will one day simply be subsumed back into other uses. Any memorial will eventually be overtaken by the undergrowth.

The precise details of what constitutes a natural burial vary at different locations. Some sites, for example, refuse any body that has been embalmed in case the small quantities of formaldehyde typically used by British undertakers poison the soil and get into the water system, but others take the view that the risk is slight, and is more than offset by the comfort afforded to grieving families because low-level embalming slows decomposition and allows for a longer interval between death and burial. That is how they approach things here at Chiltern, as Peter Taylor, the manager explains. 'The amounts of formaldehyde are so small that any environmental impact will be negligible. We try not to have rules, but we do insist that everything is biodegradable, so no lead caskets, no plastic linings. But mostly what we try to do is give relatives choice'.

'Choice' is a word that crops up often in our conversation. It has become a mantra in other spheres of human activity: for politicians, service providers and consumers. Until recently funerals have been curiously exempt. Convention – whether social or religious – has trumped choice. Wanting something different has been taken as dishonouring the dead.

Quite why this is so is hard to discern. The law says remarkably little about how the dead must be treated – a death certificate is required, notification must go to the next of kin, and the body must be disposed of in a way that doesn't damage public health. Somehow, though, a society that everywhere else has delighted in ditching and debunking accepted norms of what is acceptable – the 'proper' way of doing things – has interpreted these simple rules in a fussy way that is substantially unchanged from Victorian times. Until now.

Here at Chiltern, Taylor reports, they have welcomed coffins shaped as mobile phones, guitars or even Ferraris. There has been a Hell's Angels wake, another with music provided by an ice-cream van, with liquorice allsorts in one case, and tea bags in another, scattered on the grave instead of earth as mourners pronounce the words 'ashes to ashes'. Increasingly popular too are coffins where mourners can write or draw on the surface as part of the *ad hoc* funeral rites. 'It is that austerity, the hushed tones that traditionally surround death that we are helping people get away from', says Taylor, himself a former vicar. And the large bills. 'If relatives want to turn up with the body in the back of an estate car and bury it in a shroud, all they have to pay for is the plot'.

We are sitting in one of the burial ground's bright, simply-furnished meeting rooms. My experience of funeral parlours is, thank God, slight, but even brief acquaintance has left an indelible memory of their sombre atmosphere and faint chemical smells. Here, the traditional dark colours and pungent odours of death have also been laid to rest. Behind Taylor as we talk is a bookcase displaying a variety of paper urns. Most eye-catching of all is the brown and red acorn, like a prop from the movie *Ice Age* resprayed in robin livery. 'That is one of the most popular', he says. The others are simpler and duller, the sort of container that might also contain fancy notepaper and envelopes.

But elsewhere time-honoured norms have been discarded. The urn market, once dominated by a one-type-fits-all nondescript vase, with vague allusions to a Graeco-Roman temple, now thrives on variety.

One provider offers a container made of sea salt in which cremains can be placed on the shoreline at low tide and then slowly absorbed as the waves come in and dissolve the casket, dispersing its contents on the current. Another supplies a receptacle of cast concrete that, once filled, is attached to an underwater coral reef so that sea life can grow on and over it.

If you prefer to go up towards the heavens rather than down into the depths, there is a specially-designed biodegradable balloon and container available that take the ashes up to 100,000 feet before releasing them into the atmosphere. For those wanting to keep their loved ones forever close, there is a specially-designed necklace which incorporates a container for cremains – rather as previous generations preserved locks of hair.

In the early days of local authority-run crematoria, most urns were routinely placed in niches in specially-built walls around flower-beds of leggy roses and brightly coloured bedding plants intended to dispel the gloom, but for many this was an unappealing option. If the gardens were unimaginative, the crematoria buildings rarely rose above the mundane. Usually they are odd hybrids, somewhere between a church, a town hall and a nursery. Unlike the competitions of the 1830s to create Victorian cemeteries, architects have rarely been inspired by these commissions. That may be the profession responding to the wider unease and lack of interest in death that exists in society at large. There may also be a specific problem at crematoria with the age-old link between building and burial being routinely broken. The funeral takes place, mourners leave, and then some days or weeks later a handful of them return to signal their assent after staff have placed the urn in a niche in the wall of remembrance.

Whatever the causes, the ritual of scattering of ashes in the deceased's favourite spot has taken over. Its appeal is timeless – that idea of landscape as sacred and a human desire to be forever part of it – but this recent fashion can have its drawbacks. So much so that, in our health and safety culture, government regulations have been issued banning the practice on windy days, lest an unpredictable gust showers passers-by with burnt human remains. This seems rather killjoy, as presumably the whole point of scattering is for them to blow away on the breeze. And quite how it is policed is unclear. But for those fearful of ruining their loved one's last farewell, there are now professional 'scatterers' available.

Also prohibited is scattering on rivers where people are swimming, or near sources of drinking water. It is not just public health, though, that is the worry. On the summits of some celebrated peaks, scattering has been outlawed after it was discovered that the unusually high levels of phospherous and calcium found in the soil there was causing bizarre plant growth. The eco-cycle was being distorted. And sheer demand can prove troublesome. Among those to have banned scattering altogether are several leading football stadia, and the curators at Jane Austen's house in Hampshire. The Vatican, in April 2012, issued a warning that consigning ashes back to nature by any means other than burying them in the ground 'raises considerable doubts as to their coherence to Christian faith, especially when they conceal pantheist or naturalistic beliefs'.

*

We've moved out of the office and are walking slowly through the woods. The longer-term plan of the three-person maintenance team here is to reduce the number of imported pines and spruces, and re-introduce the native varieties they have forced out. Older notions of favouring evergreens as a symbol of eternal life play no part here.

The park is divided into different sections, named after whatever plants grow there in abundance: Foxglove Walk, Bluebell Glade, High Oaks, Moss Grove. I can't help thinking they sound like suburban cul-de-sacs, but the reality is far from conventional. The 'burial circles' that spread out from trees like a full skirt are limited to five plots for 'full burial' (as opposed to ashes) in any five-year period. With so much space, there is no need to crowd everyone in one place. As well as being clumsy and insensitive, such clustering would disturb the carefully maintained visual balance: between park and cemetery; between nature and manicure; between a countryside city of the living in their hiking boots and on their bikes, and a city of the dead; and between the overwhelming sense of untrammelled space and the desire of families to erect a memorial.

Among the few rules at Chiltern are directions concerning how graves can be marked. Cut flowers can be left, but any other items – pictures, CDs dangling from overhanging branches, statuettes – will be removed. Those wanting to plant on graves are offered bulbs harvested from the naturally-occurring bluebells and foxgloves elsewhere in the woods. These can be dispersed on and around 'their' grave. And any carved memorial plaques, posts and vases must be of wood and within strict size restrictions that makes them more akin to the explanatory tags found in formal gardens open to the public than the angels, obelisks and scrolls of a typical nineteenth century graveyard.

Many grieving families, Taylor says, respond to the natural landscape by electing not to leave anything at all on the grave. It is enough that their loved one is part of the woods, and they need have none of the old anxiety that, if not marked, the location of an individual grave will be lost forever. Every new burial is registered on a GPS (satnav) system. This new trend towards leaving no visible marker disturbs some, such as the historian James Stevens Curl. In his monumental study, *Death and Architecture*, he writes of it as 'suggestive of emotional amnesia. For the first time in the history of mankind, the disposal of the dead is treated as unceremoniously as possible'.

Which brings us back to choice. In this context, an unmarked grave no longer speaks of neglect. It is simply a question of people making a choice about how they remember, rather than wanting to forget. There are also options for what are deemed 'living memorials' – sponsoring a tree, a bird box or a bat box as a keepsake of a loved one buried here. In line with its eco-credentials, the park is very proud of what has been achieved already in reviving wildlife habitats. The dead and the hikers share these woods with winter moths, rare breeds of butterfly and Red Kites, rarely seen in these parts for years (the latter contributing to the constant level of birdsong that covers the faintest of rumbles from the not-too-far-distant M40).

The human animal is not the only priority here. There is even a flock of 19 Jacob sheep that they have introduced into an area known as the Glade towards the western end of the park, in an enclosed meadow where their grazing will help keep down the nettles and brambles, improve soil quality and ultimately encourage wildflowers.

But many, Taylor explains, still feel the need for a specific something on the grave itself, with details of the person buried there. We've arrived at a larger old ash tree with a rare fully-occupied burial circle around it. The effect is initially curious. Coming across graves in a wood should be chilling, bringing back childhood associations of dark, terrifying places, marauding wolves and other malign predators cutting off the route out to the light. But it isn't. It may be something to do with the simple symbolism of a circle – a journey shared, life coming round full circle. The messages are familiar but in this context comforting. Or it may be because of the way the woodland has been nurtured to allow as much light as possible in through the canopy of branches above, as once stained glass windows threw comforting patterns across churches. Or perhaps it is just the logical effect of the dual purpose of this slice of the countryside, pleasure park and place of remembrance as tangled together as the undergrowth. The graves lose their horror and the overall effect is benign. Nature and its mysteries combine here with death and its conundrums to make the need for answers redundant. It is enough to be.

If I wasn't looking for the small, carved wooden grave-markings, I might almost miss them. Or more to the point dismiss them, as distractions from the views. With five around one tree, though, they inevitably draw the eye in a way that a solitary post would not. On most of the plots the undergrowth has started to creep back, and the process of the plaque becoming mulch and being swallowed up by the earth is already under way. These are not my relatives, so I am not qualified to judge, but the parallels are there with the slow but inevitable fading of memory, not in one fell swoop in the moment of death, nor endlessly prolonged by a great stone memorial that will last for centuries and long outlive anyone who remembers the deceased, but rather in harness with the cycle of our own grieving from the initial acute physical pain of loss.

My instinct about these transitory markers that lie in front of me is positive, yet I like reading graveyard inscriptions and embroidering stories on the details which the more intriguing provide. A wholesale switch to memorial posts that rot away within a decade or two will rob me and future generations of that pleasure. It could be the equivalent of disposable emails taking the place of saved and stored letters and leaving the biographers of the future with nothing to go on when researching the lives of great figures in the worlds of politics, the arts, science and human progress. But already biographers are finding alternatives, and so, I suppose, will we.

*

As we amble along, Peter Taylor talks me through the business side of this park. And for all his evident concern to accommodate and console those who have cause to use these facilities, profit is also part of the equation, another balance to strike. The natural burial movement has adopted the language of 'pre-need' and 'at-need' to describe the point at which individuals reserve plots. For those who opt for 'pre-need', there is the chance to walk these paths, take in the views, choose a favourite spot, and nominate a tree under which one day to lie. It introduces a welcome note of frankness in thinking about and preparing for our own death.

'Pre-need' and 'at-need', though, are terms that have a slightly odd ring. They were first bandied about in the American funeral industry. It had followed the lead of Père-Lachaise in facilitating individual burial regardless of denomination, then added the commercial model of the Victorian pioneers. In the second half of the nineteenth century it went on to develop its own distinctive take on the formal garden design seen at London's 'magnificent seven'. The 'lawn cemetery' was first seen in 1855 when Adolph Straunch, a German-born horti-culturalist, redesigned Spring Grove Cemetery in Cincinnati. His inspiration was to smooth the rough edges off death by favouring horizontal, divan-like memorials at ground level with each grave subordinated to the softened, serene overall look of the place.

Once again, the ambition was to disguise the landscape of death as a public park. In this experiment, there was to be no one-upmanship in building ever bigger and grander mausoleums to dominate the skyline and bombard visitors with reminders of their inevitable fate. Instead, gravestones as well as graves were turned into beds, empha-sising that gentler and enduring notion of death as a falling asleep.

The grandest lawn cemetery of them all was opened by Hubert Eaton in 1913 at Glendale, California. Forest Lawn, behind gates that were twice as big as those of Buckingham Palace, would be, Eaton promised, 'devoid of misshapen monuments and other customary signs of earthly Death'. He wanted, he said, to take the sting out of the burial process. So no lumps in the ground, no stones, no fences, no railings. There were, above all, to be extremely high standards of maintenance so that there were no reminders of decay. Eaton aspired, he wrote, to create something that was full of 'light and colour, and redolent of the world's best history and romances. I believe these things educate and uplift a community'.

Others see Forest Lawn, rather differently. 'At Forest Lawn', writes Ken Worpole in his architectural tour of graveyards, *Last Landscapes*, 'nobody died, they simply got translated'. Evelyn Waugh derides it in his satirical 1948 novel, *The Loved One*, his ghastly Whispering Glades Memorial Park based firmly on Forest Lawn. Every grave is 'certified proof against fire, earthquake and nuclear fission' (as if they had the power to worry the dead), funerals are renamed 'the leave-taking', and undertakers 'grief therapists'. Mr Joyboy, the resident embalmer and self-styled artist par excellence, is rushed off his feet preparing corpses for their last goodbye in 'the slumber room' where they are propped up on chairs and sofas, as if hosting a party.

The widespread and intensive use of embalming in the States also raised the hackles of his fellow Brit, Jessica Mitford, in her celebrated 1963 polemic, *The American Way of Death*. The communist among the celebrated Mitford sisters, she was horrified by the process, but her objections had less to do with its environmental consequences (little understood when she penned her book) but with the cost and hypocrisy of America's wholesale addiction to a process that had last been so popular in Egypt in the second millennium BC. 'The drama begins to unfold with the arrival of the corpse at the mortuary. Alas, poor Yorick! How surprised he would be to see how his counterpart today is whisked off to a funeral parlour and in short order sprayed, sliced, pierced, pickled, trussed, trimmed, creamed, waxed, painted, rouged and neatly dressed – transformed from a common corpse into a Beautiful Memory Picture'.

If the lawn cemetery developed out of the garden cemetery, there is one more step on the path before we arrive at natural burial grounds – the forest cemetery. In southern Europe, where a Catholic culture means that the proportion of cremations remains low, architects have concentrated on designing more space-efficient above-ground wall-tombs, stacked like storage units on the outskirts of every town. But in the north of the continent, they have tried something different. The forest cemetery is another effort to sink death into the landscape and so tame it.

One of the most admired examples of this movement is the Stockholm Woodland Cemetery, completed in the 1940s. It was the work of two of the country's leading architects, Erik Gunnar Asplund and Sigurd Lewerentz. It is not a garden in any shape or form, and boasts no neat lawns. There is no question of humankind imposing itself and its vision of death onto the natural landscape, but instead graves are sprinkled at what seem to be irregular intervals in a pine forest that has been planted in a former quarry. This is a subtle manipulation of nature. There are symbols here and there – notably a giant cross that manages, consciously or not, to emphasize the similarities between its shape and that of a tree. The historian Simon Schama explores what he has dubbed 'Christian vegetable theory' in *Landscape and Memory*. '[The] scriptural and apocryphal traditions of the "Tree of Life"', he suggests, 'were grafted onto the cult of the Cross' by the early Church.

*

There is an essential difference between the forest cemetery and the natural burial ground. The former is a specifically created cemetery with trees. Here, in Buckinghamshire, an existing forest has been adapted to include graves. And that on-going process of adaptation is seen elsewhere in what it still feels awkward to call the funeral industry. Crematoria, for example, are coming up with new schemes to justify their prodigious use of fossil fuels. One in Worcestershire is planning to link up with a neighbouring municipal swimming pool to use its output to warm the water. Another in Durham has proposed installing turbines in its burners to generate extra electricity, which can be sold into the National Grid. Elsewhere, the waste of natural resources represented by burning a heavy, polished wooden coffin as well as a dead body is being tackled by funeral directors offering 'rental caskets' to be used for the pre-cremation service, but then the corpse is removed and put into the furnace wrapped only in a protective sheet, with the coffin recycled. This arrangement now accounts for 85 per cent of cremations in America.

Again, there is an element of looking back to look forward in these efforts to modernize. In Tibet, for example, Buddhists have been

practising 'sky burials' since at least the twelfth century (when they are recorded in 'Books of the Dead'). The origin of the rite was just as ecological as today's woodland burial grounds. Since most of Tibet is at such an altitude that the ground is either very hard or sheer rock, space for burial plots is scarce. And since most of the country is above the tree line, there is very little wood for pyres to burn the dead. What is available is reserved for lamas or other significant figures. For the rest there is 'sky burial' or *jhator*. The corpse is taken to the upper reaches of a mountain where it is either laid out on the ground, or dismembered. Then it is left, to feed the vultures and other wildlife. *Jhator* means 'giving alms to the birds' and is seen as a religious duty. The dead sustain the living.

The practice was for a time banned by Tibet's Chinese overlords in the 1960s, but has since been allowed to restart. It is thought that these ancient, mountain-top charnel grounds may have existed for thousands of years. That, at least, is what archaeological surveys of the region have suggested, based on the bones they have discovered. Either that, or an abnormally high number of mountain climbers have come to grief.

It raises an intriguing thought, as I prepare to take my leave of Chiltern Woodland Burial Park. In 500 or 1,000 years, will archaeologists be digging in this forest and wonder why they found so many bones in the ground, without the more usual signs to indicate the presence of death that they have found elsewhere in the small fragments of rubble left from what were once cemeteries? Hopefully the fact that the bones are in patterns round trees may alert them to the real purpose. And from that deduction, they will learn a little about our own civilization and its attitudes to the dead.

Grave Matters:
a last word

'Just about the time we were bringing the making of water and the movement of bowels into the house, we were pushing the birthing and marriage and sickness and dying out.'

THE UNDERTAKING: LIFE STUDIES FROM THE DISMAL TRADE BY
THOMAS LYNCH (1997)

A final story from Italy. In 1996, Gianni Agnelli, multi-millionaire boss of the car manufacturers, Fiat, heard of the death of his great friend, Greek shipping tycoon Stavros Niarchos. Agnelli insisted that he wanted to see the body of 'the Golden Greek'. Niarchos' widow assumed this sprang from a desire to pay his last respects, in the time-honoured fashion, but she looked on puzzled as the Italian first took his friend's hand and checked for a pulse. Then he pressed his finger on the corpse's temple, searching out signs of life. 'This is crazy', Agnelli moaned. 'Men like us don't die'.

It has no doubt been exaggerated in the telling, but this tale makes an essential point: progress, economic, scientific and social, has tempted us to believe we can somehow cheat death. The illusion of immortality – whether as a result of wealth, celebrity or technological advances – beguiles us today just as much as it did Achilles in ancient Greece or Gilgamesh, the Babylonian king whose tale is told in the epic that bears his name, thought to be the oldest surviving book in history, dating back to the twentieth century BC. Our particular way, at the start of the twenty first century, is to avoid ever looking death in the eye. If we don't fix it with a glance, we fool ourselves, it won't see us and claim us. And so, despite history's lesson that it is inevitable, death still manages to take us by surprise.

'Death awareness', writes Kenneth Vail, a psychology lecturer at the University of Missouri, in a research paper published in 2012, 'is seen as a bleak force of social destruction'. Conventional wisdom, he reports, therefore equates thinking about death with being morose, fearful, aggressive and even violent. And hence best avoided. There is truth in this accumulation of negatives, his study concludes, but also in the opposite. 'We were surprised', he continues, 'how much research showed positive outcomes from awareness of mortality'. So in the aftermath of the 9/11 attacks in the United States, for example, there was anger and hostility towards 'foreigners', but researchers also found evidence that people expressed 'higher degrees of gratitude, hope and kindness' towards each other.

That particular context was unprecedented, and might then be set aside as atypical, but in one sense, none of this should come as a surprise. If organised religion is – in part at least – about our desire to fit death into some kind of pattern, and about our craving to live on eternally, then religious organizations have long preached gratitude, hope and kindness in the face of death.

Vail's study also has specific points to make about cemeteries. It talks of 'non-conscious' thinking about death, and uses the example of a walk in a graveyard. And it extols its benefits. 'Subtle, day-to-day death awareness is capable of motivating attitudes and behaviours that can minimize harm to oneself and others, and can promote well-being'. As evidence, it highlights a 2008 study by social psychologist Matthew Gailliot of Florida State University. He attempted to quantify how visiting a cemetery, or living next door to one, affects behaviour. Actors engaged with those they found walking in graveyards, or in the streets around them, and sought their help with a practical dilemma. They then repeated the exercise well away from the burial ground. They reported that the first group was 40 per cent more likely to show a willingness to offer assistance than the second.

In which case, after these journeys around graveyards, I should be the epitome of public spiritedness, the ultimate Good Samaritan. The truth, I'm afraid, is rather different. The benefits of my travels are more modest, and more selfish. This voyage has provided me with a rare opportunity to think about death – my death – in the midst of life. Or at least I hope it is the midst. Fifty is the new 40 and all that. Certainly I have had none of the urgency of, say, the political pollster, Philip Gould, a key figure in the governments of Tony Blair, who made *When I Die*, a short film released online in 2012, in the period leading up to his death from cancer. 'In six weeks time, I will be dead, I will be cremated, I will face huge fear', Gould begins.

His courage is profoundly moving. I hope I will be able to summon up one iota of it when my time comes. When he is filmed standing in Highgate Cemetery, one of the 'magnificent seven', his knowledge that this is the ground that will soon embrace him for eternity is tangible. By contrast, my visit to Saint Margaret's, Burnham Norton, feels like an act of whimsy.

And that will always be the case for all of us, until the doctor in the white coat has told us there is nothing more that medicine can do to save us. If we are lucky, that is, and death doesn't come in an instant. There is that line in John Webster's *The Duchess of Malfi*: 'I know death hath 10,000 several doors/For men to take their exits'. The manner of our dying has, in fairness, become less of a taboo of late. The hospice movement and the debate around issues of assisted suicide have sidelined that reluctance to talk about the how and when and where. But dying is not the same as death. And on that second subject the stillness of a cemetery allows us to consider, reflect, take a peep, yield an inch to the restlessness inevitably aroused by the experience of the death of others close to us.

In Islam, the Prophet Muhammad recommends that it is more fitting to walk alongside a body on its last journey than to ride. In practical terms his suggestion has been largely discarded in the age of the internal combustion engine, or taken as simply meaning that there should be no show of ostentation in funeral corteges. But perhaps there is a deeper wisdom in his words. Was what he was getting at the need to take our time in thinking about death, not do it all in a rush? A walk round a cemetery once in a while seems to fit that recipe.

And it isn't necessarily a single-issue activity or act of selfishness. For the curious, there is much to learn from these neglected ritual spaces in our midst. The history of different societies and civilizations is there, as archaeologists demonstrate when they excavate ancient burial sites. In more recent graveyards, we amateurs can still examine the past without necessarily touching on our own mortality. Likewise, there is plenty on tombstone markings to whet our insatiable appetite for details about others' lives. And for the plain curious, even though the cemetery stands apart from daily life, it can still provide an unusual snapshot of social change. Such as the revival in paupers' graves.

A 2010 newspaper investigation revealed that around one child a day is being buried in communal pits in south London cemeteries. Often they are stillborn infants, or those who have died shortly after birth, with the grieving parents so distraught that they are guided by hospital about burial and abdicate responsibility. But there are others in these pits who are older. The return of such medieval methods seems to be driven principally by cost. In tough economic times, some relatives just do not have sufficient financial resources to pay undertakers the estimated £3,000 it costs for the simplest of funerals. One-off grants from the government's Social Fund come nowhere near covering the bill. So in the absence of friends and relatives to chip in, or direct them towards cheaper alternatives in the eco-burial movement (where a cardboard coffin can be had for £200), there is no alternative to their local council's offer of a communal pit with 20 or 30 others.

The hole is often left open for up to two years, protected in some places by a locked metal cover, a modern-day mortsafe, but in others left sufficiently open for foxes to prey like vultures on the bones of the dead. It was one such incident that brought the whole shameful and insanitary practice to light. The Victorians would be astonished that we have apparently learned so little.

But we don't have to limit ourselves to social studies or historical investigation when in the company of the dead on a visit to a cemetery. Or to morbidity, as I hope what has gone before demonstrates. I plan to keep on visiting, first of all for the dog – that is certainly what I tell the children – but really for me, for that reassuring sense my walks give me that I am part of a human chain, going through the same cycle of birth and death as those who came before, and will come after me.

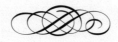

An A-Z of how to read a graveyard

I'm afraid the same rules apply – a very personal selection, not a comprehensive list, but nevertheless enough, I hope, to provide that same overview, historical, religious and cultural. There will be an overlap with what has gone before, but this is not an index.

A = *Ars Moriendi* ('The Art of Dying')
A strain of popular, pious literature on dying a 'good death' that thrived between the early fifteenth century and Victorian times, the *Ars Moriendi*, began with an anonymous Dominican friar around 1415. His writings proved popular but were beyond the pocket, or the literacy skills, of most. A shorter version, accompanied by many more illustrations, started circulating in 1450. By 1500 there were over 100 different editions available. The texts laid a heavy emphasis on a prayerful preparation for eternal life, a thorough examination of conscience, and the need for repentance. Most offered a checklist of 'temptations in death' that included lack of faith, succumbing to despair, impatience, spiritual pride and avarice (worrying more about what you were leaving behind on earth than considering what was to come in the after-life). Arguably the most notable of the *Ars Moriendi* – because of the quality of its prose – was that produced by Bishop

Jeremy Taylor in England in 1651. *Holy Dying* had many admirers, including John Wesley, the founder of Methodism. Its author was sometimes referred to as 'the Shakespeare of the divines'.

B = The Deid Bell

The Deid – or dead – Bell was rung to announce funerals, and then again during the funeral procession, both to summon mourners and to ward off evil spirits. It existed at the time of the Norman Conquest. The Bayeux Tapestry shows a 'dead bell' being rung at the funeral of Edward the Confessor. And it was still in use in northern England and especially Scotland in the nineteenth century, where it was also known as the 'passing bell' and the 'skellet bell'. It can sometimes be seen as part of the decorations on tombstones; there is one in Greyfriars' Kirkyard. John Donne, in the essay 'Devotions Upon Emergent Occasions' that contains the famous line 'no man is an island', is referring to the Deid Bell when he concludes, 'never send to know for whom the bell tolls, it tolls for thee'.

C = Catafalque

An elaborate word, taken from the Italian for scaffolding, and a favourite in my childhood spelling tests, it refers to what can be a simple object. The catafalque is the stand on which a coffin is placed, usually when standing on the altar during a funeral mass. The rough-hewn platform on which Abraham Lincoln's coffin lay in state after his assassination in 1865 has now become part of the iconography of America as 'Lincoln's Catafalque'. Covered by a black cloth, it is on display under the Capitol Rotunda in Washington DC, and is called into use as a mark of the significance of individuals whose coffins are allowed to stand on it. The honour has been accorded in recent decades to John F. Kennedy, Lyndon Johnson and Ronald Reagan, but is by no means standard for former presidents.

D = Dakhma

Zoroastrianism, the ancient religion of Iran and Iraq which profoundly influenced Judaism and Islam, before being displaced by the latter, had its own distinctive form of burial, the *dakhma* or 'tower of silence'. Zoroastrians saw the world as a perpetual battle between good and evil. So once the spirit had left the body at death, the corpse was deemed evil, and was believed to be infested by demons; it is from the Zoroastrians that Christianity drew one of the principal role models for its devil. So since the body could not therefore be laid in the earth, because it would pollute it, or be destroyed by flames since fire – *atar* – was regarded as holy, it was laid out on a circular platform at the top of a tower, open to the elements and to birds of prey. There would be three rings on the platform – one for men, on the outside, one for women, and in the centre one for children. After a year, the bones were removed and put in an ossuary inside the tower, which traditionally was located on a mountain or in the desert. The small number of modern Zoroastrians – mainly among the Parsi people of India – have largely abandoned this practice, but dotted around the Middle East and Indian sub-continent are ancient *dakhmas*.

E = Exedra

The exedra was the original memorial bench. In ancient Greece, decorated ornamental benches, often curved, were found in public places, and would play host to philosophers and their disciples when they gathered to discuss and debate. In their graveyards too, the Greeks would erect exedra next to the burial mound of family members. It was a monument to their dead loved ones, a sign of their family wealth, and a place to sit when, on annual feast days, the custom was to gather for a feast. Often the exedra was semi-circular, shaped round the grave as if protecting it. Victorian cemetery builders copied the design, but tended to position these elaborate benches in public areas of their graveyards, rather than next to individual plots.

F = Flame

The flame in a modern cemetery is a traditional symbol of either eternal life or of eternal vigilance. The flame in medieval churchyards, by contrast, was maintained to drive away evil spirits. It is found engraved on many tombs, and in Christianity in particular can also signify that an individual was particularly fervent in their beliefs. The Eternal Flame burned at Delphi, home to the most important oracle in the classical Greek world, and a shrine to the god Apollo. In China, the eternally lit lamp is a visible aspect of ancestor veneration on a family shrine. In Judaism, the *menorah*, or seven branched candelabra, recalls the flame that burned in the Temple in Jerusalem before its final destruction in AD 70, and is commonly seen on Jewish graves, including those at Deane Road in Liverpool. Since the First World War, a light has been kept burning at national memorials to the Unknown Soldier as a sign that the sacrifice of so many has not been forgotten.

G = the Grim Reaper

With his outsized scythe, the Grim Reaper's image abounds in many older graveyards, often skeletal (as opposed to his less popular and plumper alternative, Father Time, with his trademark hourglass), and wrapped loosely in a cowl. Rooted in Greek myth and the figure of Charon, who ferried the dead over the River Styx into the underworld, the Grim Reaper was interchangeable in medieval times with the 'Angel of Death' and was linked in some descriptions to the devil.

H = Halicarnassus

The tomb at Halicarnassus (modern-day Bodrum in Turkey) was built in the fourth century BC to commemorate an ambitious local ruler, Mausolus. His wife – also his sister – Artemisia suffered a terrible grief after his death in 353 BC. She is said to have mixed his ashes with her daily drink, and faded away two years later. She had, however, been determined that his memorial should remind subsequent ages of his importance, and so recruited the greatest craftsmen and artists of the time. The result – 140 feet high, resplendent in white marble, with nine columns on each of its four sides, a roof in the shape of a 24-step Egyptian pyramid, all crowned by a chariot and four horses – was one of the Seven Wonders of the Ancient World. Its reputation was such that many grand memorials thereafter were known after Mausolus as a mausoleum.

I = Isola Sacra Necropolis

For those who suffer from claustrophobia – or who don't trust the piers that support Saint Peter's Basilica in Rome to stop the whole vast church from collapsing into the pagan mausoleum underneath – the health and safety option is the Isola Sacra Necropolis. Lying to the south of Rome, on the artificial island created by the Emperor Trajan when he built a canal to link his capital to the sea at the port of Ostia, it was the burial ground of the local community in the second and third centuries AD. Based on the model of an Etruscan necropolis, it contains house-tombs and streets. Excavated in the 1920s and 1930s, today it stands on either side of the old Via Severiana. The only risk is the rumble of planes landing at the nearby main airport of Rome.

J = Jacob's Ladder

The ladder is a common engraving on Christian gravestones, usually shown as ascending into clouds, prefacing the deceased's rise, body and soul, into heaven. The source of the image is Jacob's Ladder in the Book of Genesis. The biblical patriarch, Jacob, is sleeping, his head resting on stone pillows, when he has a dream. He sees a ladder that connects heaven and earth, with angels ascending and descending.

It was only in later Jewish and Christian depictions that angels were assumed to have wings so the ladder did indeed represent the principal thoroughfare between the two realms.

K = Knowth Passage Grave

The Neolithic burial mound needed an entrance, and the 5000-year-old passage-grave at Knowth, in the valley of the River Boyne in Co. Meath boasts not one but two, running on an east-west axis, but leading to separate chambers within. What makes Knowth so special, though, is its location, surrounded by 18 smaller barrows or mounds, and its carvings. The ancient decorated stones that line the chambers, and the passageways, are among the finest surviving examples of Neolithic art.

L = Laurel Wreath

Another familiar sight in graveyards, the laurel wreath, has a variety of associations in this context. Like other evergreens, its leaves do not fade, and so it has become an additional symbol of immortality. However, it has an extra connotation, at least in the ancient world, as the sign of chastity. The laurel was consecrated to the Vestal Virgins. More generally, beyond the cemetery walls, it was the trophy of the victor. In Greece and Rome, that victory was on earth, and usually in battle, but in his First Letter to the Corinthians, Saint Paul contrasts the hollowness of such triumphs with the laurels that await those in heaven. In Christian imagery, the laurel on a grave is usually a complete circle – again signifying eternal life – whereas in more secular applications, both in the ancient world and today (it is, for example, the logo of car manufacturer, Alfa Romeo), it is typically horseshoe shaped.

M = Memento Mori

A memento mori can take many forms. All are artistic expressions of the need to 'remember thy death', the translation of the Latin phrase.

That message can be conveyed by books (see Ars Moriendi, above), in paintings of subjects such as the *danse macabre*, in gravestone engravings, in the poems of the Graveyard Poets, in inscriptions on clocks and watches, and in rings or lockets which contain a lock of hair of a dead relative. The practice is largely Christian – though Buddhism does have something roughly similar – but dates back to ancient Rome, where a victorious general would be accompanied on a triumphal parade through the city by an individual (usually a slave) whose 'memento mori' role it was to remind him of the prospect of death in the next battle. The concept of memento mori was especially popular in medieval Europe, in the wake of the Black Death, but the tradition continued on into the twentieth century, with the invention of photography making popular the habit of carrying around pictures of dead loved ones (again often in a locket) as a memento mori.

N = Nabatean Tombs

The extraordinarily elaborate tombs cut into the rock face at Petra, the capital of the Nabatean kingdom that thrived from the sixth century BC, are a UNESCO site of world heritage. This 'rose-red city half as old as time', in present-day Jordan, shows the influence of Rome and Greece on the Persian habit of burying the dead in chambers hewn into the rock. Elaborate façades were erected over the graves at Petra in classical, Roman and even Baroque styles. Behind them would be placed sarcophagi – another Roman custom adopted after the Nabateans had been subjugated to the Empire on its eastern margins. Prior to that cremation had been the custom.

O = Ouroboros

Images of the snake, especially the cobra, were a symbol of death in Egyptian art, but the *ouroboros*, or coiled serpent, its head biting its tail to complete a circle, was a reminder of immortality and rejuvenation. The Victorians borrowed it as a motif on their tombs to suggest a new life starting in eternity. In earlier centuries, though, the presence of an uncoiled serpent on a gravestone would have been a reminder that the devil was always close. In the Book of Genesis, it is the serpent in the Garden of Eden that Christianity later took to be the devil in disguise. One popular carving was of the serpent slithering its way through a human skull – a warning that there may be no safety from Satan and his temptations even in the grave.

P = Pomegranate

Grapes, apples (symbol of Eden) and vines are often to be spotted on gravestones, but the pomegranate is an altogether rarer sight. In pagan mythology, it was the sign of the goddess Persephone who ushered in spring and rejuvenation. Christianity adopted it, redesignated it an expression of the hope of immortality, and even renamed it 'the holy apple'. When the pomegranate is shown as burst open, its symbolism is of the fullness of Jesus' suffering and resurrection. In Islam, it is regarded as one of the fruits that grow in the heavenly garden (*jannah*).

Q = Quatremère de Quincy

In the late eighteenth century, the French architectural writer Quatremère de Quincy was one of the principal voices promoting a revival in interest in ancient Egypt and its pyramids. His essay, *De l'Architecture Égyptienne*, was written for a competition at the Académie des Inscriptions et Belles-Lettres in 1785 and published in 1803. It is thought to have influenced the plans for the new Père-Lachaise, which was originally to have had a pyramid-style main chapel. Though he insisted that landscape gardening could not be admitted among the fine arts, Quatremère de Quincy was also a key influence on John Claudius Loudon and the landscaped Victorian cemetery.

R = Aldo Rossi

The latter part of the twentieth century boasts few architects who have excelled in designing for the dead, but a notable exception is the Italian Aldo Rossi and his partner, Gianni Braghieri. Their modernist San Cataldo Cemetery in Modena, northern Italy, was completed in 1984. Its pastel-coloured medium-rise apartment blocks, each containing several floors of spaces (*loculi*, the same word as in the catacombs) where the coffins or urns of the dead can be sealed in, stand amid green lawns. This is mass scale burial above the ground, southern European style, but done with a contemporary flourish. In the centre of the 'grave-blocks', where once the chapel would have been, there is a single, taller tower, with windowless frames, no roof and no floors, a piece of public sculpture for a godless age.

S = Shell

The cockle or scallop shell is usually the sign of pilgrimage in Christianity, seen in particular on the *camino* or pilgrim route across northern Spain to the shrine of Santiago de Compostela. When included on a gravestone, it indicates life's journey from birth to death (the shell is also the symbol of Christian baptism), and additionally the voyage that lies ahead, to eternal life. Placing a shell on a gravestone when visiting the site is a more ancient custom than Christianity. Its origins are obscure, but there may be a link with the Jewish habit of laying stones. The shell may also refer to the belief that the after-life is reached by crossing a great sea – to the Isle of the Blest on the far horizon, as the Celtic saints of the fourth and fifth century AD believed, or by navigating the River Styx in Greek mythology.

T = Treestones

Sculpted tree stumps – also known as treestones – were popular in late Victorian times, especially in America, where they could be obtained from mail-order catalogues. They were a rustic variation on the broken Greek pillar, and often were used to symbolize a life cut short. In the United States, they also conveyed that the deceased was a member of the Woodmen of the World, a not-for-profit mutual insurance society, set up in the 1890s in Nebraska. Until the 1920s, when the offer was discontinued on the grounds of cost, all members were entitled as part of their package to the distinctive tree-stump memorial at the time of their death.

U = Urban VIII's Tomb

Bernini's design for the tomb of Pope Urban VIII, his great patron, in Saint Peter's Basilica is a Baroque feast, part of the one-upmanship that occasionally broke out amongst admirers of a recently dead pontiff who wanted to ensure that their man's legacy lived on by erecting for him the most spectacular tomb bar none. All bronze and marble, Urban VIII's memorial is perched on a high podium, with a figure of the dead pope giving a benediction.

V = Vacant Chair

Another familiar gravestone engraving, or monument, is the empty or vacant chair, expressing the space the deceased has left in the home and family life. Traditionally it is placed on the grave of a child, and will have a small pair of shoes, sculpted in stone, next to it. In my local cemetery recently, a family from Ghana left a large, gold-painted wooden chair next to the grave of their pater familias. There was some debate with the authorities there as to whether it could remain, but the family explained the symbolism and so far it has survived, though the weather has started to take its toll.

W = Woking's Brookwood Cemetery

When it opened in 1854 as the London Necropolis, this tract of Surrey was the largest cemetery in the world. It soon lost that distinction, but what makes it stand out in the history of graveyards is the London Necropolis Railway, its very own branch line all the way up to a specially-designed station terminal underneath London's Waterloo. Bodies could be brought to the terminal, often by boat, carried into the arches under the mainline station, and dispatched by this special rail link, via tunnels and deep cuttings, out of sight, out of mind, to Brookwood. There were special waiting rooms at Waterloo, and funerals could even be held there. It carried on operating until 1941 when it was damaged in a Second World War bombing raid and closed down.

X = Xanthos Tombs

The ruined Greek city of Xanthos, at Kinik in modern-day Turkey, provides an insight into the Greek way of burying their dead in the Hellenistic period, the zenith of Greek influence in the ancient world from 323 BC to about 146 BC. There are elaborate burial chambers, including domestic furniture (usually a couch), all resting on raised, decorated bases, fronted by columns and with vaulted roofs. They were rediscovered in the nineteenth century and some of what was unearthed was sent to the British Museum in London, where it can still be seen.

Y = Yahrtzeit

The *Yahrtzeit*, originally an oil-filled basin with a floating wick, more recently a candle, is used by Jews to commemorate the dead. It is lit on the anniversaries of the deaths of members of the family, and on Yom Kippur and Holocaust Remembrance Day. It is popular with both religious and secular Jews. The *yahrtzeit* is also placed on graves as a mark of respect. The tomb of the murdered Israeli Prime Minister, Yitzhak Rabin, for example, is usually covered with *yahrtzeit* candles.

Z = Zoser

The famous step-pyramid at Zoser dates back to 2770 BC and allows visitors to trace the development of Egyptian funerary monuments. It began life as a *mastaba* – a flat-roofed structure, with sloping sides, containing above ground chambers and an underground tomb for the pharaoh. Subsequently first three, then five steps were added, giving it its more familiar shape, at just over 200 feet high.

Acknowledgements

My thanks to all who have helped me on this journey with thoughts, recommendations, pointers and practical assistance: Simon Banner, Rachel Cooke, Lucinda Coxon, Kevin Crossley-Holland, Fiona Fraser, Peter Francis at the Commonwealth War Graves Commission, Arnold Lewis at Deane Road Cemetery, Natasha Maw, Cristina Odone, Nicholas Stanley-Price and Amanda Thursfield at the Cimitero Acattolico in Rome, Peter Taylor at Chiltern Woodland Burial Park, Angus Trumble and David Young. I am grateful to my publishers, Robin Baird-Smith and Caroline Chartres, for their continuing faith in me, and to my agent Derek Johns for his constant support and guidance over two decades. Particular thanks go to the Authors' Foundation, administered by the Society of Authors, for the award they made to help me to complete this book. And, finally to my brother, Martin, for playing host during my various trips to Rome, and to my children, Kit and Orla, and to Siobhan, also my first reader, for their companionship on part of this peculiar journey, and for their constant support, encouragement and unwavering belief in me. Without it, I would be lost.

Peter Stanford
London
May 2012

Index